Southern Living®

Christmas Cookbook

Southern Living®

Christmas Cookbook

All-New Ultimate Holiday Entertaining Guide

Oxmoor House®

Book Division of Southern Progress Corporation
P. O. Box 2262, Birmingham, Alabama 35201-2262

ISBN-13: 978-0-8487-3229-5
ISBN-10: 0-8487-3229-4
Library of Congress Control Number: 2007941807

Printed in the United States of America
Second Printing 2009

Southern Living® Christmas Cookbook
Editor: Rebecca Brennan
Project Editor: Vanessa Rusch Thomas
Copy Chief: L. Amanda Owens
Director, Test Kitchens: Elizabeth Tyler Austin
Assistant Director, Test Kitchens: Julie Christopher
Test Kitchens Professionals: Jane Chambliss; Patricia Michaud; Kathleen Royal Phillips; Catherine Crowell Steele; Ashley T. Strickland; Kate Wheeler, R.D.
Photography Director: Jim Bathie
Senior Photo Stylist: Kay E. Clarke
Associate Photo Stylist: Katherine G. Eckert
Director of Production: Laura Lockhart
Production Manager: Theresa Beste-Farley

Contributors
Designers: Carol O. Loria, Amy Heise Murphree
Compositor: Rick Soldin
Copy Editor: Julie Gillis
Proofreader: Stacey B. Loyless
Indexer: Mary Ann Laurens
Editorial Assistants: Amelia Heying, Kevin Pearsall
Interns: Erin Loudy, Lauren Wiygul

Cover: Coconut-Glazed Baby Bundt Cakes (page 228)
Back Cover: Italian-Stuffed Pork Loin Roast (page 136)

Lemon Curd Pound Cake (page 232)

Contents

Green Beans With Mushrooms and Bacon (page 178)

Chunky Apple Cake With Cream Cheese Frosting (page 67)

YOU'RE *Invited*

Lemon-Vinaigrette Marinated Antipasto (page 85)

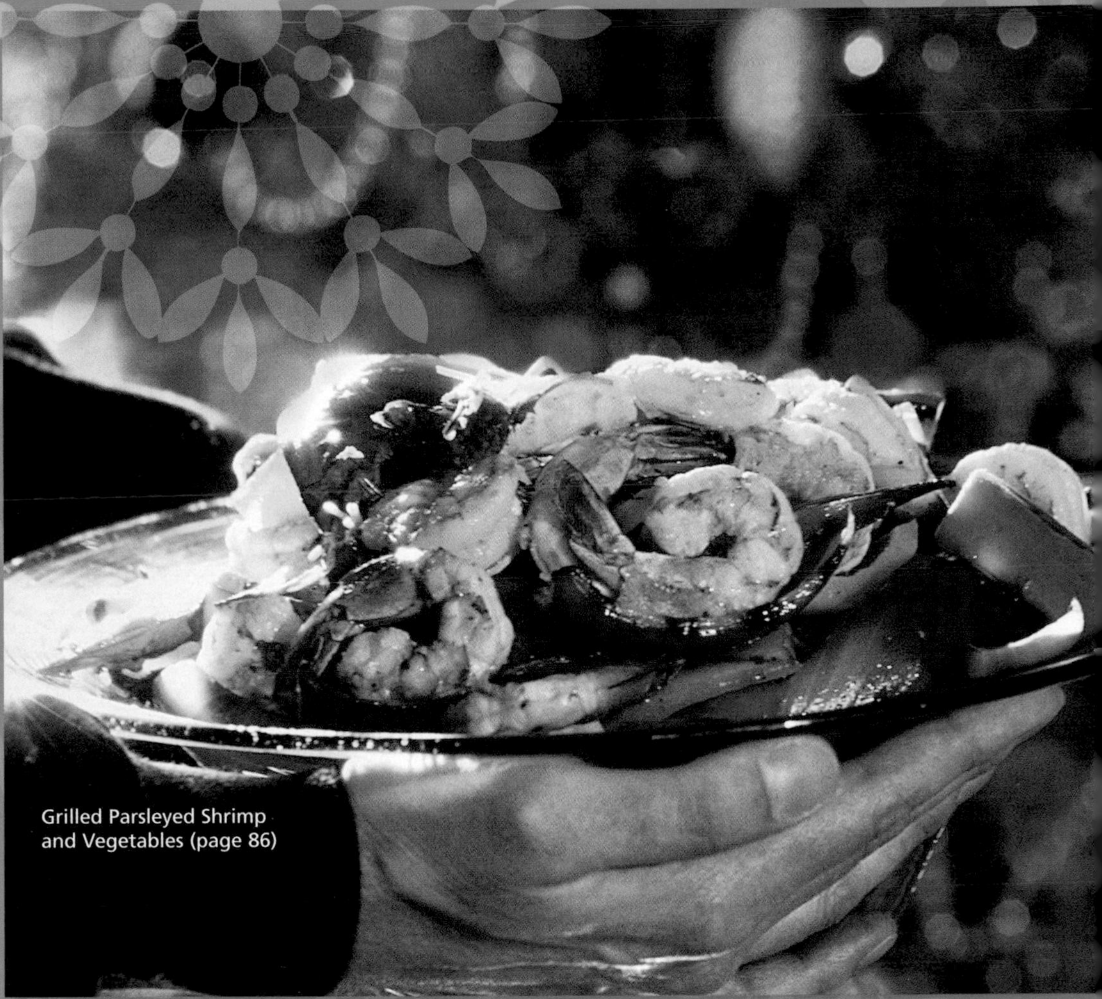

Grilled Parsleyed Shrimp and Vegetables (page 86)

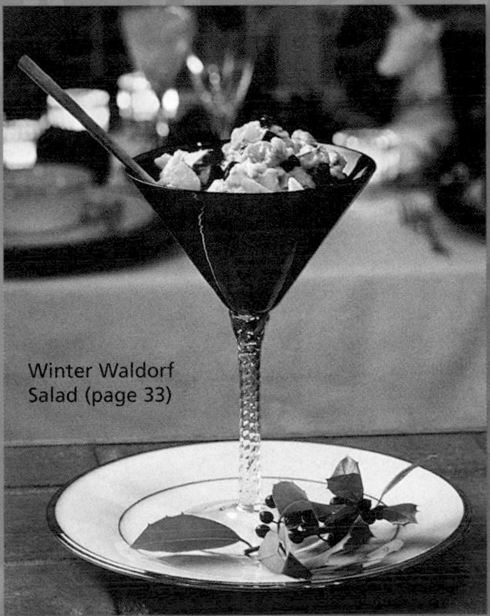

Winter Waldorf Salad (page 33)

MENUS FOR EVERY HOLIDAY GATHERING ARE OFFERED HERE—ALL YOU HAVE TO DO IS CHOOSE YOUR FAVORITE!

Bourbon-Glazed Ham, Petite Orange Carrots (page 12), Out-of-This-World Scalloped Potatoes (page 12)

HARVEST *Fare*

Plan a stress-free meal with this selection of recipes that can be easily prepared ahead.

MENU FOR 8

Bourbon-Glazed Ham

Out-of-This-World Scalloped Potatoes

Petite Orange Carrots

Bing Cherry-and-Cranberry Salad

Pumpkin Roll

Menu Prep Plan

1 DAY AHEAD:

- Prepare Bing Cherry-and-Cranberry Salad; chill.
- Prepare Pumpkin Roll; chill.
- Prepare but do not bake Out-of-This-World Scalloped Potatoes. Cover with foil, and refrigerate.

4 HOURS AHEAD:

- Bake Bourbon-Glazed Ham.

3 HOURS AHEAD:

- Let potatoes stand at room temperature 30 minutes. Bake as directed.

45 MINUTES AHEAD:

- Carve ham.
- Prepare Petite Orange Carrots; keep warm.

LAST MINUTE:

- Unmold salad onto serving platter.
- Garnish Pumpkin Roll.

editor's favorite

Bourbon-Glazed Ham

It's best to bake the ham the day you plan to serve it, but it takes only a moment to wrap the meat in foil and prepare for baking; then you have 2 hours of hands-off time.

Prep: 20 min. Bake: 2 hr., 20 min. Stand: 15 min.

1 (10-lb.) fully cooked smoked ham
2 Tbsp. whole cloves
¾ cup bourbon or apple juice
¼ cup orange juice
2 cups dark brown sugar
1 Tbsp. dry mustard

Wrap ham in aluminum foil, and place in a lightly greased 13- x 9-inch pan.

Bake at 325° for 2 hours. Remove ham from oven, and increase temperature to 450°.

Unwrap ham; discard foil. Remove skin and excess fat from ham. Make ¼-inch-deep cuts in a diamond design, and insert cloves at 1-inch intervals.

Stir togther ½ cup bourbon and orange juice; brush ham evenly with mixture. Stir together remaining ¼ cup bourbon, sugar, and mustard in a small bowl. Pat sugar mixture evenly over ham. Lightly baste with drippings; bake for 15 to 20 minutes or until a meat thermometer inserted into thickest portion registers 140° and sugar has melted and formed a glaze. Let stand 15 minutes before slicing. **Yield:** 8 to 10 servings.

Out-of-This-World Scalloped Potatoes

(pictured on page 10)

Prep: 30 min. Cook: 10 min. Bake: 2 hr., 30 min.

¼ cup butter or margarine
¼ cup all-purpose flour
3 cups milk
1 (10-oz.) block Cheddar cheese, shredded
½ cup thinly sliced green onions
1 tsp. salt
¼ tsp. freshly ground pepper
4 lb. red potatoes, peeled and thinly sliced
1½ cups soft breadcrumbs
¼ cup butter or margarine, melted
¼ cup grated Parmesan cheese

Melt ¼ cup butter in a large saucepan over medium heat. Whisk in flour, and cook, whisking constantly, 2 to 3 minutes or until flour is lightly browned. Whisk milk into butter mixture; bring to a boil. Reduce heat, and simmer 6 minutes or until thickened. Stir in Cheddar cheese and next 3 ingredients, stirring until cheese melts.

Spread ¼ cup cheese sauce evenly in a lightly greased 13- x 9-inch baking dish. Layer half of potatoes over sauce; top with half of remaining cheese sauce. Repeat with remaining potatoes and cheese sauce.

Bake at 325°, covered, 1½ to 2 hours. Stir together breadcrumbs, melted butter, and Parmesan cheese; spread evenly over potatoes. Bake, uncovered, 20 to 30 more minutes or until potatoes are tender. **Yield:** 8 to 10 servings.

Petite Orange Carrots

(pictured on page 10)

Prep: 5 min. Cook: 10 min.

5 cups water
1½ (1-lb.) packages baby carrots
¼ cup butter or margarine
4 tsp. fresh orange juice
1 tsp. grated fresh orange rind
1 tsp. salt
¼ tsp. ground red pepper

Bring 5 cups water to a boil in a 3-qt. saucepan; add carrots, and return to a boil. Cook 5 minutes or until tender; drain.

Melt butter in a large nonstick skillet over medium heat; add carrots, orange juice, and remaining ingredients, tossing to combine. Cook just until heated through. **Yield:** 8 servings.

make ahead

Bing Cherry-and-Cranberry Salad

This salad adds color to the table and a sweet-tart flavor to the meal.

Prep: 15 min. Cook: 5 min. Chill: 8 hr.

2½ cups water
3 (3-oz.) packages black cherry-flavored gelatin
2 cups cola soft drink (see note)
1 (16-oz.) can whole-berry cranberry sauce
1 (15-oz.) can pitted Bing cherries, drained and quartered
2 cups chopped pecans, toasted

Bring 2½ cups water to a boil in a large saucepan over high heat; remove from heat. Add gelatin, stirring 2 minutes or until gelatin dissolves.

Stir cola, cranberry sauce, cherries, and chopped pecans into gelatin mixture; pour into a lightly greased 13- x 9-inch baking dish. Cover and chill 8 hours or until firm. Cut into squares. **Yield:** 10 to 12 servings.

Note: For testing purposes only, we used Coca-Cola for cola soft drink.

GET A HEAD START

Plan your make-ahead menu starting with the table. Set the table a day or two ahead. Use ribbon as inexpensive napkin rings, and tuck in some greenery just before the meal for a finishing touch.

Pumpkin Roll

editor's favorite

Pumpkin Roll

Prep: 25 min. Bake: 15 min. Chill: 3 hr.

Vegetable cooking spray
3 large eggs
1 cup granulated sugar
¾ cup all-purpose flour
2 tsp. cinnamon
1 tsp. baking soda
1 tsp. baking powder
1 tsp. ground ginger
½ tsp. salt
½ tsp. ground nutmeg
⅔ cup canned unsweetened pumpkin
½ cup finely chopped pecans, toasted
1 tsp. lemon juice
1½ cups powdered sugar, divided
2 (3-oz.) packages cream cheese, softened
¼ cup butter or margarine, softened
1 tsp. vanilla extract
1 tsp. lemon juice
Garnishes: powdered sugar, chocolate-coated pecan halves

Coat bottom and sides of a 15- x 10-inch jelly-roll pan with cooking spray; line with wax paper. Coat wax paper with cooking spray; set aside.

Beat eggs at medium speed with an electric mixer 5 minutes or until thick and lemon-colored; gradually add granulated sugar, beating until well combined. Combine flour and next 6 ingredients. Gradually add to egg mixture, beating well. Combine pumpkin, pecans, and 1 tsp. lemon juice, and gradually add to mixture, beating well. Spread batter evenly into prepared pan.

Bake at 375° for 15 minutes or until a wooden pick inserted in center comes out clean.

Sift ½ cup powdered sugar in a 15- x 10-inch rectangle on a clean, dry dish towel. Run a knife around edges of pan to loosen cake; turn cake out onto prepared towel. Peel wax paper off cake. Starting at narrow end, roll up cake and towel together; place, seam side down, on a wire rack to cool completely.

Beat cream cheese and butter at medium speed with an electric mixer until creamy; gradually add remaining 1 cup powdered sugar, beating until smooth. Stir in vanilla and 1 tsp. lemon juice.

Unroll cake; remove towel. Spread cream cheese mixture on cake, leaving a 1-inch border around edges. Reroll cake without towel, and place, seam side down, on a serving platter. Cover and chill at least 3 hours. Garnish, if desired. **Yield:** 8 servings.

Breakfast Pizza, fresh fruit,
Cheesy Baked Grits (page 16)

EASYGOING FAMILY *Breakfast*

This laid-back meal is perfect for a relaxed weekend morning. Most of the ingredients can be kept on hand in the pantry or freezer.

MENU FOR 8

Breakfast Pizza

Cheesy Baked Grits

fresh cut fruit

Toffee-Apple Dip

Brown Sugar-Pecan Coffee Cake

Menu Prep Plan

UP TO 5 DAYS AHEAD:

- Prepare Toffee-Apple Dip; store in refrigerator.

1 DAY AHEAD:

- Prepare crust, sausage, hash browns, and cheese for Breakfast Pizza. (Do not add egg mixture or bake pizza.)
- Bake Brown Sugar-Pecan Coffee Cake.

2 HOURS AHEAD:

- Prepare Cheesy Baked Grits; keep warm.
- Slice apples; soak 1 hour in pineapple juice.

1 HOUR AHEAD:

- Complete preparation of Breakfast Pizza; bake.
- Cut fresh fruit as desired.

LAST MINUTE:

- Slice coffee cake.
- Arrange apples and dip on serving platter.

make ahead

Breakfast Pizza

Instead of baking this pizza in a casserole dish, you can also use a 12-inch deep-dish pizza pan.

Prep: 15 min. Bake: 40 min. Cook: 10 min.

1 (8-oz.) can refrigerated crescent rolls
1 lb. hot ground pork sausage
1 (28-oz.) package frozen hash browns with onions and peppers
1 cup shredded Cheddar cheese
4 large eggs
½ cup milk
1 tsp. salt
½ tsp. freshly ground pepper

Unroll crescent roll dough, and press on bottom and partially up sides of a 13- x 9-inch baking dish; press perforations to seal. Bake at 375° for 5 minutes.

Cook sausage in a large skillet over medium-high heat, stirring until sausage crumbles and is no longer pink. Drain well, and sprinkle evenly over crust.

Prepare frozen hash browns according to package directions, and spoon evenly over sausage. Sprinkle shredded cheese evenly over hash browns. (Cover and chill up to 24 hours, if desired.) Whisk together eggs and next 3 ingredients; pour evenly over shredded cheese.

Bake, uncovered, at 350° for 30 to 35 minutes or until set. **Yield:** 8 servings.

Cheesy Baked Grits

If you're lucky enough to have leftovers, reheat them in the microwave. *(pictured on page 14)*

Prep: 15 min. Bake: 50 min.

1 cup uncooked regular grits
1 (16-oz.) package pasteurized prepared cheese product, cubed (see note)
½ cup butter
6 large eggs
¼ cup milk
½ tsp. salt
Paprika

Prepare 1 cup grits according to package directions; remove from heat, and stir in three-fourths of cheese and butter until blended.

Whisk together eggs, milk, and salt. Gradually whisk about one-fourth of hot grits mixture into egg mixture; add to the remaining hot grits mixture, whisking constantly. Spoon mixture evenly into a lightly greased 13- x 9-inch baking dish. Bake at 350° for 30 minutes. Sprinkle with remaining chesse and paprika; bake 10 to 20 minutes or until set. **Yield:** 8 servings.

Note: For testing purposes only, we used Velveeta.

quick & easy

Toffee-Apple Dip

One recipe makes enough dip for six large apples or pears. To prevent the cut fruit from turning brown, soak the slices for an hour in canned pineapple juice.

Prep: 5 min.

1 (8-oz.) package cream cheese, softened
1 (8-oz.) package toffee bits
¾ cup firmly packed light brown sugar
½ cup granulated sugar
1 tsp. vanilla extract

Stir together all ingredients until well blended. Serve immediately, or store in an airtight container in the refrigerator up to 5 days. **Yield:** about 3 cups.

editor's favorite

Brown Sugar-Pecan Coffee Cake

A crisp, buttery crust makes this a tasty morning pick-me-up.

Prep: 15 min. Bake: 30 min.

2 cups all-purpose flour
2 cups firmly packed light brown sugar
¾ cup butter, cubed
1 cup sour cream
1 large egg, lightly beaten
1 tsp. baking soda
3 Tbsp. granulated sugar
1 tsp. ground cinnamon
1 cup chopped pecans

Stir together flour and brown sugar in a large bowl. Cut ¾ cup butter into flour mixture with a pastry blender or 2 forks until crumbly. Press 2¾ cups crumb mixture evenly on the bottom of a lightly greased 13- x 9-inch pan.

Stir together sour cream, egg, and baking soda; add to remaining crumb mixture, stirring just until dry ingredients are moistened. Stir together granulated sugar and cinnamon. Pour sour cream mixture over crumb crust in pan; sprinkle evenly with cinnamon mixture and pecans.

Bake at 350° for 25 to 30 minutes or until a wooden pick inserted into center comes out clean. **Yield:** 12 servings.

COFFEE TIPS

Nothing complements coffee cake like a hot cup of joe. Here are suggestions for the perfect brew:

- Start with cold (preferably filtered) water.
- Grind only as much coffee as you plan to brew.
- Use 2 Tbsp. of coffee for 6 oz. (¾ cup) of water.
- After brewing, serve coffee immediately or transfer to a thermal carafe for up to 15 minutes. Don't leave in coffeemaker where it can develop a scorched taste.
- Don't boil coffee; boiling destroys flavor and makes coffee bitter.

Brown Sugar-Pecan
Coffee Cake

Pineapple-Nut Cheese
With Cranberry Chutney

SIMPLE SUPPER FOR *Friends*

Busy schedule? Not a problem. With this undemanding menu, planning get-togethers for a holiday meal is a joy.

MENU FOR 6

Pineapple-Nut Cheese With Cranberry Chutney

Belgian Wassail

Orange-Cranberry-Glazed Pork Tenderloin

wild rice

Mandarin-Almond Salad

Menu Prep Plan

1 DAY AHEAD:
- Prepare chutney; chill.
- Prepare almonds for salad; store in airtight container.
- Prepare dressing for salad; chill.

MORNING OF:
- Prepare Pineapple-Nut Cheese; chill.
- Prepare clove-studded orange slices for wassail.
- Prepare Belgian Wassail; chill if serving cold.
- Tear salad greens; chill in zip-top plastic bag.

1½ HOURS AHEAD:
- Prepare Orange-Cranberry-Glazed Pork Tenderloin.

1 HOUR AHEAD:
- Prepare wild rice according to package directions.

30 MINUTES AHEAD:
- Combine ingredients for Mandarin-Almond Salad except dressing; chill.

LAST MINUTE:
- Arrange Pineapple-Nut Cheese With Cranberry Chutney and crackers in serving dish.
- Reheat Belgian Wassail if serving warm.
- Slice pork tenderloin; arrange on serving platter with cranberry mixture.
- Drizzle dressing over salad.

Pineapple-Nut Cheese With Cranberry Chutney

Prep: 20 min. Chill: 1 hr.

2 (8-oz.) packages cream cheese, softened
1 (8½-oz.) can crushed pineapple, well drained
¼ cup finely chopped green bell pepper
2 Tbsp. finely chopped onion
1 tsp. seasoned salt
1½ cups chopped pecans, toasted and divided
Cranberry Chutney
Assorted crackers

Beat cream cheese at medium speed until smooth. Gradually stir in next 4 ingredients and 1 cup pecans. Transfer to a serving bowl. Sprinkle with remaining pecans. Chill 1 hour. Serve with chutney and crackers. **Yield:** 10 to 12 appetizer servings.

Cranberry Chutney:

Prep: 15 min. Cook: 15 min.

1 cup water
¾ cup sugar
3 cups fresh cranberries (12 oz.)
1 pink grapefruit, peeled, seeded, and chopped
1 orange, peeled, seeded, and chopped
1 Granny Smith apple, peeled and diced
1 Anjou pear, peeled and diced
1½ cups mixed dried fruit
1 tsp. ground cinnamon
½ tsp. ground nutmeg
¼ tsp. ground cloves
⅛ tsp. salt

Bring 1 cup water to a boil over medium heat; add sugar, stirring until dissolved. Reduce heat to medium-low; stir in cranberries and remaining ingredients, and simmer, stirring constantly, 10 minutes. Remove from heat, and let cool. **Yield:** about 4½ cups.

Orange-Cranberry-Glazed Pork Tenderloin

Belgian Wassail

Float clove-studded orange slices atop the wassail for a festive touch. To make them, poke small holes around the edges of each orange slice with a fork or knife, and insert whole cloves.

Prep: 15 min. Cook: 30 min.

2 oranges
2 lemons
1 gal. apple cider
1 cup sugar
2 (3-inch) cinnamon sticks
1 tsp. whole allspice
Garnish: clove-studded orange slices

Squeeze juice from oranges and lemons into a bowl, reserving rinds.

Bring citrus juice, rinds, apple cider, and next 3 ingredients to a boil over medium-high heat. Reduce heat, and simmer 25 minutes. Pour mixture through a wire-mesh strainer into a container, discarding solids. Garnish, if desired. **Yield:** about 1 gal.

Note: Enjoy this hot or cold. To serve warm, keep the beverage in coffee carafes or a slow cooker.

Belgian Wassail

Orange-Cranberry-Glazed Pork Tenderloin

This tenderloin is basted with a mixture of canned cranberry sauce, orange zest and juice, balsamic vinegar, and spices.

Prep: 10 min. Cook: 30 min. Bake: 25 min. Stand: 5 min.

1 (16-oz.) can whole-berry cranberry sauce
1 tsp. grated fresh orange rind
⅔ cup fresh orange juice
2 tsp. balsamic vinegar
½ tsp. freshly ground pepper
¼ tsp. ground allspice
⅛ tsp. salt
⅛ tsp. ground cinnamon
⅛ tsp. ground cloves
1½ lb. pork tenderloin, trimmed
1½ Tbsp. olive oil
Garnishes: halved oranges slices, fresh thyme sprigs

Bring first 9 ingredients to a boil over medium heat. Reduce heat, and simmer, stirring occasionally, 20 minutes. Remove half of mixture, and set aside.

Brown pork in hot oil in a large nonstick skillet over medium-high heat 3 minutes on each side or until golden brown. Place pork in a lightly greased, shallow roasting pan.

Bake at 425° for 25 minutes or until a meat thermometer inserted into thickest portion registers 155°, basting occasionally with half of cranberry mixture. Remove pork from oven, and cover with aluminum foil; let stand 5 minutes or until thermometer registers 160°. Slice pork, garnish if desired, and serve with reserved cranberry mixture. **Yield:** 6 servings.

DON'T LET BUSY SCHEDULES KEEP YOU FROM GETTING TOGETHER WITH FRIENDS. A *simple menu* MAKES IT HAPPEN.

EASY GRATING

The grated rind from some citrus fruits adds bold flavor, but it's important not to grate into the bitter white pith. A microplane grater, available at any superstore, can help. It delicately grates certain foods, lending a finer grate with more volume than a box grater can produce. Use it for zesting fruits or for grating cinnamon sticks, chocolate, nutmeg, fresh ginger, and such hard cheeses as Parmesan.

Mandarin-Almond Salad

Prep: 15 min. Cook: 10 min. Cool: 20 min.

½ cup slivered almonds
¼ cup sugar
¼ cup vegetable oil
2 Tbsp. red wine vinegar
1 Tbsp. minced fresh parsley
½ tsp. salt
⅛ tsp. freshly ground pepper
3 drops hot pepper sauce
1 Tbsp. sugar
1 bunch green leaf lettuce, torn (8 cups)
1 (11-oz.) can mandarin oranges, drained
½ small red onion, thinly sliced

Place almonds and ¼ cup sugar in a small saucepan over medium heat. Cook, stirring constantly, 10 minutes or until sugar coats almonds and turns golden. Spread in a single layer on lightly greased wax paper; cool 20 minutes. Break into pieces, and set aside.

Combine oil and next 6 ingredients in a jar with a lid. Tightly close lid, and shake well. Chill until ready to serve.

Toss together lettuce, oranges, onion, and almonds. Shake dressing, and drizzle over salad. **Yield:** 6 servings.

Festive Pork Roasts, Au Gratin Potato Casserole (page 24), Brussels sprouts, Cranberry Relish Salad (page 24)

MAKE-AHEAD *Dinner*

You can look forward to a relaxing meal thanks to recipes that are prepared the day before.

MENU FOR 8 TO 10

Festive Pork Roasts

Au Gratin Potato Casserole

steamed Brussels sprouts

Cranberry Relish Salad

Coconut Layer Cake

Menu Prep Plan

1 DAY AHEAD:
- Prepare Cranberry Relish Salad; chill.
- Marinate pork roasts in refrigerator.
- Prepare Coconut Layer Cake. Store in refrigerator.
- Place hash browns in refrigerator to thaw.

MORNING OF:
- Assemble Au Gratin Potato Casserole; refrigerate but do not bake.

2½ HOURS AHEAD:
- Prepare sauce for pork roasts.
- Let roasts stand at room temperature 30 minutes; bake as directed.

2 HOURS AHEAD:
- Let Au Gratin Potato Casserole stand at room temperature 30 minutes; bake as directed.

30 MINUTES AHEAD:
- Steam Brussels sprouts.

LAST MINUTE:
- Carve pork roasts.

editor's favorite

Festive Pork Roasts

Prep: 15 min. Chill: 8 hr. Broil: 5 min. Bake: 1 hr., 30 min. Stand: 10 min.

1½ cups dry red wine
⅔ cup firmly packed brown sugar
½ cup water
½ cup ketchup
¼ cup vegetable oil
4 garlic cloves, minced
3 Tbsp. soy sauce
2 tsp. curry powder
1 tsp. ground ginger
½ tsp. freshly ground pepper
2 (2½- to 3-lb.) boneless rolled pork roasts
4 tsp. cornstarch
1½ cups water

Combine first 10 ingredients in a large shallow dish or zip-top plastic freezer bag; add pork. Cover or seal, and chill 8 hours, turning occasionally.

Remove pork from marinade, reserving marinade to equal 2½ cups, adding water if necessary. Place pork on a rack in a shallow roasting pan lined with aluminum foil. Whisk reserved marinade into cornstarch in a small saucepan. Place pan over medium-high heat, and bring sauce to a boil, whisking constantly. Cook, whisking constantly, 2 to 3 minutes or until thickened. Remove and reserve ¼ cup sauce. Set remaining sauce in saucepan aside.

Broil pork 6 inches from heat for 5 minutes. Pour 1½ cups water into bottom of pan. Reduce oven temperature to 325°, and bake 1 hour and 15 minutes to 1 hour and 30 minutes or until a meat thermometer inserted into thickest portion registers 155°, basting with reserved ¼ cup sauce during the last 15 minutes. Remove roast, and let stand at least 10 minutes or until meat thermometer inserted into thickest portion registers 160°. Serve with remaining warm sauce. **Yield:** 8 to 10 servings.

Au Gratin Potato Casserole

(pictured on page 22)

Prep: 10 min. Bake: 1 hr., 20 min.

1 (32-oz.) package frozen Southern-style hash browns
1 (16-oz.) container sour cream
2 cups (8 oz.) shredded Cheddar cheese
1 (10¾-oz.) can cream of mushroom soup
1 small onion, finely chopped
¼ tsp. freshly ground pepper
2 cups crushed cornflakes cereal
¼ cup melted butter

Stir together first 6 ingredients in a large bowl. Spoon potato mixture into a lightly greased 13- x 9-inch baking dish. Sprinkle evenly with crushed cornflakes, and drizzle evenly with butter.

Bake at 325° for 1 hour and 20 minutes or until bubbly. **Yield:** 10 to 12 servings.

Cranberry Relish Salad

This congealed salad is softly set and can be spooned out as a relish or cut into squares and served over lettuce leaves. *(pictured on page 22)*

Prep: 28 min. Chill: 8 hr.

2 cups boiling water
2 (3-oz.) packages cherry-flavored gelatin
¾ cup sugar
3 Red Delicious apples, peeled and quartered
3 navel oranges, peeled and sectioned
1 cup pecan halves, toasted
1 (12-oz.) package fresh or frozen cranberries
1 (8-oz.) can crushed pineapple in juice

Stir 2 cups boiling water into gelatin in a lightly greased 13- x 9-inch baking dish until gelatin is completely dissolved. Add sugar, stirring until completely dissolved.

Process apples and oranges in a food processor until chopped; stir into gelatin mixture. Process pecans and cranberries in food processor until chopped; stir into apple mixture.

Drain pineapple in a wire mesh strainer, pressing out juice with the back of a spoon; reserve juice for another use. Add drained pineapple to cranberry mixture, stirring until fruit and nuts are thoroughly distributed in gelatin mixture. Cover and chill 8 hours. Spoon out as a relish or cut into squares. **Yield:** 10 servings.

Coconut Layer Cake

Prep: 45 min. Bake: 20 min.

⅔ cup butter or shortening, softened
1⅔ cups sugar
3 large eggs
2½ cups all-purpose flour
1½ tsp. baking powder
1 tsp. salt
1½ cups milk
1 tsp. vanilla extract
¼ cup freshly squeezed orange juice (juice of 1 orange)
2 tsp. sugar
Satin Icing
2 (6-oz.) packages frozen grated coconut, thawed

Beat butter at medium speed with an electric mixer until fluffy; gradually add 1⅔ cups sugar, beating well. Add eggs, 1 at a time, beating until blended after each addition. Combine flour, baking powder, and salt; add to butter mixture alternately with milk, beating at low speed, beginning and ending with flour mixture. Stir in vanilla. Pour into 3 greased and floured 8-inch cake pans.

Bake at 350° for 18 to 20 minutes or until a wooden pick inserted in center comes out clean. Cool in pans on wire racks 10 minutes; remove from pans, and cool completely on racks.

Stir together orange juice and 2 tsp. sugar. Microwave at HIGH 1 minute or until sugar dissolves. Drizzle over layers.

Spread ½ cup Satin Icing between layers. Spread remaining icing on top and sides of cake. Lightly press coconut between layers of paper towels to remove excess moisture. Sprinkle coconut on top and sides of cake; press slightly. **Yield:** 12 servings.

Satin Icing:

Prep: 10 min. Cook: 7 min.

2 large egg whites
1 cup sugar
¼ cup water
3 Tbsp. light corn syrup
¼ tsp. cream of tartar
⅛ tsp. salt
1 tsp. vanilla extract

Combine first 6 ingredients in top of a large double boiler; beat at low speed with a handheld electric mixer until blended. Place over boiling water, beating at high speed 7 minutes; remove from heat. Add vanilla, and beat to spreading consistency. Spread immediately over cooled cake. **Yield:** about 5½ cups.

EASY WEEKNIGHT *Favorites*

Short ingredients lists make these recipes convenient to prepare for a flavorful meal that's also healthy.

MENU FOR 4

Crispy Oven-Fried Catfish

Ranch Potatoes

Pecan Broccoli

Rosemary-Roasted Cherry Tomatoes

S'mores Sundaes

Menu Prep Plan

1 DAY AHEAD OR MORNING OF:

- Freeze ice-cream mixture for S'mores Sundaes.
- Cook bacon for potatoes; store in refrigerator.

1½ HOURS AHEAD:

- Prepare Ranch Potatoes; keep warm.
- While potatoes cook, prepare Crispy Oven-Fried Catfish.

45 MINUTES AHEAD:

- Prepare Rosemary-Roasted Cherry Tomatoes; bake 15 minutes in oven with catfish.
- Prepare Pecan Broccoli; keep warm.

LAST MINUTE:

- Transfer broccoli to serving dish.
- Arrange catfish on serving platter.

AFTER DINNER:

- Complete preparation of S'mores Sundaes.

Crispy Oven-Fried Catfish

Using a salt-free seasoning allows you to control the amount of sodium in this dish, while adding flavor at the same time. *(pictured on following page)*

Prep: 10 min. Chill: 20 min. Bake: 35 min.

1 cup low-fat buttermilk
4 (6-oz.) catfish fillets
2½ tsp. salt-free Creole seasoning (see note)
½ tsp. salt
3 cups cornflakes cereal, crushed
Vegetable cooking spray
Lemon wedges

Place 1 cup low-fat buttermilk in a large zip-top plastic freezer bag; add 4 (6-oz.) catfish fillets, turning to coat. Seal and chill 20 minutes, turning once.

Remove catfish fillets from buttermilk, discarding buttermilk. Sprinkle fillets evenly with 2½ tsp. salt-free Creole seasoning and ½ tsp. salt.

Place 3 cups crushed cornflakes in a shallow dish. Dredge catfish fillets in cornflakes, pressing cornflakes gently onto each fillet. Place fillets on a rack coated with cooking spray in a roasting pan.

Bake catfish fillets at 425° for 30 to 35 minutes or until fish flakes with a fork. Serve fillets immediately with lemon wedges. **Yield:** 4 servings.

Note: For testing purposes only, we used The Spice Hunter Cajun Creole Seasoning Salt Free.

Crispy Oven-Fried Catfish (page 25), Rosemary-Roasted Cherry Tomatoes, Pecan Broccoli, Ranch Potatoes

Ranch Potatoes

It is possible to fit rich and creamy mashed potatoes into a healthful diet. Light butter and reduced-fat dressing keep this recipe lighter than traditional versions, without sacrificing flavor.

Prep: 10 min. Cook: 25 min.

1½ lb. Yukon gold potatoes (about 4 medium)
2 Tbsp. light butter
¼ tsp. salt
½ tsp. freshly ground pepper
⅓ cup reduced-fat Ranch dressing
2 turkey bacon slices, cooked and crumbled

Bring potatoes and water to cover to a boil in a large Dutch oven; boil 15 to 20 minutes or until tender. Drain; peel, if desired.

Beat potatoes at low speed with an electric mixer just until mashed. Add butter, salt, and pepper, beating until butter is melted. Gradually add dressing, beating just until smooth. Top with crumbled bacon; serve immediately. **Yield:** 4 servings.

Pecan Broccoli

Pecans contribute a heart-healthy crunch to this recipe.

Prep: 5 min. Cook: 15 min.

1 (12-oz.) package fresh broccoli florets
1 Tbsp. light butter
3 Tbsp. chopped pecans, toasted
¼ tsp. salt
¼ tsp. freshly ground pepper

Arrange broccoli in a steamer basket over boiling water. Cover and steam 4 minutes or until crisp-tender. Plunge broccoli into ice water to stop the cooking process; drain.

Heat butter in a large nonstick skillet over medium heat 2 to 3 minutes or until melted. Add broccoli, pecans, salt, and pepper. Cook, stirring gently, 2 to 3 minutes or until thoroughly heated. **Yield:** 4 servings.

quick & easy

Rosemary-Roasted Cherry Tomatoes

Fragrant rosemary boosts the flavor of these juicy tomatoes. If you can't find cherry tomatoes, substitute winter tomatoes such as Roma.

Prep: 5 min. Bake: 15 min.

2 pints cherry tomatoes
1 tsp. olive oil
1½ tsp. chopped fresh rosemary
2 garlic cloves, minced
¼ tsp. salt
¼ tsp. freshly ground pepper
Vegetable cooking spray

Combine first 6 ingredients in a zip-top plastic freezer bag. Gently shake until tomatoes are well coated. Transfer to an aluminum foil-lined jelly-roll pan coated with cooking spray.

Bake at 425°, stirring occasionally, 15 minutes or until tomatoes begin to burst. **Yield:** 4 servings.

editor's favorite

S'mores Sundaes

Prep: 10 min. Freeze: 1 hr.

2 cups low-fat chocolate chunk ice cream, slightly softened (see note)
20 graham cracker sticks, crushed (see note)
¼ cup marshmallow crème
4 tsp. semisweet chocolate mini-morsels
8 whole graham cracker sticks

Stir together softened ice cream and crushed graham crackers in a small bowl. Freeze 1 hour or until firm.

Spoon ice-cream mixture into 4 bowls; top evenly with marshmallow crème and chocolate morsels. Serve each with 2 graham cracker sticks. **Yield:** 4 servings.

Note: For testing purposes only, we used Healthy Choice Chocolate Chocolate Chunk Premium Low Fat Ice Cream and Honey Maid Grahams Honey Sticks.

Cream of Curried Peanut Soup

AUTUMN *Feast*

Take dinner outside, and enjoy this harvest menu complete with bright pansies, pumpkins, and rustic-colored leaves.

MENU FOR 8

Cream of Curried Peanut Soup

Roast Turkey With Sage and Thyme

Baked Sweet-and-Savory Mashed Potatoes

Garlic Green Beans

Elegant Pumpkin-Walnut Layered Pie

Menu Prep Plan

3 DAYS AHEAD:
- Place turkey in refrigerator to thaw, if frozen.

2 DAYS AHEAD:
- Prepare Elegant Pumpkin-Walnut Layered Pie; chill.

1 DAY AHEAD:
- Prepare Cream of Curried Peanut Soup; chill.
- Chop onion, bell pepper, mushrooms, pecans, and green onion for dressing; chill.
- Trim green beans; chill.
- Cook and crumble bacon for mashed potatoes; chill.

4½ HOURS AHEAD:
- Prepare Roast Turkey With Sage and Thyme.

2½ HOURS AHEAD:
- Prepare Baked Sweet-and-Savory Mashed Potatoes; keep warm.

1 HOUR AHEAD:
- Prepare Garlic Green Beans; keep warm.
- Carve turkey.

LAST MINUTE:
- Reheat soup.
- Whip cream to garnish pumpkin pie; chill.

Cream of Curried Peanut Soup

Curry powder and peanut butter enhance this warm, creamy soup and offer an unusual Thai flavor. Make it a day ahead of time, and chill; reheat in the microwave or on the cooktop before serving.

Prep: 15 min. Cook: 35 min.

2 Tbsp. butter
1 small onion, minced
3 celery ribs, minced
1 garlic clove, minced
2 Tbsp. all-purpose flour
2 Tbsp. curry powder
⅛ to ¼ tsp. ground red pepper
3½ cups chicken broth
1 cup creamy peanut butter
2 cups half-and-half
Garnish: chopped peanuts

Melt butter in a large saucepan over medium heat; add onion and celery, and sauté 5 minutes. Add garlic; sauté 2 minutes. Stir in flour, curry powder, and red pepper until smooth; cook, stirring constantly, 1 minute. Stir in broth, and bring to a boil; reduce heat to low, and simmer 20 minutes.

Stir in peanut butter and half-and-half; cook, stirring constantly, 3 to 4 minutes or until thoroughly heated. Cool slightly.

Process mixture, in batches, in a food processor or blender until smooth. Serve immediately; garnish, if desired. **Yield:** 6 cups.

Roast Turkey With Sage and Thyme

editor's favorite

Roast Turkey With Sage and Thyme

Prep: 20 min. Bake: 2 hr., 30 min. Stand: 20 min.

1 (14-lb.) fresh or thawed frozen whole turkey
¼ cup butter, softened
½ tsp. salt
½ tsp. freshly ground pepper
¼ cup fresh sage leaves
4 fresh thyme sprigs
1 pear or apple, cut into eighths
2 celery ribs, cut into 2-inch pieces
1 large onion, quartered
2 large garlic cloves, peeled
Garnishes: flat-leaf parsley, pecans, pears, muscadines, fresh sage leaves, fresh thyme sprigs

Lightly grease broiler pan rack and broiler pan. Set aside.

Remove giblets and neck from turkey; discard. Rinse turkey with cold water; pat dry. Loosen skin from turkey breast without totally detaching skin. Stir together butter, salt, and pepper. Rub half of butter mixture evenly over turkey breast under skin. Carefully place sage leaves and thyme sprigs evenly on each side of breast under skin. Replace skin.

Divide pear, celery, onion, and garlic evenly between body cavity and neck cavity. Tuck neck skin under bird; tuck wing tips under neck skin to secure it to back. Place turkey, breast side up, on rack of prepared pan. Rub entire turkey evenly with remaining half of butter mixture.

Bake at 325° for 2 hours to 2 hours and 30 minutes or until a meat thermometer inserted into thigh registers 168° or desired doneness. Remove turkey from pan. Remove and discard pear, celery, onion, and garlic. Let stand 20 minutes before slicing. Garnish, if desired. **Yield:** 12 servings.

Baked Sweet-and-Savory Mashed Potatoes

Cook and crumble a few extra slices of bacon, and add to the top of the potatoes for a fancy finish. Substitute turkey bacon for a lighter touch.

Prep: 20 min. Cook: 35 min. Bake: 20 min.

3½ lb. baking potatoes, peeled and cut into 1-inch pieces
3 tsp. salt, divided
1 (29-oz.) can sweet potatoes in syrup, drained and mashed
1 (8-oz.) package ⅓-less-fat cream cheese, softened
6 bacon slices, cooked and crumbled
¾ cup light sour cream
⅔ cup chicken broth
½ tsp. freshly ground pepper

Bring potatoes, 1 tsp. salt, and water to cover to a boil in a Dutch oven; cook 30 minutes or until tender. Drain.

Return potatoes to Dutch oven. Add sweet potatoes and cream cheese; mash with a potato masher until smooth. Stir in bacon, next 3 ingredients, and remaining 2 tsp. salt. Spoon mixture into a lightly greased 11- x 7-inch baking dish. Bake, uncovered, at 350° for 20 minutes. **Yield:** 6 to 8 servings.

Garlic Green Beans

To trim fresh green beans, simply snap off the stem of each bean; or gather beans in small handfuls with the stems facing the same direction, and cut them off all at once with a sharp kitchen knife.

Prep: 10 min. Cook 15 min.

2 lb. fresh green beans, trimmed
3 Tbsp. butter
4 garlic cloves, pressed
1 tsp. lemon pepper
¼ tsp. salt
¼ cup chopped fresh parsley

Arrange green beans in a steamer basket over boiling water. Cover and steam 8 to 10 minutes or until crisp-tender; drain.

Melt butter in a Dutch oven over medium heat; add garlic, and sauté 1 minute. Add beans, lemon pepper, and salt; sauté 3 minutes. Toss with parsley. Serve immediately. **Yield:** 8 servings.

editor's favorite • make ahead

Elegant Pumpkin-Walnut Layered Pie

This pie received our Test Kitchens' highest rating because of its luscious flavor and easy preparation. Make it up to 2 days ahead, cover, and store in the refrigerator until ready to serve.

Prep: 20 min. Bake: 57 min.

1 (15-oz.) package refrigerated piecrusts, divided
1 large egg, lightly beaten
1¼ cups firmly packed light brown sugar, divided
1 cup walnuts, finely chopped and toasted
3 Tbsp. butter, softened
¼ tsp. vanilla extract
1 (16-oz.) can pumpkin
1 (8-oz.) package cream cheese, softened
2 large eggs
2 Tbsp. all-purpose flour
1 tsp. ground cinnamon
½ tsp. ground ginger
½ tsp. ground allspice
½ tsp. ground nutmeg
Whipped cream (optional)

Unroll 1 piecrust; cut out leaves from crust with a leaf-shaped cutter. Brush leaves with lightly beaten egg, and place on a baking sheet; set leaves aside.

Fit remaining piecrust into a 9-inch pieplate according to package directions; fold edges under, and crimp.

Bake leaves at 350° for 10 to 12 minutes or until golden; bake piecrust for 6 minutes or until lightly browned. Remove leaves and piecrust from oven; let cool completely. Increase oven temperature to 425°.

Combine ½ cup brown sugar, walnuts, butter, and vanilla; spread evenly on the bottom of baked piecrust.

Beat pumpkin, cream cheese, eggs, and remaining ¾ cup brown sugar at medium speed with an electric mixer. Add flour and next 4 ingredients, beating until blended. Spoon pumpkin mixture over walnut mixture in piecrust.

Bake at 425° for 15 minutes. Reduce temperature to 350°, and bake 30 more minutes or until set. Remove pie to a wire rack; slightly cool. Arrange leaves on top of pie. Serve warm or chilled with whipped cream, if desired. **Yield:** 10 servings.

Winter Waldorf Salad

FAMILY *Comfort Food*

The classic clove-studded ham entrée makes a spectacular centerpiece. To add more merriment to the holiday table, serve the Waldorf salad in martini glasses.

MENU FOR 8 TO 10

Winter Waldorf Salad

Peach Holiday Ham

Sweet Potato Casserole

Garlic-Tarragon Green Beans

Ground Pecan Torte

Menu Prep Plan

1 DAY AHEAD:
- Bake Ground Pecan Torte; store in refrigerator.

MORNING OF:
- Combine ingredients for Winter Waldorf Salad except walnuts; chill.
- Wash and trim green beans; chill.

3 HOURS AHEAD:
- Prepare Peach Holiday Ham.
- Cook sweet potatoes; assemble casserole.

1 HOUR AHEAD:
- Bake Sweet Potato Casserole; keep warm.
- Carve ham; keep warm.
- Prepare Garlic-Tarragon Green Beans; keep warm.

LAST MINUTE:
- Add walnuts to Winter Waldorf Salad.

Winter Waldorf Salad

If you'd like to offer this as an appetizer salad, serve it in decorative glasses and add crunchy breadsticks to garnish.

Prep: 25 min. Chill: 1 hr.

¾ cup mayonnaise
¾ cup sour cream
⅓ cup honey
1 Tbsp. grated fresh lemon rind
1½ Tbsp. fresh lemon juice
¾ tsp. ground ginger
3 large Granny Smith apples, chopped
3 large Red Delicious apples, chopped
3 large Golden Delicious apples, chopped
1½ cups diced celery
1½ cups seedless red grapes, halved
½ cup raisins*
1 to 1¼ cups chopped walnuts, toasted
Garnishes: pomegranate seeds, breadsticks

Whisk together first 6 ingredients in large bowl. Stir in Granny Smith apples and next 5 ingredients. Cover and chill 1 hour.

Stir in walnuts just before serving. Garnish, if desired. **Yield:** 12 servings.

*½ cup dried cranberries may be substituted for raisins.

Peach Holiday Ham

Prep: 25 min. Bake: 1 hr., 30 min. Stand: 10 min.

1 (8-lb.) smoked fully cooked ham
Whole cloves
1 cup peach preserves
1 cup peach nectar
3 Tbsp. coarse-grained mustard
¼ tsp. ground cloves

Remove skin and excess fat from ham. Score fat on ham in a diamond pattern; insert clovves in center of diamonds. Place ham, fat side up, in a heavy-duty aluminum foil-lined roasting pan.

Stir together peach preserves and next 3 ingredients; pour mixture evenly over ham.

Bake at 325° for 1½ hours or until a meat thermometer inserted in ham registers 140°, basting every 20 minutes. Shield with foil after 30 minutes to prevent excess browning. Let stand 10 minutes before slicing. **Yield:** 8 to 10 servings.

Sweet Potato Casserole

This golden-baked favorite is sure to please your holiday guests. Make two recipes for a larger crowd.

Prep: 20 min. Cook: 40 min. Bake: 35 min.

8 medium-size sweet potatoes (6 lb.)
1 cup milk
¼ cup butter
3 Tbsp. sugar
1 tsp. vanilla extract
1 Tbsp. orange juice
¼ tsp. ground cinnamon
¼ tsp. ground nutmeg
¼ tsp. salt
1 (10.5-oz.) package miniature marshmallows

Bring sweet potatoes and water to cover to a boil, and cook 20 to 30 minutes or until tender; drain. Peel potatoes, and place in a mixing bowl.

Peach Holiday Ham

Heat milk and next 3 ingredients in a saucepan over medium heat, stirring until butter melts and sugar dissolves. (Do not boil.) Stir in orange juice, spices, and salt.

Beat potatoes at medium speed with an electric mixer until mashed. Add milk mixture, beating until smooth. Spoon half of mashed sweet potatoes into a lightly greased 13- x 9-inch baking dish; top evenly with half of marshmallows. Spread remaining mashed potatoes over marshmallows.

Bake, uncovered, at 350° for 25 minutes. Top with remaining half of marshmallows, and bake 8 to 10 more minutes or until marshmallows are golden. **Yield:** 8 to 10 servings.

Garlic-Tarragon Green Beans

Prep: 20 min. Cook: 15 min.

2 qt. water
2 Tbsp. salt
2 lb. thin fresh green beans
2 garlic cloves, minced
½ tsp. dried tarragon leaves
2 Tbsp. olive oil
½ tsp. salt
½ tsp. freshly ground pepper

Bring 2 qt. water and 2 Tbsp. salt to a boil in a Dutch oven; add beans. Cook 6 minutes or until crisp-tender; drain. Plunge into ice water to stop the cooking process; drain.

Sauté garlic and tarragon in hot oil in Dutch oven over medium heat 2 to 3 minutes or until garlic is tender. (Do not brown garlic.) Add beans, salt, and pepper, and cook, stirring constantly, 2 minutes or until thoroughly heated. **Yield:** 10 to 12 servings.

FEATURED ATTRACTION

Use this garnishing idea to make your ham a spectacular centerpiece: Place the ham on a large serving tray; encircle with kale and an assortment of seasonal fruits. To make pastry leaves, unroll a refrigerated piecrust onto a lightly floured surface. Cut leaves from piecrust using leaf-shaped cutters. Mark leaf veins using the tip of a small paring knife. In a small bowl, whisk together 1 egg and 1 Tbsp. water; brush onto leaves. Place leaves on a parchment paper-lined baking sheet, and bake at 425° for 6 to 8 minutes or until golden.

Ground Pecan Torte

Prep: 25 min. Bake: 30 min. Cool: 35 min.

1 cup butter or margarine, softened
1 cup sugar
3 large eggs
3 cups pecan meal (see note)
1 Tbsp. grated fresh lemon rind
⅓ cup cake flour
Cream Cheese Filling
½ cup raspberry preserves

Beat butter and sugar at medium speed with an electric mixer until creamy. Add eggs, 1 at a time, beating just until blended after each addition; add in pecan meal and lemon rind, and beat at low speed until blended.

Add flour, and beat at low speed just until blended. Spread into 2 buttered and floured 9-inch round cake pans.

Bake at 350° for 25 to 30 minutes or until a wooden pick inserted in center comes out clean. Cool in pans on wire racks 5 minutes; remove from pans, and cool for 30 minutes.

Spread half of Cream Cheese Filling on top of 1 cake layer; top evenly with half of raspberry preserves. Top with remaining cake layer; repeat procedure with remaining Cream Cheese Filling and preserves. **Yield:** 8 to 10 servings.

Note: Commercially ground pecans have a very fine texture and are often sold as pecan meal. We found this to be more economical than grinding whole or halved pecans. To make your own pecan meal, place 2½ cups pecan halves in a food processor, and pulse about 45 seconds or until pecans are finely ground.

Cream Cheese Filling:

Prep: 5 min.

1 (8-oz.) package cream cheese, softened
½ cup sugar
1 tsp. vanilla extract

Beat cream cheese at medium speed with an electric mixer until creamy; gradually add sugar and vanilla, beating well. **Yield:** 1⅓ cups.

Marinated Cornish Hens, Broccoli-and-Cauliflower Gratin (page 38), Sweet Potatoes With Rosemary-Honey Vinaigrette (page 39)

CLASSIC CHRISTMAS *Dinner*

This mix-and-match menu makes preparing the Christmas feast easier than ever. Choose the recipes that suit your palate as well as your pocketbook.

MENU FOR 6

Marinated Cornish Hens or Marinated Turkey Breast

Cheesy Mashed Potatoes

Broccoli-and-Cauliflower Gratin

Sweet Potatoes With Rosemary-Honey Vinaigrette

Individual Fudge Cakes

Menu Prep Plan

2 DAYS AHEAD:

- Prepare marinade for Cornish hens or turkey breast; chill.
- Thaw Cornish hens or turkey breast in refrigerator, if frozen.

1 DAY AHEAD:

- Marinate Cornish hens or turkey breast in refrigerator.
- Shred cheeses for potatoes and gratin; chill.

6 HOURS AHEAD:

- Prepare Individual Fudge Cakes, but do not bake; chill.

4 HOURS AHEAD:

- Prepare turkey breast. (For Cornish hens, wait to prepare 1 hour ahead.)

2 HOURS AHEAD:

- Prepare Sweet Potatoes With Rosemary-Honey Vinaigrette.
- Prepare Cheesy Mashed Potatoes; keep warm.
- Prepare Broccoli-and-Cauliflower Gratin; keep warm.

1 HOUR AHEAD:

- Prepare Cornish hens.

LAST MINUTE:

- Reheat sweet potatoes.
- Carve turkey; arrange turkey or Cornish hens on platter.

DURING DINNER:

- Bake fudge cakes; sprinkle with powdered sugar.

make ahead

Marinated Cornish Hens

If your roasting pan won't fit under the broiler, transfer hen halves and roasting rack to an aluminum foil-lined jelly-roll pan.

Prep: 25 min. Cook: 6 min. Chill: 8 hr. Bake: 35 min. Broil: 10 min. Stand: 5 min.

2 celery ribs with tops, quartered
2 large garlic cloves, minced
1 small onion, quartered
½ cup lemon juice
½ cup white wine vinegar
2 Tbsp. dried Italian seasoning
1 Tbsp. salt
2 tsp. freshly ground pepper
4 tsp. lite soy sauce
4 tsp. Worcestershire sauce
⅓ cup vegetable oil
4 (1¼-lb.) frozen Cornish hens, thawed

Bring first 10 ingredients to a boil over medium-high heat in a small saucepan, stirring occasionally; reduce heat to medium, and simmer, stirring often, 2 minutes. Remove from heat; cool completely. Stir in oil (see note).

Rinse hens under cold water, and pat dry. Using kitchen shears, cut down each side of backbone; remove and discard backbone. Cut down middle of breastbone to form two halves. Place hen halves in a large zip-top plastic freezer bag or shallow dish; add lemon juice mixture. Cover or seal, and chill, turning occasionally, 8 hours.

Remove hen halves from marinade, discarding marinade. Place halves, breast sides up, on a lightly greased rack in an aluminum foil-lined roasting pan.

Bake at 375° for 30 to 35 minutes or until meat thermometer inserted in thickest portion of breast registers 165°. Broil 5 inches from heat 5 to 10 minutes or until hens are browned. Remove from oven; cover with foil, and let stand 5 minutes. **Yield:** 6 to 8 servings.

Marinated Turkey Breast: Prepare Marinated Cornish Hens recipe on page 37 as directed, substituting 1 (6-lb.) bone-in turkey breast for Cornish hens (see note). Marinate turkey breast in a large dish or extra-large 2-gallon zip-top plastic freezer bag. Cover or seal, and chill 8 hours, turning occasionally. Remove turkey from marinade, reserving marinade. Place turkey in an aluminum foil-lined roasting pan. Bring reserved marinade to a boil in a small saucepan over medium heat; boil 3 minutes. Remove from heat. Bake at 325° for 2½ to 3 hours or until meat thermometer inserted into thickest portion registers 165°, brushing occasionally with reserved cooked marinade. Remove from oven; cover with aluminum foil, and let stand 15 minutes before serving. Yield: 12 servings.

Note: Marinade may be prepared and refrigerated up to 2 days ahead. Our Foods staff tested Marinated Turkey Breasts with both a fresh and frozen turkey. To our surprise, we liked the frozen one better. Shop for specials on fresh or frozen whole turkeys or turkey breasts.

Cheesy Mashed Potatoes

Prep: 15 min. Cook: 30 min.

2 lb. russet potatoes, peeled and cut into chunks
¼ cup butter, melted
⅔ cup room-temperature half-and-half
¼ tsp. salt
¼ tsp. freshly ground pepper
1 (10-oz.) block sharp Cheddar cheese, shredded*

Bring potatoes and salted water to cover to a boil in a large saucepan over medium-high heat; reduce heat to medium-low, and cook 15 to 20 minutes or until tender. Drain and return to saucepan.

Mash potatoes; stir in melted butter until blended. Stir in half-and-half, salt, and pepper. Add cheese, and stir until cheese melts. Spoon mixture into 6 (8-oz.) ramekins or a 2-qt. baking dish. Serve immediately. **Yield:** 4 to 6 servings.

*2 (5.2-oz.) packages garlic-and-herb spreadable cheese, cut into pieces, may be substituted.

Broccoli-and-Cauliflower Gratin

(pictured on page 36)

Prep: 15 min. Bake: 20 min.

2 (12-oz.) packages fresh broccoli and cauliflower florets (see note)
1 cup (4 oz.) shredded 2% reduced-fat Cheddar cheese
1 cup shredded Parmesan cheese
¾ cup light mayonnaise
¾ cup light sour cream
⅓ cup sliced green onions
2 Tbsp. Dijon mustard
¼ tsp. ground red pepper
3 Tbsp. Italian-seasoned breadcrumbs

Pierce floret packages multiple times with a fork. Microwave at HIGH 5 minutes or until vegetables are crisp-tender. Carefully remove florets from packages, and arrange in a lightly greased 2-qt. baking dish.

Stir together Cheddar cheese and next 6 ingredients. Spoon evenly over florets. Sprinkle with breadcrumbs. Bake at 375° for 20 minutes or until golden. **Yield:** 6 to 8 servings.

Note: For testing purposes only, we used Mann's Broccoli & Cauliflower.

WHETHER YOUR FAMILY'S *holiday meal* IS FANCY WITH HEIRLOOM CRYSTAL OR A MORE CASUAL AFFAIR USING EVERYDAY LINENS, REMEMBER THAT THE IMPORTANT FACTOR IS THE *precious time* YOU SPEND TOGETHER.

Sweet Potatoes With Rosemary-Honey Vinaigrette

(pictured on page 36)

Prep: 20 min. Bake: 30 min.

Vegetable cooking spray
8 cups peeled, cubed sweet potato (about 3 large)
4 Tbsp. olive oil, divided
⅓ cup honey
¼ cup white wine vinegar
3 garlic cloves, minced
2 Tbsp. chopped fresh rosemary
1¼ tsp. salt
¾ tsp. freshly ground pepper

Line a 15- x 10-inch jelly-roll pan with aluminum foil. Coat foil evenly with cooking spray.

Place cubed sweet potatoes in prepared pan. Drizzle evenly with 2 Tbsp. oil, stirring to coat.

Bake at 450° for 30 minutes or until tender, stirring after 15 minutes. Place sweet potatoes in a serving bowl.

Whisk together honey, white wine vinegar, minced garlic, rosemary, salt, pepper, and remaining 2 Tbsp. oil in a small bowl. Pour over sweet potatoes; toss well. Cool slightly (see note). Serve with a slotted spoon. **Yield:** 6 servings.

Note: Serve this festive sweet potato dish warm or at room temperature.

NAPKIN ACCENTS

Add a casual touch of color to the holiday table by tying napkins with lengths of bright ribbon or encircling them with rings made from sprigs of rosemary. For a dressed-up look, use jeweled or embellished napkin rings. Personalize the place setting by writing guests' names on magnolia leaves using a metallic pen, and tucking leaves under the napkin rings.

Individual Fudge Cake

freezer friendly • make ahead

Individual Fudge Cakes

Prep: 15 min. Bake: 20 min. Cool: 10 min.

1 Tbsp. instant espresso powder
¼ cup hot water
1 cup semisweet chocolate morsels
1 (19.5-oz.) package fudge brownie mix (see note)
6 Tbsp. butter, melted and slightly cooled
¾ cup egg substitute
Unsweetened cocoa
12 bite-size caramel-filled chocolate nuggets (see note)
Powdered sugar
Garnish: fresh mint sprigs

Combine instant espresso powder and ¼ cup hot water, stirring until dissolved; set aside.

Microwave chocolate morsels in a small glass bowl at HIGH 1 minute; stir until smooth.

Combine brownie mix, espresso, melted chocolate, melted butter, and egg substitute in a large bowl, beating with a wooden spoon until well blended.

Grease 12 muffin pan cups generously, and dust with unsweetened cocoa. Spoon 2 rounded Tbsp. batter into each prepared muffin cup. Top batter with 1 chocolate nugget. Spoon remaining batter evenly over chocolate nuggets.

Bake at 350° for 18 to 20 minutes or until cakes are puffed and centers are almost set. Let cool in pans 5 to 10 minutes. Carefully remove from pans, and transfer to serving plates. Sprinkle with powdered sugar, and garnish, if desired. Serve immediately. **Yield:** 12 cakes.

Note: For testing purposes only, we used Pillsbury Brownie Classics Traditional Fudge Brownie Mix and Nestlé Signatures Creamy Caramel Treasures.

Make-Ahead Note: Prepare batter and fill muffin pans as directed. Cover and chill filled muffin pans up to 6 hours. Uncover and bake at 350° for 30 to 35 minutes or until cakes are puffed and centers are almost set. Proceed with recipe as directed.

Individual Fudge Cakes With Coffee Frosting: Prepare and bake cakes as directed, increasing bake time to 20 to 22 minutes or just until set. Cool in pans on wire racks 5 minutes. Remove from pans, and cool completely. Frost with Coffee Frosting. Top with toasted chopped pecans, if desired.

Coffee Frosting:

Prep: 10 min.

2 tsp. instant espresso powder
2 tsp. hot water
½ cup butter, softened
2 cups powdered sugar

Combine instant espresso powder and 2 tsp. hot water, stirring until dissolved.

Beat butter at medium speed with an electric mixer until creamy; gradually add powdered sugar, beating well. Add espresso, beating until smooth. **Yield:** about 1 cup.

Make-Ahead Note: Cool cakes completely; freeze unfrosted up to 1 month. Let stand, covered, at room temperature 3 hours or until thawed. For Individual Fudge Cakes With Coffee Frosting, frost as directed. To serve Individual Fudge Cakes, microwave each serving at MEDIUM-LOW (40% power) 20 seconds or until cake is heated and center is bubbly.

INDIVIDUAL FUDGE CAKES

• To make Individual Fudge Cakes, generously grease 12 muffin pan cups and dust with unsweetened cocoa.

• Spoon 2 rounded Tbsp. batter into prepared muffin cups. Top with chocolate nuggets.

• Spoon remaining batter evenly over candy, and bake as directed.

• For a less formal presentation, slather Coffee Frosting on Individual Fudge Cakes after they have cooled.

Sugar-and-Spice-Cured Turkey, gravy, Fresh Cranberry Sauce (page 44)

THANKSGIVING WITH ALL THE *Trimmings*

This harvest menu is complete with all the traditional favorites: roasted turkey and dressing with gravy, buttery mashed potatoes, and chunky cranberry sauce. Just add your favorite dessert.

MENU FOR 8

Sugar-and-Spice-Cured Turkey

Crabmeat-and-Oyster Dressing

Fresh Cranberry Sauce

Creamy Mashed Potatoes

Honey-Orange-Glazed Acorn Squash

Roasted Brussels Sprouts With Brown Butter and Almonds

assorted dinner rolls

Menu Prep Plan

4 DAYS AHEAD:
- Thaw turkey in refrigerator, if frozen.

1 DAY AHEAD:
- Rub brown sugar mixture over turkey; cover and chill.
- Prepare cranberry sauce; chill.

4 HOURS AHEAD:
- Bake turkey.
- Prepare Brussels sprouts.

1½ TO 2 HOURS AHEAD:
- Prepare mashed potatoes, acorn squash, and dressing; keep warm.

30 MINUTES AHEAD:
- Prepare gravy for turkey; carve turkey.

LAST MINUTE:
- Reheat mashed potatoes in microwave.
- Reheat Brussels sprouts in microwave.
- Transfer acorn squash to serving platter.
- Heat bread; arrange in bread basket.
- Transfer cranberry sauce to serving dish.

make ahead

Sugar-and-Spice-Cured Turkey

Prep: 10 min. **Chill:** 8 hr. **Bake:** 3 hr. **Stand:** 15 min. **Cook:** 5 min.

1 (12-lb.) whole turkey
¼ cup firmly packed light brown sugar
2 Tbsp. kosher or coarse-grain sea salt
2 tsp. Caribbean jerk seasoning
1 tsp. onion powder
½ tsp. garlic powder
1 large onion, quartered
2 (14-oz.) cans low-sodium fat-free chicken broth
3 Tbsp. all-purpose flour
Garnishes: fresh basil sprigs, pears, Swiss chard leaves

Remove giblets and neck; rinse turkey with cold water. Pat dry. Tie legs together with string; tuck wing tips under. Combine brown sugar and next 4 ingredients. Rub evenly over outside of turkey. Cover with plastic wrap; chill 8 hours.

Place turkey on a rack in a roasting pan, breast side up. Arrange onion quarters around turkey. Pour 2 cans broth in bottom of pan.

Bake, loosely covered with aluminum foil, at 325° for 1½ hours. Uncover and bake 1 to 1½ more hours or until a meat thermometer registers 170°, basting with pan juices the last 30 minutes. (Cover with foil to prevent excessive browning, if necessary.) Remove and discard onion; reserve pan drippings. Let turkey stand 15 minutes before carving.

Place 2 cups pan drippings in a saucepan over medium heat. Whisk in flour, and cook, whisking constantly, 5 minutes or until thickened. Serve gravy with turkey. Garnish, if desired. **Yield:** 8 to 10 servings.

Crabmeat-and-Oyster Dressing

Crabmeat-and-Oyster Dressing

Oyster dressing is a classic Southern holiday dish. Fresh vegetables, rice, and crabmeat enhance this version.

Prep: 25 min. Cook: 25 min.

1 (6.2-oz.) package long-grain and wild rice mix
¼ cup butter
1 medium onion, chopped
½ medium-size green bell pepper, chopped
1 cup chopped fresh mushrooms
1 lb. fresh crabmeat, drained, picked, and flaked
1 (12-oz.) container fresh oysters, drained
1 (10¾-oz.) can cream of celery soup
1 cup chopped pecans, toasted
½ cup Italian-seasoned breadcrumbs
1 green onion, chopped
¼ tsp. salt
¼ tsp. freshly ground black pepper
⅛ tsp. ground red pepper

Prepare rice mix according to package directions. Set rice aside.

Melt butter in a large nonstick skillet over medium heat; add onion, bell pepper, and mushrooms, and sauté 8 minutes or until tender.

Stir in crabmeat and oysters, and cook 4 minutes. Stir in rice, soup, and remaining ingredients; cook, stirring occasionally, 5 to 10 minutes or until thoroughly heated. **Yield:** 8 servings.

Fresh Cranberry Sauce

Serve this sauce with turkey, or spoon it over cream cheese for an appetizer. (pictured on page 42)

Prep: 5 min. Cook: 15 min. Chill: 1 hr.

1 cup sugar
1 cup water
1 (12-oz.) package fresh cranberries
1 Tbsp. grated fresh orange rind
1 Tbsp. orange liqueur (see note)
¼ cup toasted chopped pecans or sliced almonds (optional)

Bring sugar and 1 cup water to a boil in a saucepan, stirring until sugar dissolves. Add cranberries, rind, and liqueur; return to a boil, reduce heat, and simmer 10 minutes. If desired, stir in toasted pecans. Cover and chill 1 hour or until firm. **Yield:** about 2 cups.

Note: For testing purposes only, we used Cointreau for orange liqueur.

make ahead

Creamy Mashed Potatoes

Prep: 10 min. Cook: 45 min.

5 lb. baking potatoes (about 5 large potatoes)
1 (8-oz.) package ⅓-less-fat cream cheese, softened
1½ cups half-and-half
1½ tsp. salt
½ tsp. freshly ground pepper
Pats of butter (optional)

Bring potatoes and cold water to cover to a boil in a large Dutch oven; boil 35 minutes or until tender. Drain; peel, if desired.

Mash potatoes and cream cheese with a potato masher until smooth or to desired consistency. Microwave half-and-half in a microwave-safe bowl at HIGH 1½ minutes. Stir into potatoes; stir in salt and pepper. Top with pats of butter, if desired, and let melt. Serve immediately. **Yield:** 8 to 10 servings.

Make-Ahead Note: These potatoes can be made up to 2 hours ahead. When ready to serve, microwave at HIGH 2 to 3 minutes, stirring at 1-minute intervals or until thoroughly heated.

Honey-Orange-Glazed Acorn Squash

Prep: 15 min. Cook: 5 min. Bake: 50 min.

½ cup butter, softened
2 Tbsp. brown sugar
2 Tbsp. honey
4 medium acorn squash
2 tsp. grated fresh orange rind
¼ cup fresh orange juice

Stir together butter, brown sugar, and honey until smooth.

Cut squash in half. Scoop out seeds and membrane. Arrange squash, cut sides up, on a roasting pan. Spread half of butter mixture evenly on cut sides of squash.

Bake squash, uncovered, at 400° for 30 minutes.

Stir together remaining butter mixture, grated orange rind, and orange juice in a small saucepan. Cook over low heat until butter melts, and brush half of orange-butter mixture evenly on squash.

Bake, uncovered, 20 more minutes or until squash is tender and golden, basting occasionally with remaining orange-butter mixture.

Carefully transfer to a large serving platter; drizzle with any remaining orange-butter mixture. **Yield:** 8 servings.

make ahead

Roasted Brussels Sprouts With Brown Butter and Almonds

Skip the green beans this year, and opt for another green vegetable: Brussels sprouts. Our staff agreed that this dish by far surpassed even their favorite green bean recipes. We hope you'll try it, too!

Prep: 15 min. Bake: 20 min. Cook: 5 min.

2½ lb. fresh Brussels sprouts (about 6 cups)*
3 Tbsp. olive oil
1 (2-oz.) package slivered almonds (⅓ cup)
3 Tbsp. butter
2 garlic cloves, minced
¼ tsp. salt
¼ tsp. freshly ground pepper

Wash Brussels sprouts thoroughly; remove discolored leaves. Cut off stem ends, and discard; cut in half. Toss Brussels sprouts with oil in a shallow roasting pan, coating well. Remove and discard any loose leaves.

Bake at 425° for 20 minutes. Transfer to a serving bowl, and keep warm.

Brown almonds in butter in a small skillet over medium heat, stirring often, just until golden brown. Add garlic, and cook 1 more minute; stir in salt and pepper. Pour garlic mixture over Brussels sprouts; toss gently. Serve immediately. **Yield:** 8 servings.

*4 (8-oz.) packages frozen Brussels sprouts, thawed, may be substituted for fresh Brussels sprouts.

Make-Ahead Note: Prepare recipe several hours before meal. To reheat, place in a microwave-safe dish; cover with heavy-duty plastic wrap. Microwave at HIGH 2 to 4 minutes or until thoroughly heated, stirring after 2 minutes.

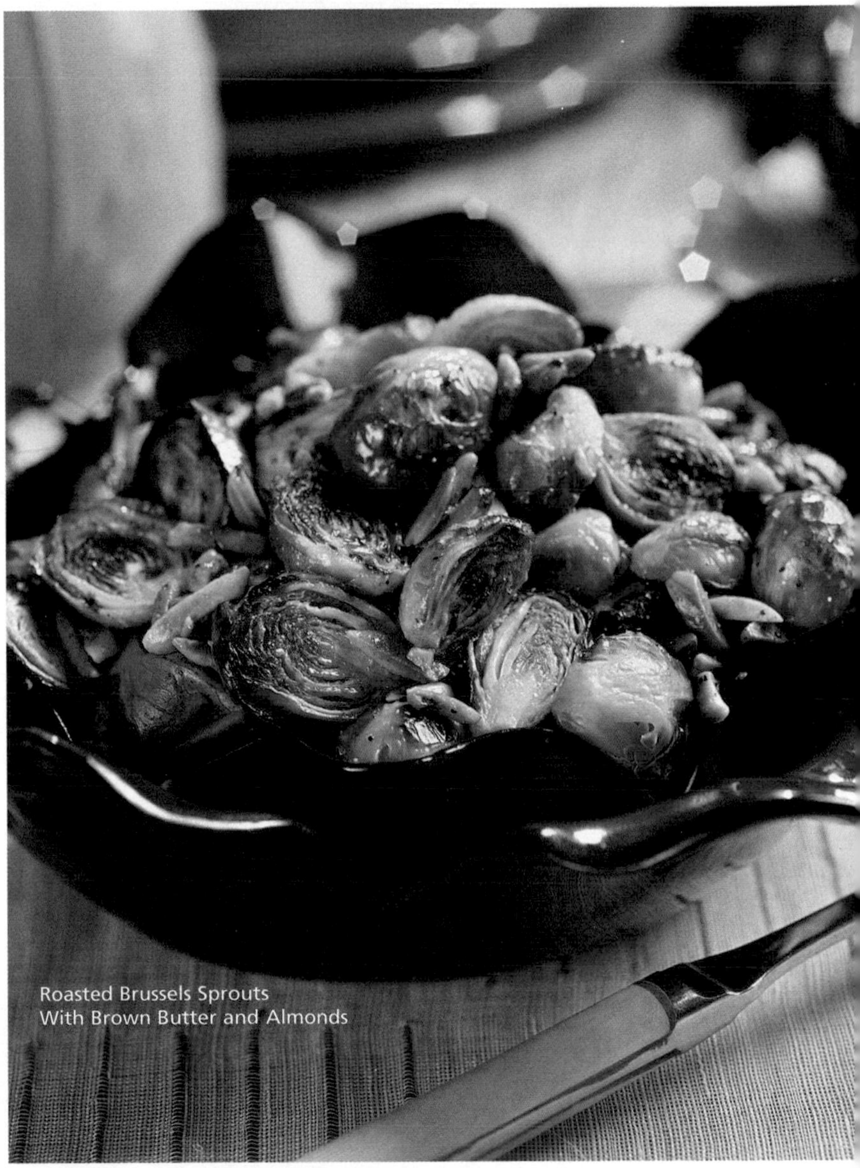

Roasted Brussels Sprouts With Brown Butter and Almonds

Citrus Blush Sunrises, Black Bean and Black-eyed Pea Salad (page 48)

HOLIDAY BRUNCH WITH *Southwestern Style*

The secret to this easy-to-serve casual menu is make-ahead recipes spiked with the robust flavors of the Southwest.

MENU FOR 6

Citrus Blush Sunrise

Black Bean and Black-eyed Pea Salad

Fresh Citrus-Mint Fruit Salad

Creamy Poblano Chicken With Cornbread Waffles

Coconut-Cream Cheese Pound Cake

Menu Prep Plan

1 DAY AHEAD:
- Cut fruit for salad; chill.
- Bake Coconut-Cream Cheese Pound Cake.
- Prepare Black Bean and Black-eyed Pea Salad; chill.
- Bake Cornbread Waffles; store in zip-top plastic freezer bag in refrigerator.
- Prepare Creamy Poblano Chicken; chill.

2 HOURS AHEAD:
- Complete preparation of fruit salad; chill.

30 MINUTES AHEAD:
- Combine orange juice and lemonade for Citrus Blush Sunrise; prepare rims of glasses.

LAST MINUTE:
- Reheat Creamy Poblano Chicken and Cornbread Waffles.
- Arrange Black Bean and Black-eyed Pea Salad in serving dish.
- Slice pound cake.
- Prepare Citrus Blush Sunrise.

quick & easy

Citrus Blush Sunrise

Prep: 10 min.

Lime juice
Colored sugar
1 (15¼-oz.) can crushed pineapple, undrained
3 cups orange juice
3 cups lemonade
4 tsp. grenadine
Garnish: fresh mint sprigs

Coat rims of glasses with lime juice; dip in colored sugar.

Spoon 2 Tbsp. pineapple into each 12-oz. glass; fill glasses with ice cubes. Stir together orange juice and lemonade; pour ¾ cup mixture into each glass. Slowly add ½ tsp. grenadine, forming a pink layer in bottom. Do not stir. Garnish, if desired, and serve immediately. **Yield:** 8 servings.

GREET EACH GUEST WITH A *twinkling glass* OF CITRUS BLUSH SUNRISE. YOU'RE ALL IN FOR A *wonderful time.*

Black Bean and Black-eyed Pea Salad

Black Bean and Black-eyed Pea Salad

Chili powder and cumin spice up this salad that doubles as an appetizer when served with tortilla chips.

Prep: 20 min. Chill: 30 min.

½ cup fresh lime juice (about 4 limes)
¼ cup olive oil
1 tsp. brown sugar
1 tsp. chili powder
1 tsp. grated fresh lime rind
½ to 1 tsp. salt
½ tsp. ground cumin
1 (15-oz.) can black beans, rinsed and drained
1 (15.5-oz.) can black-eyed peas, rinsed and drained
1½ cups frozen whole kernel corn, thawed
⅓ cup chopped fresh cilantro
½ small green bell pepper, chopped
Bibb lettuce
Garnish: Chile peppers

Whisk together first 7 ingredients in a large bowl. Add black beans and next 4 ingredients, tossing to coat. Cover and chill 30 minutes.

Arrange lettuce around salad. Garnish, if desired. **Yield:** 6 servings.

quick & easy

Fresh Citrus-Mint Fruit Salad

Prep: 15 min.

1 (8-oz.) can pineapple tidbits, drained
¼ cup coarsely chopped fresh strawberries
1 cup coarsely chopped cantaloupe
1 cup coarsely chopped honeydew
1 cup coarsely chopped mango
3 kiwifruit, peeled and chopped
3 Tbsp. chopped fresh mint
2 Tbsp. fresh lime juice

Combine all ingredients in a large bowl. Chill before serving. **Yield:** 3½ cups.

editor's favorite

Creamy Poblano Chicken With Cornbread Waffles

Prep: 20 min. Cook: 23 min.

3 Tbsp. butter or margarine
1 large sweet onion, chopped
2 poblano chile peppers, seeded and diced
3 garlic cloves, minced
8 skinned and boned chicken breast halves, cut into bite-size pieces
1 tsp. salt
½ tsp. freshly ground black pepper
1 (10¾-oz.) can cream of chicken and mushroom soup, undiluted
1 (8-oz.) container sour cream
1 (8-oz.) package shredded sharp Cheddar cheese
Cornbread Waffles

Melt butter in a Dutch oven. Add onion, chile pepper, and garlic; sauté 5 minutes. Add chicken, salt, and black pepper; cook, stirring often, 8 to 10 minutes or until chicken is done. Stir in soup and sour cream until smooth. Add cheese, and cook 7 to 8 minutes or until cheese is melted. Serve over Cornbread Waffles. **Yield:** 6 to 8 servings.

Cornbread Waffles:

Prep: 15 min. Bake: 10 min.

1½ cups yellow cornmeal
½ cup all-purpose flour
2 Tbsp. sugar
2½ tsp. baking powder
¾ tsp. salt
1 large egg
1½ cups frozen white shoepeg corn, thawed
1½ cups milk
¼ cup butter or margarine, melted

Stir together first 5 ingredients in a large bowl. Stir together egg and next 3 ingredients; add to cornmeal mixture, stirring just until dry ingredients are moistened.

Bake waffles in a preheated, oiled waffle iron just until crisp. **Yield:** 12 (4-inch) waffles.

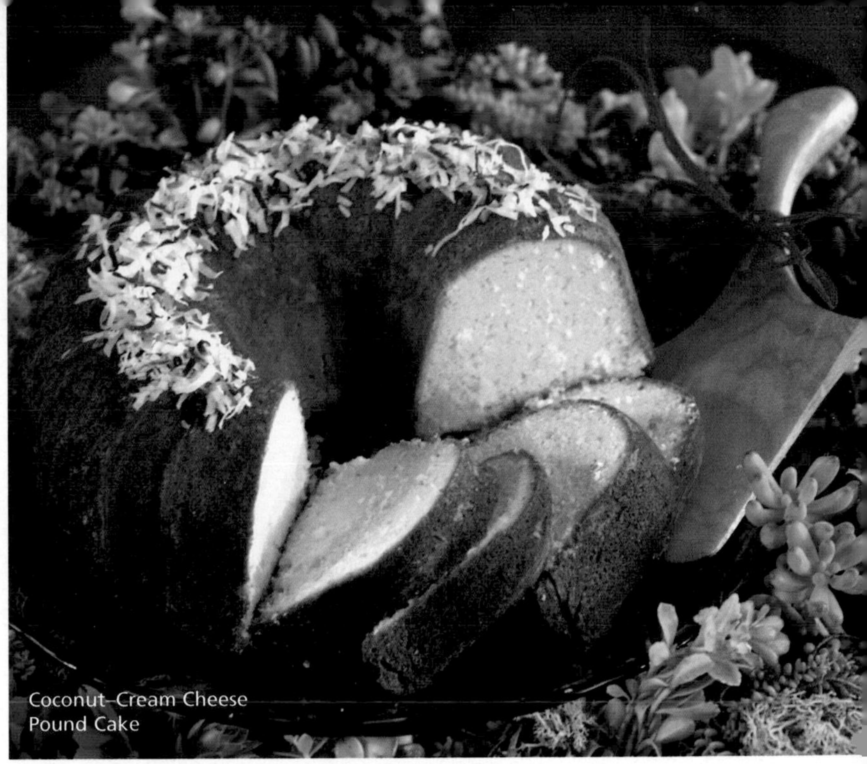
Coconut-Cream Cheese Pound Cake

Coconut-Cream Cheese Pound Cake

Look for frozen grated coconut in the freezer section of your supermarket.

Prep: 15 min. Bake: 1 hr., 30 min.

½ cup butter or margarine, softened
½ cup shortening
1 (8-oz.) package cream cheese, softened
3 cups sugar
6 large eggs
3 cups all-purpose flour
¼ tsp. baking soda
¼ tsp. salt
1 (6-oz.) package frozen grated fresh coconut, thawed
1 tsp. vanilla extract
1 tsp. coconut extract
Garnish: toasted coconut

Beat first 3 ingredients at medium speed of an electric mixer 2 minutes or until soft and creamy; gradually add sugar, beating at medium speed 5 to 7 minutes. Add eggs, one at a time, beating just until yellow disappears.

Combine flour, soda, and salt; add to butter mixture. Mix at low speed just until blended. Stir in coconut and flavorings. Pour batter into a greased and floured 10-inch Bundt or tube pan.

Bake at 325° for 1 hour and 30 minutes or until a wooden pick inserted in center comes out clean. Cool in pan on a wire rack 15 minutes. Remove from pan; cool completely on wire rack. Garnish, if desired. **Yield:** 16 to 18 servings.

Pork-Filled Biscuits With Cranberry Chutney Butter

SOUTHERN *Brunch*

A casual midmorning gathering is a terrific way to entertain. What's more, all of the recipes can be made at least a couple hours ahead.

MENU FOR 6

Pork-Filled Biscuits With Cranberry Chutney Butter

Shrimp and Grits

Cheese Buttons

Ambrosia

Milk Punch

Menu Prep Plan

2 DAYS AHEAD:

- Prepare chutney butter; chill.

1 DAY AHEAD:

- Prepare Milk Punch; chill.
- Peel and devein shrimp; chill.
- Chop onion and bacon, and shred cheese for grits; chill.
- Prepare Cheese Buttons; store in airtight container.
- Section oranges and grapefruit for Ambrosia.

5 HOURS AHEAD:

- Marinate pork tenderloin in refrigerator.
- Combine ingredients for Ambrosia except whipped cream; chill.

1 TO 2 HOURS AHEAD:

- Bake pork tenderloin.
- Prepare Shrimp and Grits.
- Bake biscuits.
- Carve pork, and assemble Pork-Filled Biscuits with Cranberry Chutney Butter.

LAST MINUTE:

- Whip cream for Ambrosia, and spoon Ambrosia into serving dish.
- Stir Milk Punch; pour into punch bowl.
- Spoon Shrimp and Grits into serving dish.
- Transfer Cheese Buttons to serving dish.

Pork-Filled Biscuits With Cranberry Chutney Butter

Prep: 30 min. Chill: 2 hr., 30 min. Cook: 10 min. Bake: 30 min. Stand: 10 min.

3 cups apple cider
1 cup water
1 Tbsp. salt
1 (1-lb.) pork tenderloin, trimmed
2 Tbsp. olive oil, divided
½ tsp. ground sage
½ tsp. freshly ground pepper
¼ tsp. salt
1 (26.4-oz.) package frozen Southern-style biscuits
Cranberry Chutney Butter (following page)
Garnish: fresh rosemary sprigs

Combine first 3 ingredients in a shallow dish or large zip-top plastic freezer bag; add pork. Cover or seal, and chill, turning occasionally, 2½ hours.

Remove pork from marinade, discarding marinade. Pat pork dry with a paper towel. Combine 1 Tbsp. olive oil, sage, pepper, and ¼ tsp. salt; rub evenly over pork.

Brown pork in remaining 1 Tbsp. olive oil in a nonstick skillet over medium-high heat. Place pork on the lightly greased rack of a foil-lined broiler pan.

Bake at 350° for 30 minutes or until a meat thermometer inserted into thickest portion registers 155°. Cover with aluminum foil, and allow to stand for 10 minutes or until temperature reaches 160°.

Bake biscuits according to package directions; cool and split in half.

Cut pork diagonally across the grain into 12 even slices. Place 1 pork slice on bottom half of each split biscuit. Top each slice with 2 tsp. Cranberry Chutney Butter and 1 biscuit top. Garnish, if desired. **Yield:** 6 servings.

Cranberry Chutney Butter:

This recipe can be made up to 2 days ahead. Bring it to room temperature, and give it a quick stir before serving.

Prep: 5 min.

½ cup butter, softened
¼ cup cranberry chutney*
Pinch of ground red pepper

Stir together all ingredients in a small bowl until blended. Serve at room temperature. **Yield:** ¾ cup.
*¼ cup whole-berry cranberry sauce may be substituted for cranberry chutney. For testing purposes only, we used Crosse & Blackwell Cranberry Chutney.

Shrimp and Grits

Shrimp and Grits

You can prepare this recipe up to two hours ahead. Add an extra 2 cups chicken broth to keep the grits from becoming too dry. We prefer to transfer the grits to a slow cooker and keep them warm over low heat until ready to serve.

Prep: 30 min. Cook: 35 min.

1 lb. unpeeled, medium-size raw shrimp, cooked*
3 bacon slices, chopped
1 medium onion, finely chopped
2 garlic cloves, minced
2 cups low-sodium chicken broth
1 cup water
1 cup whipping cream
½ tsp. salt
¼ tsp. ground red pepper
1 cup quick-cooking grits, uncooked
1 cup (4 oz.) shredded extra-sharp Cheddar cheese
Garnish: chopped fresh chives

Peel shrimp, and devein, if desired. Set aside.

Cook bacon in a 3½-qt. saucepan over medium heat until crisp. Drain bacon on paper towels, reserving 1 Tbsp. bacon drippings in saucepan. Crumble bacon.

Sauté onion in hot drippings over medium-high heat 5 minutes or until tender. Add garlic, and sauté 1 minute. Add chicken broth and next 4 ingredients; bring to a boil. Reduce heat to medium, and whisk in grits. (When you're done whisking, tap whisk on saucepan to remove excess grits.) Cook, stirring constantly, 7 to 8 minutes or until mixture is smooth. Stir in shrimp and cheese, and cook 1 to 2 minutes or just until shrimp turn pink. Sprinkle each serving evenly with bacon. Garnish, if desired. **Yield:** 6 servings.
*1 lb. frozen uncooked, unpeeled medium-size shrimp, thawed, may be substituted.

Cheese Buttons

If you use preshredded cheese, the wafers will have a more rounded shape. Shredding your own cheese produces wafers with crispy edges reminiscent of lace cookies.

Prep: 25 min. Bake: 10 min. per batch Stand: 2 min. per batch

1 (8-oz.) package shredded sharp Cheddar cheese*
1 cup all-purpose flour
½ cup butter, softened
⅛ tsp. salt
¼ tsp. ground red pepper

Combine all ingredients in a food processor; process until mixture forms a ball.

Shape dough into 1-inch balls; place 2 inches apart on parchment paper-lined baking sheets (see note).

Bake, in batches, at 400° for 8 to 10 minutes or until edges are golden. Let stand 2 minutes; remove to wire racks to cool. **Yield:** 3 dozen.

*1 (8-oz.) block sharp Cheddar cheese may be substituted. Cut cheese into pieces; shred in a food processor. Replace shredding disc with knife blade, and proceed as directed.

Make-Ahead Note: Freeze dough balls before baking; place frozen dough in zip-top plastic freezer bags, and seal. Store in freezer up to 1 month, if desired. Bake frozen dough balls on parchment paper-lined baking sheets at 400° for 15 to 17 minutes or until edges are golden.

Ambrosia

A fresh and delightful end to a holiday meal, Ambrosia makes a lovely statement when served in tall, pretty glasses that allow its many colors to show through.

Prep: 35 min. Chill: 2 hr.

6 large navel oranges
1 red grapefruit
2 (20-oz.) cans pineapple chunks in juice, drained, or 1 fresh pineapple, peeled, cored, and cut into chunks
1 cup frozen freshly grated coconut*
⅓ cup whole red maraschino cherries, stemmed and halved
2 Tbsp. powdered sugar, divided
1 cup whipping cream
Garnishes: orange rind curls, cherries

Peel and section oranges and grapefruit over a bowl, reserving juices.

Toss together reserved juices, orange and grapefruit sections, pineapple, coconut, ⅓ cup cherries, and 1 Tbsp. powdered sugar in a large bowl. Cover and chill 2 hours.

Beat whipping cream until foamy; gradually add remaining 1 Tbsp. powdered sugar, beating until soft peaks form. Serve fruit mixture with whipped cream. Garnish, if desired. **Yield:** 6 servings.

*1 cup sweetened flaked coconut may be substituted; omit 1 Tbsp. powdered sugar. For testing purposes only, we used Tropic Isle Fresh Frozen Coconut.

make ahead

Milk Punch

Prepare up to 1 day ahead; stir just before serving.

Prep: 10 min.

5 cups milk
1 cup sugar
1 cup whipping cream
1 cup bourbon
1 tsp. vanilla extract
½ tsp. ground cinnamon
Sweetened cocoa (optional)
Cinnamon sticks (optional)

Whisk together first 6 ingredients in a large pitcher until well combined. Cover and chill until ready to serve. Stir well, and pour into pitcher or punch bowl. Serve with sweetened cocoa and cinnamon sticks, if desired. **Yield:** 8 cups.

Ambrosia

Chocolate Cake With Truffle Filling (page 56),
Chocolate Reindeer (page 57)

FESTIVE *Ladies' Luncheon*

An elegant entrée that takes only five minutes of hands-on prep time sets the tone for a special seasonal get-together.

MENU FOR 8

Baked Salmon With Caribbean Fruit Salsa

Dill Mini-Muffins **green salad**

Peppermint Nog Punch

Chocolate Cake With Truffle Filling

Chocolate Reindeer

Menu Prep Plan

UP TO 1 MONTH AHEAD:
- Bake Dill Mini-Muffins; freeze in airtight container.

1 DAY AHEAD:
- Cut fruit and vegetables for Caribbean Fruit Salsa; chill.
- Bake chocolate cake; chill.
- Prepare Chocolate Reindeer; store in airtight container.
- Wash lettuce, and prepare desired green salad ingredients; chill in airtight plastic bags.

2½ HOURS AHEAD:
- Sprinkle salmon with seasoning and oil; chill 2 hours.
- Complete preparation of fruit salsa; chill 2 hours.

2½ HOURS AHEAD:
- Thaw Dill Mini-Muffins.

1 HOUR AHEAD:
- Combine eggnog, club soda, and ice cream for punch; chill.

30 MINUTES AHEAD:
- Bake salmon.

LAST MINUTE:
- Reheat muffins.
- Put punch in bowl; sprinkle with crushed candies.
- Arrange salmon and fruit salsa in serving dishes.
- Toss salad.

Baked Salmon With Caribbean Fruit Salsa

A whole salmon fillet is perfect for serving. If necessary, ask the butcher at your grocery store to remove the skin.

Prep: 5 min. Chill: 2 hr. Bake: 25 min.

1 (3-lb.) whole skinless salmon fillet
1 Tbsp. Caribbean jerk seasoning*
1½ Tbsp. olive oil
Caribbean Fruit Salsa
Garnish: lime wedges

Place salmon fillet in a roasting pan; sprinkle evenly on 1 side with jerk seasoning. Drizzle with oil. Cover and chill 2 hours.

Bake salmon at 350° for 20 to 25 minutes or until fish flakes with a fork. Serve with Caribbean Fruit Salsa. Garnish, if desired. **Yield:** 8 to 10 servings.

*Jamaican jerk seasoning may be substituted. Caribbean jerk seasoning has a hint of sweetness.

Caribbean Fruit Salsa:

This salsa is also great as an appetizer served with tortilla chips.

Prep: 20 min. Chill: 2 hr.

1 mango (about ½ lb.), peeled and diced*
1 papaya (about ½ lb.), peeled and diced*
1 medium-size red bell pepper, diced
1 medium-size green bell pepper, diced
1 cup diced fresh pineapple
1 small red onion, diced
3 Tbsp. chopped fresh cilantro
2 Tbsp. fresh lime juice
1 Tbsp. olive oil

Stir together all ingredients. Cover and chill at least 2 hours. **Yield:** 5 cups.

*May substitute 1 cup each diced, jarred mango and papaya.

make ahead

Dill Mini-Muffins

Baked muffins may be frozen in an airtight container up to 1 month.

Prep: 10 min. Bake: 25 min.

1 cup butter, softened
1 (8-oz.) container sour cream
2 cups self-rising flour
1 Tbsp. dill seed
2 Tbsp. dried parsley flakes
¼ tsp. onion powder

Beat softened butter at medium speed with an electric mixer until creamy; add sour cream, and beat mixture at low speed until blended.

Combine flour and next 3 ingredients. Stir flour mixture into butter mixture until blended. Spoon dough into greased miniature muffin pans, filling three-fourths full.

Bake at 375° for 22 to 25 minutes or until golden. **Yield:** about 3 dozen.

make ahead

Peppermint Nog Punch

Prep: 10 min.

1 qt. eggnog
½ gal. peppermint ice cream, softened
1 (1-liter) bottle club soda, chilled
Hard peppermint candies, crushed

Stir together first 3 ingredients in a punch bowl or large bowl. Sprinkle with peppermint candy, and serve immediately. **Yield:** about 16 cups.

Make-Ahead Note: Stir together first 2 ingredients; cover and store in refrigerator. Add club soda, and sprinkle with candy just before serving.

editor's favorite

Chocolate Cake With Truffle Filling

You'll need 3 (8-oz.) packages semisweet chocolate squares to make this rich, decadent dessert. (pictured on page 54)

Prep: 30 min. Cook: 10 min. Bake: 30 min. Chill: 30 min.

8 (1-oz.) semisweet chocolate squares
2½ cups milk
1 cup butter, softened
3 large eggs
2 tsp. vanilla extract
2⅔ cups all-purpose flour
2 cups sugar
1¼ tsp. baking soda
½ tsp. salt
Truffle Filling, divided (opposite page)
10 (1-oz.) semisweet chocolate squares, coarsely chopped
½ cup plus 2 Tbsp. whipping cream
1 to 2 (1-oz.) semisweet chocolate squares, finely grated

Stir together first 3 ingredients in a large heavy saucepan over low heat, and cook, stirring constantly, 8 to 10 minutes or until chocolate melts and mixture is smooth. Remove from heat, and let mixture cool slightly (about 10 minutes).

Whisk together eggs and vanilla in a large bowl. Gradually whisk in melted chocolate mixture until blended and smooth.

Combine flour and next 3 ingredients; whisk into chocolate mixture until blended and smooth.

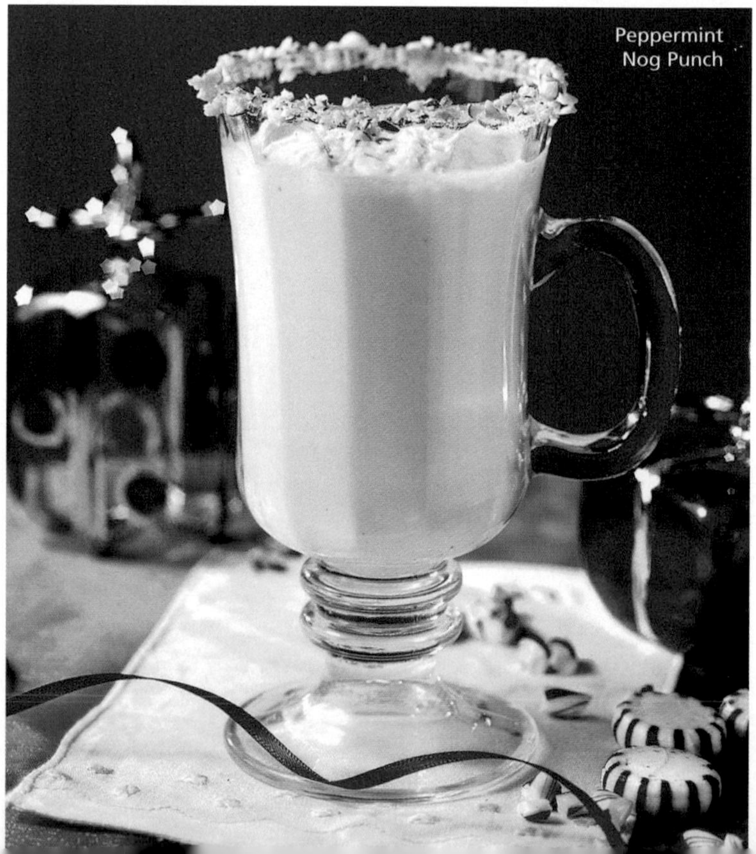

Peppermint Nog Punch

Pour batter into 3 greased and floured 9-inch round cakepans.

Bake at 325° for 25 to 30 minutes or until a wooden pick inserted in center comes out clean. Cool cake layers in pans on wire racks 10 minutes. Remove from pans, and let cool completely on wire racks.

Spread ½ cup plus 2 Tbsp. Truffle Filling evenly on top of 1 cake layer. Top with 1 cake layer; spread ½ cup plus 2 Tbsp. Truffle Filling evenly on top, reserving remaining ½ cup Truffle Filling. Top with remaining cake layer.

Microwave coarsely chopped semisweet chocolate squares and cream in a 2-qt. microwave-safe bowl at HIGH 1½ to 2 minutes, stirring after 1 minute and then every 30 seconds until chocolate melts and mixture is smooth and slightly thickened. Let cool slightly (about 15 minutes).

Spread warm semisweet chocolate mixture over top and sides of cake. Chill cake 30 minutes or until chocolate glaze is firm. Pipe border using a rosette tip around bottom of cake with remaining ½ cup Truffle Filling. Sprinkle finely grated semisweet chocolate evenly over top of cake. **Yield:** 12 servings.

Truffle Filling:

Prep: 10 min.

4 (1-oz.) semisweet chocolate squares
6 Tbsp. butter
½ cup whipping cream, divided
2½ cups powdered sugar, sifted

Microwave semisweet chocolate squares and 6 Tbsp. butter in a large microwave-safe bowl at HIGH 1½ to 2 minutes or until melted and smooth, stirring every 30 seconds. Stir in ¼ cup whipping cream. Stir in 2½ cups powdered sugar, adding remaining ¼ cup whipping cream, 1 Tbsp. at a time, if necessary, until mixture is smooth and creamy. Let mixture cool completely. **Yield:** 1¾ cups.

Chocolate Reindeer

(pictured on page 54)

Prep: 30 min. Freeze: 30 min. Stand: 15 min.

12 (2-oz.) chocolate bark coating squares, divided
4 plastic deer candy molds (2 deer shapes per mold; deer are about 5½ inches tall)
8 mini-pretzel twists
1 (2-oz.) white vanilla bark coating square
8 red cinnamon candies
Thin red satin ribbon

Microwave 6 (2-oz.) chocolate bark coating squares in a 4-cup glass measuring cup at HIGH 1½ minutes, stirring at 30-second intervals. Stir until smooth. Pour melted chocolate evenly into 4 deer shapes (in 2 candy molds), filling each just over top.

Level chocolate with a small spatula, scraping excess back into measuring cup. Gently tap candy molds on kitchen counter 2 or 3 times to remove air bubbles, if necessary. Freeze 20 minutes or until firm. Repeat procedure with remaining 6 (2-oz.) chocolate bark coating squares and 2 candy molds.

Break curved sides away from the center of each pretzel twist to form antlers. Dip tops of antlers into remaining melted chocolate bark in measuring cup, and place on a wax paper-lined baking sheet; freeze 10 minutes or until firm.

Invert chocolate deer from molds onto wax paper; carefully trim any rough edges around bottom flat sides with a paring knife, if necessary.

Microwave vanilla bark coating square in a small glass measuring cup at HIGH 1 minute, stirring after 30 seconds. Stir until smooth. Dip a small wooden pick into melted vanilla bark; dot eyes onto reindeer.

Reheat chocolate in measuring cup in microwave at HIGH in 15-second intervals, stirring until smooth, if necessary. Dip a small wooden pick into melted chocolate bark. Dot melted chocolate bark onto head of 1 deer; attach 1 red cinnamon candy for nose, holding candy in place until adhered. Repeat procedure with remaining candies and remaining deer. Dip bottom of 1 set of antlers into melted chocolate bark, and attach to forehead of 1 deer, holding in place until adhered. Repeat procedure with remaining antlers.

Let reindeer stand 15 minutes on wax paper before handling. Tie ribbon around neck of each reindeer. **Yield:** 8 reindeer.

CHOCOLATE REINDEER TIPS

- Try to hold the outside edges of the reindeer, using just a few fingers, to prevent getting prints on the decorative side.
- To stand the reindeer, lean the flat side against a cake plate or decorative item.
- Wrap individually in cellophane, and give as party favors.
- Deer candy molds are available at www.cakeartpartystore.com or from Cake Art in Tucker, GA, (770) 493-1305.

Bourbon-Lime Spritzers

COCKTAILS AT *Five*

These signature drinks and satisying nibbles impart a hearty dose of holiday cheer. Double or triple the beverage recipes as needed for your crowd.

MENU FOR 12

Bourbon-Lime Spritzers
Champagne and Cranberries
Sour Apple Martinis
Chocolate Martinis
Cape Codder Punch
Sausage-Stuffed Mushrooms
Bacon-Wrapped Water Chestnuts
Buttery Blue Cheese-and-Walnut Spread
Asparagus With Tomato-Basil Dip

Menu Prep Plan

1 DAY AHEAD:

- Prepare Tomato-Basil Dip; chill.
- Chill Champagne and ginger ale. Prepare ice cubes for spritzer.
- Prepare spread; chill.
- Prepare mushrooms, but do not bake; chill.
- Cook asparagus; chill.

2 HOURS AHEAD:

- Prepare punch up to ginger ale, and prepare garnish; chill.
- Hollow out bread loaf. Bring spread to room temperature.
- Soak apple and pear slices in pineapple juice, if desired.
- Wrap chestnuts with bacon.

1 HOUR AHEAD:

- Chill martini glasses; prepare rims of martini glasses.
- Complete preparation of water chestnuts; bake and keep warm.
- Bake mushrooms; transfer to a serving platter and keep warm.

LAST MINUTE:

- Arrange asparagus dip in serving dish.
- Spoon spread into bread shell.
- Arrange fruit and baguette slices around bread loaf.
- Stir ginger ale into punch.
- Prepare martinis, spritzer, and Champagne beverages.

quick & easy

Bourbon-Lime Spritzers

For a nonalcoholic version, omit bourbon and proceed as directed.

Prep: 5 min.

1 (12-oz.) can frozen limeade concentrate, thawed
1 cup bourbon
1 (2-liter) bottle ginger ale, chilled
Lime Ice Cubes
Garnish: lime wedges

Stir together limeade concentrate and bourbon in a large bowl or pitcher, stirring well. Stir in ginger ale. Add Lime Ice Cubes to spritzer in bowl, or serve spritzer over Lime Ice Cubes in individual glasses and garnish, if desired. **Yield:** about 11 cups.

Lime Ice Cubes: Place 2 thin lime rind curls in each section of ice cube trays; add water, and freeze until firm.

SPRITZER TIPS

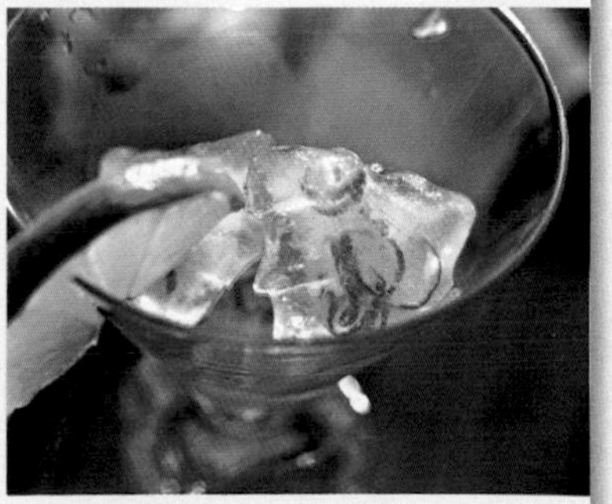

Whether making ahead or serving immediately, you can retain the most bubbles for your spritzers by first stirring together noncarbonated ingredients. Just before serving, stir in any carbonated soda or soft drinks. They'll be just right to tickle your nose—and your fancy!

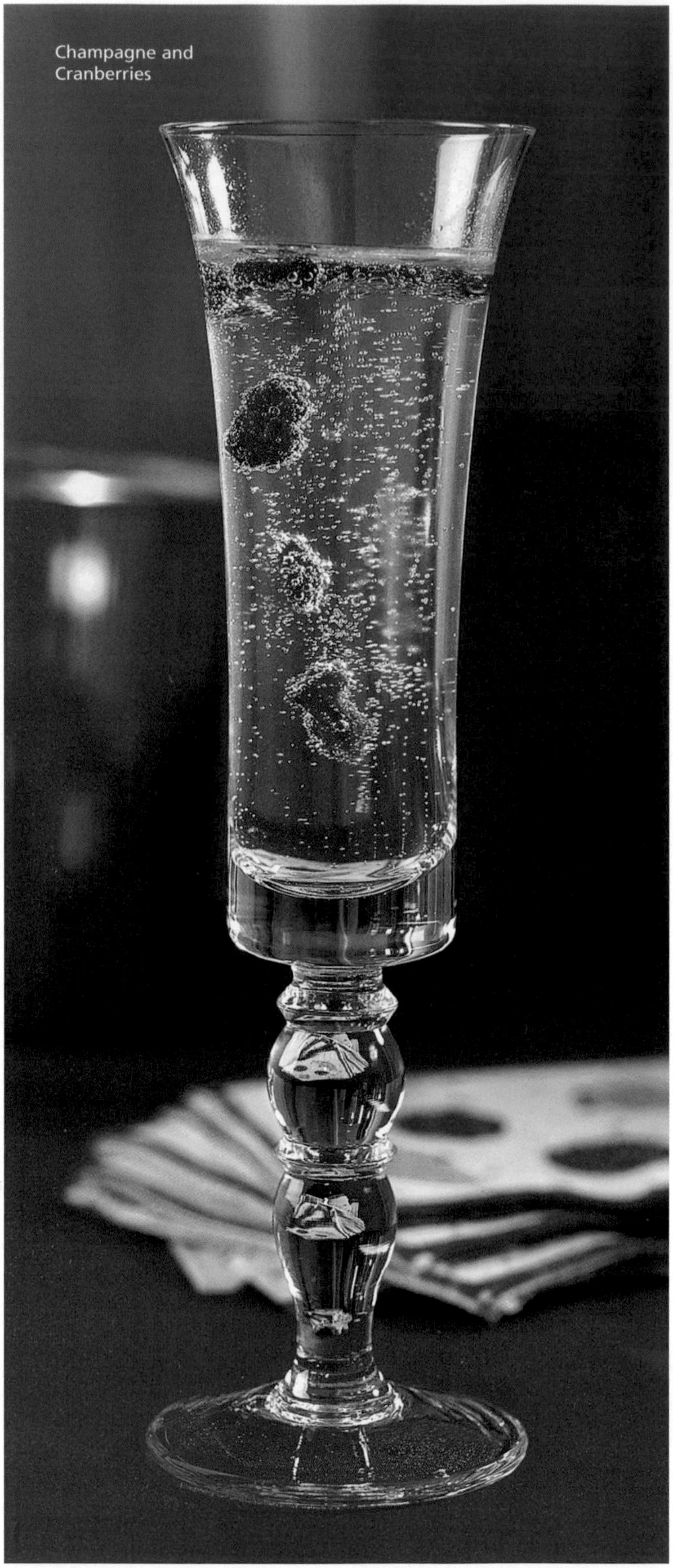

Champagne and Cranberries

Champagne and Cranberries

Prep: 5 min.

6 dried cranberries
¾ cup Champagne or sparkling wine, chilled

Place cranberries in Champagne flute. Pour Champagne over berries. Serve immediately. **Yield:** 1 serving.

quick & easy

Sour Apple Martinis

Prep: 10 min.

4 very thin Granny Smith apple wedges
Cinnamon sugar
¾ cup vodka
¾ cup sour apple Schnapps
Crushed ice cubes

Rub rims of chilled martini glasses with apple slices. Place cinnamon sugar in a saucer; spin rim of each glass in cinnamon sugar. Attach one apple slice on rim of each glass.

Stir together vodka and Schnapps. Fill half of cocktail shaker with ice. Add half of vodka mixture, cover with lid, and shake 10 seconds or until thoroughly chilled. Strain into chilled glasses. Repeat with remaining vodka mixture. Serve immediately. **Yield:** 4 servings.

quick & easy

Chocolate Martinis

Prep: 10 min.

⅓ cup chocolate liqueur
⅓ cup dark cream of cocoa
⅔ cup half-and-half
¼ cup vodka
Crushed ice cubes

Stir together first 4 ingredients.

Fill half of cocktail shaker with ice. Add half of liqueur mixture, cover with lid, and shake 8 to 10 seconds until thoroughly chilled. Strain into chilled martini glasses. Repeat with remaining mixture. Serve immediately. **Yield:** 4 servings.

quick & easy
Cape Codder Punch

Prep: 10 min.

1 (48-oz.) bottle cranberry juice cocktail
1½ cups vodka
⅓ cup sweetened lime juice (see note)
1 (1-liter) bottle ginger ale, chilled
Ice cubes
Garnish: fresh cranberries and lime wedges on swizzle sticks

Stir together first 3 ingredients. Stir in ginger ale just before serving. Serve over ice, and garnish, if desired. **Yield:** 10 to 12 servings.

Note: For testing purposes only, we used Rose's West India Sweetened Lime Juice.

make ahead
Sausage-Stuffed Mushrooms

If this appetizer is made ahead and chilled, the baking time will be closer to 30 minutes.

Prep: 25 min. Cook: 20 min. Bake: 30 min.

2 (16-oz.) packages fresh whole mushrooms
1 (12-oz.) package reduced-fat ground pork sausage
2 Tbsp. butter or margarine
1 medium onion, finely chopped (about 1½ cups)
2 cups herb stuffing mix
¾ cup mayonnaise

Clean mushrooms. Remove and finely chop stems to equal about 2 cups; set stems and mushroom caps aside.

Cook sausage in a large nonstick skillet over medium-high heat, stirring until it crumbles and is no longer pink. Remove sausage, and drain on paper towels. Set aside.

Melt butter in skillet over medium-high heat; add onion and chopped mushroom stems, and sauté 10 minutes.

Stir together onion mixture, sausage, stuffing mix, and mayonnaise in a large bowl. (Mixture will be a little stiff.) Spoon generously into mushrooms caps. If desired, cover with plastic wrap, and chill up to 8 hours.

Bake, uncovered, at 350° on a wire rack in a jelly-roll pan for 20 to 30 minutes or until thoroughly heated. Transfer to a serving platter. **Yield:** 3 dozen.

Cape Codder Punch

Bacon-Wrapped Water Chestnuts

Prep: 15 min. Bake: 25 min.

2 (8-oz.) cans whole water chestnuts, drained
14 bacon slices, cut in half
½ cup orange marmalade or plum jam
¼ tsp. crushed red pepper flakes
1 Tbsp. lite soy sauce

Wrap each water chestnut with 1 bacon slice; place seam side down on a wire rack on an aluminum foil-lined baking sheet.

Bake at 400° for 20 to 25 minutes or until bacon is brown and crisp.

Stir together marmalade, red pepper, and soy sauce in a microwave-safe glass bowl. Microwave at HIGH 30 seconds or until hot.

Brush warm bacon-wrapped water chestnuts evenly with 2 Tbsp. marmalade mixture. Serve remaining mixture as a dipping sauce. **Yield:** 14 servings.

Buttery Blue Cheese-and-Walnut Spread,
Asparagus With Tomato-Basil Dip

make ahead

Buttery Blue Cheese-and-Walnut Spread

Use bread pieces from the hollowed-out loaf to make crumbs for breading meat, topping casseroles, or mixing with ground beef for burgers or meatloaf.

Prep: 20 min.

3 (8-oz.) packages cream cheese, softened
½ cup butter, softened
1 (4-oz.) package crumbled blue cheese
½ cup diced walnuts, toasted
½ cup chopped fresh chives
1 (16-oz.) bread loaf
Apple and pear slices
French baguette slices
Garnish: toasted diced walnuts

Stir together first 5 ingredients in a large bowl.

Hollow out bread loaf, leaving a 1-inch-thick shell; reserve inside of loaf for other uses. Spoon cheese spread into shell. Serve with fruit slices and baguette slices. Garnish, if desired. **Yield:** about 3 cups.

Make-Ahead Note: Cover and chill cream cheese mixture 8 hours, if desired, before filling bread shell. Let stand at room temperature to soften; or freeze spread up to 1 month, and thaw in the refrigerator for 8 hours.

make ahead

Asparagus With Tomato-Basil Dip

Prep: 15 min. Cook: 2 min. Chill: 30 min.

1 cup mayonnaise
½ cup sour cream
½ cup chopped fresh basil
1 Tbsp. tomato paste
1 Tbsp. grated fresh lemon rind
4 lb. fresh asparagus

Whisk together first 5 ingredients. Cover and chill up to 2 days, if desired.

Snap off tough ends of asparagus spears, and discard. Cook in boiling salted water to cover 2 minutes or until crisp-tender; drain. Plunge asparagus into ice water to stop the cooking process; drain. Cover and chill 30 minutes. Serve with dip. **Yield:** 12 to 15 servings.

CHAMPAGNE BAR

Set up a Champagne bar at your next party. Fill glass bottles with such mixers as peach nectar, cassis, orange juice, and cranberry juice, and simply ice them down along with 2 (750-milliliter) bottles of Champagne or sparkling wine. Guests can help themselves to their favorite flavors by combining equal parts chilled Champagne and desired mixer in flutes or glasses.

Rosemary-Thyme Rib Roast,
Potato-and-Gruyère Casserole (page 66),
Strawberry-Cranberry-Orange Salad (page 66)

NO-FUSS DINNER FOR *10*

The rib roast and potato casserole can bake at the same time, making this menu ideal for busy schedules. Just pop the casserole in the oven during the last hour of baking the roast.

MENU FOR 8 TO 10

Rosemary-Thyme Rib Roast

Potato-and-Gruyère Casserole

Strawberry-Cranberry-Orange Salad

Chunky Apple Cake With Cream Cheese Frosting

Menu Prep Plan

UP TO 1 WEEK AHEAD:
- Prepare dressing for Strawberry-Cranberry-Orange Salad; chill.

1 DAY AHEAD:
- Prepare Chunky Apple Cake With Cream Cheese Frosting. Cover and chill.

4 HOURS AHEAD:
- Prepare Rosemary-Thyme Rib Roast.
- Prepare fruit and toast almonds for salad; chill.

3 HOURS AHEAD:
- Prepare Cream Sauce for potato casserole.
- Prepare Potato-and-Gruyère Casserole; keep warm.

30 MINUTES AHEAD:
- Combine salad ingredients except dressing.

LAST MINUTE:
- Carve roast.
- Arrange Strawberry-Cranberry-Orange Salad in serving dish.

editor's favorite

Rosemary-Thyme Rib Roast

If you can't find a boneless rib roast, purchase a 6-lb. bone-in roast and have the butcher remove the bone for you.

Prep: 25 min. Bake: 3 hr. Stand: 15 min.

1 Tbsp. salt
2 Tbsp. coarsely ground pepper
1 (4½-lb.) boneless beef rib roast
4 garlic cloves, minced
1 Tbsp. dried rosemary
1 tsp. dried thyme
1½ cups dry red wine
1½ cups red wine vinegar
½ cup olive oil
Garnishes: fresh rosemary sprigs, fresh thyme sprigs

Combine salt and pepper; rub evenly over roast.

Brown roast on all sides in a large skillet over medium-high heat. Remove skillet from heat, and let roast cool slightly.

Combine garlic, dried rosemary, and dried thyme. Rub mixture evenly over roast; place on a lightly greased rack in an aluminum foil-lined roasting pan.

Stir together wine, vinegar, and oil. Gradually pour wine mixture over roast.

Bake at 250° for 2 hours; increase oven temperature to 350°, and bake 1 more hour or until a meat thermometer inserted into thickest portion registers 145° (medium rare) or to desired degree of doneness. Remove roast from oven, and let stand 15 minutes before slicing. Garnish, if desired. **Yield:** 8 to 10 servings.

Potato-and-Gruyère Casserole

Gruyère cheese is known for its rich, nutty flavor. But if you prefer a milder tasting cheese, you can also substitute with Swiss or Cheddar. *(pictured on page 64)*

Prep: 20 min. Cook: 30 min. Bake: 1 hr., 15 min.

12 medium Yukon gold potatoes (about 4 lb.)
2 tsp. salt, divided
2 Tbsp. butter or margarine
1 large sweet onion, chopped
½ tsp. freshly ground pepper
2 cups (8 oz.) shredded Gruyère cheese*
Cream Sauce

Peel and thinly slice potatoes.

Bring potatoes, 1 tsp. salt, and water to cover to a boil in a Dutch oven; cook 8 to 10 minutes. Remove from heat; drain and set aside.

Melt butter in a large skillet over medium-high heat; add chopped onion, and sauté 12 to 15 minutes or until golden brown.

Layer half of potatoes in a lightly greased 13- x 9-inch baking dish or 2 (8-inch) square baking dishes; sprinkle with ½ tsp. salt and ¼ tsp. pepper. Top with half each of onions, Gruyère cheese, and Cream Sauce. Repeat layers once, ending with Cream Sauce.

Bake at 350° for 1 hour and 15 minutes or until golden brown. **Yield:** 10 to 12 servings.

*1 (8-oz.) block Swiss cheese, shredded, or 1 (8-oz.) block sharp white Cheddar cheese, shredded, may be substituted.

Cream Sauce:

Prep: 5 min. Cook: 25 min.

¼ cup butter or margarine
⅓ cup all-purpose flour
2½ cups milk
1 cup dry white wine
¼ tsp. salt

Melt butter in a heavy saucepan over low heat; whisk in flour until smooth. Cook, whisking constantly, 1 minute. Gradually whisk in milk and wine; cook over medium heat, whisking constantly, 18 to 20 minutes or until mixture is thickened and bubbly. Stir in salt. **Yield:** 3½ cups.

make ahead

Strawberry-Cranberry-Orange Salad

The salad dressing can be made ahead and refrigerated up to 1 week. *(pictured on page 64)*

Prep: 30 min.

½ cup olive oil
½ cup orange juice
¼ cup cranberry-orange crushed fruit (see note)
1 small shallot, peeled and chopped
2 Tbsp. balsamic vinegar
¼ tsp. salt
⅛ to ¼ tsp. ground red pepper
¼ tsp. freshly ground black pepper
2 (5-oz.) packages gourmet mixed salad greens
2 cups sliced fresh strawberries
½ cup sweetened dried cranberries, chopped
2 large navel oranges, peeled and sectioned
½ cup slivered almonds, toasted

Process first 8 ingredients in a blender until smooth, stopping to scrape down sides.

Place salad greens and next 3 ingredients in a large bowl, and gently toss. Sprinkle with slivered almonds. Serve with vinaigrette. **Yield:** 8 to 10 servings.

Note: For testing purposes only, we used Ocean Spray Cran-Fruit Crushed Fruit for Chicken (Cranberry Orange).

AS THOUGHTS OF HOLIDAY SHOPPING, DECORATING, AND TRAVELING LOOM LARGE, ***planning a quiet dinner*** WITH CLOSE FRIENDS MIGHT BE THE THING TO DO.

Chunky Apple Cake With Cream Cheese Frosting

editor's favorite

Chunky Apple Cake With Cream Cheese Frosting

Don't worry when you see the consistency of the batter for this moist spice cake—it's supposed to be thick.

Prep: 25 min. Bake: 45 min.

½ cup butter, melted
2 cups sugar
2 large eggs
1 tsp. vanilla extract
2 cups all-purpose flour
1 tsp. baking soda
1 tsp. salt
2 tsp. ground cinnamon
4 Granny Smith apples, peeled and sliced
1 cup chopped walnuts, toasted
Cream Cheese Frosting
Chopped walnuts, toasted (optional)

Stir together first 4 ingredients in a large bowl until blended. Combine flour and next 3 ingredients; add to butter mixture, stirring until blended. Stir in apple slices and 1 cup walnuts. Spread into greased 13- x 9-inch pan.

Bake at 350° for 45 minutes or until a wooden pick inserted in center comes out clean. Cool completely in pan on wire rack. Spread with Cream Cheese Frosting; sprinkle with toasted walnuts, if desired. Store in refrigerator. **Yield:** 12 to 15 servings.

Cream Cheese Frosting

Prep: 10 min.

1 (8-oz.) package cream cheese, softened
3 Tbsp. butter or margarine, softened
1½ cups powdered sugar
⅛ tsp. salt
1 tsp. vanilla extract

Beat cream cheese and 3 Tbsp. butter at medium speed with an electric mixer until creamy. Gradually add 1½ cups powdered sugar and ⅛ tsp. salt, beating until blended. Stir in vanilla. **Yield:** 1⅔ cups.

Asian Party Mix (page 70)

HOLIDAY *Buffet*

This low-key, nontraditional menu is well-suited for a casual buffet since the recipes lend themselves to using only a fork.

MENU FOR 8

Hot Cider Punch

Asian Party Mix

Meatball Lasagna

Roasted Red Onion Salad With Garlic Vinaigrette

Parmesan Crisps

Brownie Trifle Parfaits

Menu Prep Plan

UP TO 3 DAYS AHEAD:
- Prepare Asian Party Mix; store in airtight container.

1 DAY AHEAD:
- Bake brownies and prepare garnish for Brownie Trifle Parfaits.
- Prepare Parmesan Crisps; store in airtight container.
- Place meatballs in refrigerator to thaw.

4 HOURS AHEAD:
- Complete preparation of Brownie Trifle Parfaits; chill.
- Bake onion slices and make vinaigrette for salad.

2 HOURS AHEAD:
- Prepare Meatball Lasagna; keep warm.
- Prepare Hot Cider Punch; keep warm.

1 HOUR AHEAD:
- Assemble Roasted Red Onion Salad in salad bowl; prepare vinaigrette. Chill vinaigrette and salad seperately.

LAST MINUTE:
- Drizzle salad with vinaigrette.
- Garnish parfaits.
- Transfer Asian Party Mix and Parmesan Crisps to separate serving dishes.

Hot Cider Punch

Prep: 5 min. Cook: 1 hr.

1 (64-oz.) bottle apple cider
2 cups orange juice
¾ cup fresh lemon juice
¼ cup honey
10 whole allspice
5 whole cloves
1 (2½-inch) cinnamon stick
Garnish: lemon and apple slices, cloves

Bring first 7 ingredients to a boil in a Dutch oven; cover, reduce heat, and simmer 1 hour. Pour mixture through a wire-mesh strainer into a container; discard spices. Garnish, if desired. Serve warm. **Yield:** 8 servings.

Hot Cider Punch

make ahead
Asian Party Mix

Dried green peas coated with wasabi are available by the pound in the bulk-foods department of many supermarkets. If you can't find them, the mix still has plenty of snap without the peas. Rice crackers, found in the snack aisle or Asian section, are crunchy with a mild taste. *(pictured on page 68)*

Prep: 10 min. Bake: 45 min.

2 cups crispy corn cereal squares (see note)
2 cups crispy rice cereal squares (see note)
2 cups sesame rice crackers, broken
1 cup small pretzel twists
1 cup wasabi peas (optional)
¼ cup lightly salted dry-roasted peanuts
3 Tbsp. butter
1 Tbsp. sugar
1 Tbsp. curry powder
1 Tbsp. low-sodium soy sauce
1 tsp. Worcestershire sauce
½ tsp. garlic powder
½ tsp. ground cumin
¼ tsp. salt
¼ tsp. ground red pepper

Combine first 4 ingredients in a bowl. Add wasabi peas, if desired. Add peanuts; set aside.

Melt butter in a small saucepan over medium heat. Add sugar and remaining ingredients, stirring with a whisk. Pour butter mixture over cereal mixture, tossing gently to coat. Spread party mix onto a lightly greased 15- x 10-inch jelly-roll pan. Bake, uncovered, at 200° for 45 minutes. Cool completely. Store in airtight containers up to 3 days. **Yield:** 8 cups.

Note: For testing purposes only, we used Corn Chex and Rice Chex cereals.

editor's favorite
Meatball Lasagna

Prep: 15 min. Bake: 1 hr., 10 min. Stand: 15 min.

1 (15-oz.) container ricotta cheese
1 (8-oz.) container soft onion-and-chive cream cheese
¼ cup chopped fresh basil
½ tsp. garlic salt
½ tsp. seasoned pepper
1 large egg, lightly beaten
2 cups (8 oz.) shredded mozzarella cheese, divided
1 (3-oz.) package shredded Parmesan cheese, divided
2 (26-oz.) jars tomato-basil pasta sauce, divided (see note)
1 (16-oz.) package egg roll wrappers
60 to 64 frozen cooked Italian-style meatballs (see note)

Stir together first 6 ingredients until blended. Stir in ½ cup mozzarella cheese and ½ cup Parmesan cheese; set aside.

Spread 1 cup pasta sauce in a lightly greased 13- x 9-inch baking dish.

Cut egg roll wrappers in half; arrange 10 halves over pasta sauce. (Wrappers will overlap.) Top with meatballs. Spoon 3 cups pasta sauce over meatballs, and sprinkle with ¾ cup mozzarella cheese. Arrange 10 wrappers evenly over mozzarella. Spread ricotta cheese mixture over wrappers; top with remaining wrappers and pasta sauce.

Bake at 350° for 1 hour. Top with remaining ¾ cup mozzarella cheese and ½ cup Parmesan cheese. Bake 10 more minutes. Let stand 15 minutes before serving. **Yield:** 8 servings.

Note: For testing purposes only, we used Classico Tomato & Basil Pasta Sauce and Rosino Italian Style Meatballs.

Ground Sirloin Lasagna: Substitute 2 lb. ground sirloin, cooked until no longer pink, drained, and seasoned with 1 tsp. salt and 1 tsp. Italian seasoning, for frozen meatballs. Proceed as directed.

FOR EASY TRAFFIC FLOW, SET UP *individual food stations*—ONE EACH FOR BEVERAGES AND APPETIZERS, SALAD AND THE MAIN DISH, AND DESSERT.

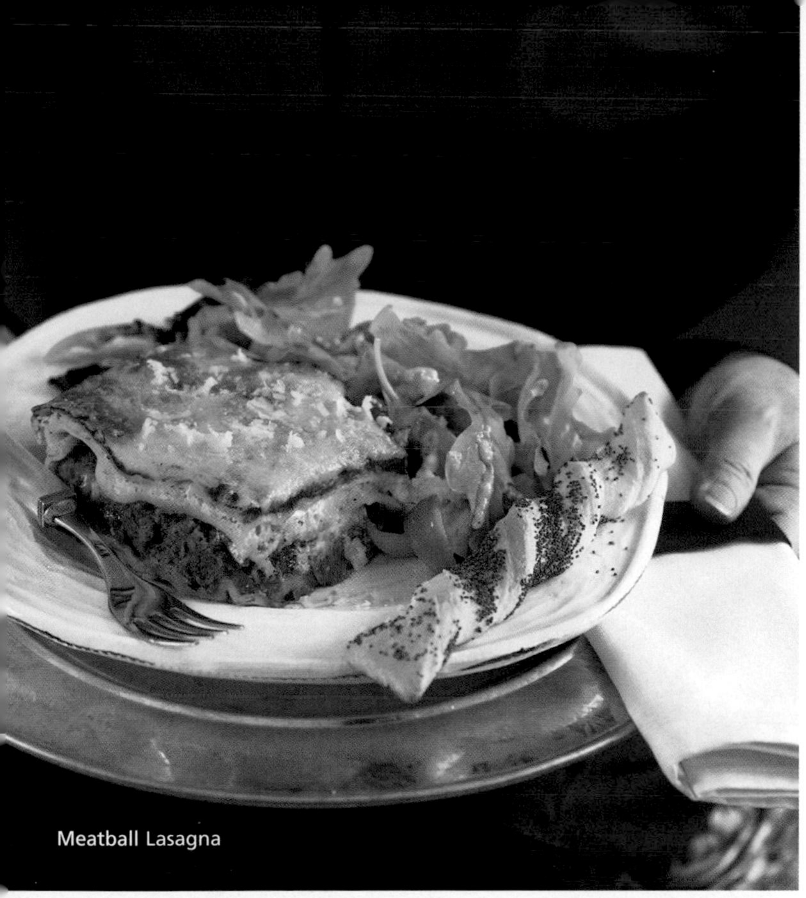
Meatball Lasagna

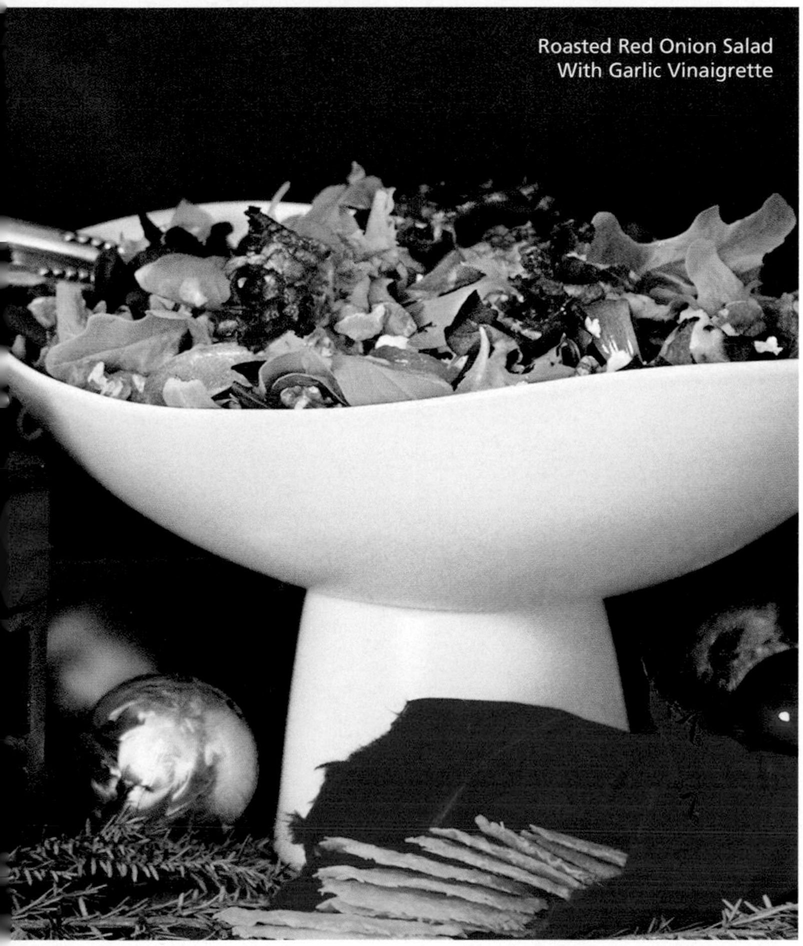
Roasted Red Onion Salad With Garlic Vinaigrette

Roasted Red Onion Salad With Garlic Vinaigrette

Prep: 15 min. Bake: 30 min. Cool: 5 min.

5 medium-size red onions, peeled and cut into ½-inch-thick slices
¼ cup olive oil
8 cups gourmet mixed salad greens
½ cup chopped walnuts, toasted
1 (4-oz.) package crumbled blue cheese
Garlic Vinaigrette

Arrange onion slices in a roasting pan. Drizzle with olive oil. Stir gently to coat onions; spread onions evenly in pan.

Bake at 450° for 25 to 30 minutes or until onion slices are lightly charred. Cool 5 minutes.

Combine salad greens, walnuts, and blue cheese; toss gently. Top with onion slices; drizzle with Garlic Vinaigrette. **Yield:** 8 servings.

Garlic Vinaigrette:

Prep: 10 min.

1 garlic clove
2 shallots
¼ cup chopped fresh parsley
2 Tbsp. white wine vinegar
½ tsp. salt
½ tsp. freshly ground black pepper
½ tsp. dried crushed red pepper
⅔ cup olive oil

Pulse garlic and shallots in a food processor 3 or 4 times. Add parsley and next 4 ingredients; process 20 seconds, stopping once to scrape down sides. With processor running, gradually pour olive oil in a slow, steady stream through food chute until blended. **Yield:** 1 cup.

Parmesan Crisps

Prep: 20 min. Bake: 8 min.

1½ cups finely grated Parmesan cheese
Vegetable cooking spray

Sprinkle 1 Tbsp. Parmesan cheese, forming 2-inch round, on an aluminum foil-lined baking sheet coated with cooking spray. Repeat with remaining cheese, leaving 1 inch between rounds.

Bake at 350° for 8 minutes or until lightly browned. Quickly remove from baking sheet with spatula. Cool on wire rack. Store in airtight containers. **Yield:** 2 dozen.

Brownie Trifle Parfaits

Prep: 1 hr., 30 min. Bake: 25 min. Chill: 1 hr.

1 (19.5-oz.) package fudge brownie mix
¼ cup coffee liqueur (optional)
½ cup corn syrup
4 (1.38-oz.) chocolate-covered toffee candy bars, finely crushed
2 (3.9-oz.) packages chocolate fudge instant pudding
1 (12-oz.) container frozen whipped topping, thawed
8 (1.4-oz.) chocolate-covered toffee candy bars, coarsely crushed
Ground nutmeg
Garnishes: 1 (16-oz.) package chocolate bark coating, fresh mint sprigs

Prepare brownie mix according to package directions in a 13- x 9-inch pan. Prick top of warm brownies at 1-inch intervals with a wooden pick; brush with coffee liqueur, if desired. Cool on a wire rack. Cut into 16 pieces.

While brownies bake, dip rims of 8 (1½-cup) stemmed glasses into a thin coating of corn syrup and then into finely crushed candy bars.

Prepare pudding according to package directions, omitting chilling. Spoon about 2 Tbsp. whipped topping in each glass; crumble 1 brownie over topping, and top evenly with pudding (about ¼ cup), coarsely crushed candy bars (about 2 Tbsp.), and whipped topping (about ¼ cup). Repeat with remaining brownies, pudding, candy bars, and topping. Sprinkle with nutmeg, if desired. Cover and chill at least 1 hour.

Melt bark coating in a saucepan over low heat; cool slightly. Place a sheet of wax paper on a large cookie sheet. Spread bark coating evenly over wax paper, about ¼ inch. Let dry 15 minutes or until almost firm. Cut star shapes using a 2-inch cutter. Garnish parfaits with stars and mint, if desired. **Yield:** 8 parfaits.

Brownie Trifle: Omit corn syrup, 4 finely crushed candy bars, chocolate bark coating, and mint. Prepare brownies as directed for Brownie Trifle Parfaits. Let cool, and crumble. Prepare pudding according to directions, omitting chilling. Layer half of crumbled brownies in a 3-qt. trifle bowl or dish; top with half of pudding, half of coarsely crushed candy bars, and half of whipped topping. Repeat with remaining brownies, pudding, and topping. Cover and chill 8 hours or overnight. Garnish with remaining crushed candy bars.

30-MINUTE DECORATING IDEAS

- Enhance a table setting with various heights and shapes of glass cylinders. Then brighten them with colored water, or spiral a long leaf inside. Punctuate with acrylic pebbles that bob on the surface or nestle on the bottom, depending on weight.
- Place a candleholder and a candle into a hurricane globe, and fill with fresh cranberries or whole nuts.
- Stack similar items, such as dinner plates and glassware, on cake plates and books, or tuck them into baskets to elevate the table presentation.
- Dress up a punch bowl with a festive wreath, or wire colorful garland around the base.
- Fashion disposable table runners, place mats, and napkin rings from colorful, heavyweight holiday wrapping paper.

Brownie Trifle

Chocolate-Dipped Strawberries (page 76), Mint Chocolate Mousse, Dark Chocolate Brownies (page 76), Chocolate Coffee (page 79), Easy Fudge (page 78)

COFFEE AND CHOCOLATE *Party*

Entice guests with a spread of delectable delights complemented by a well-supplied coffee bar. Best of all, the desserts can be made in advance. Double or triple the coffee beverages as needed to suit your guests.

MENU FOR 8 TO 12

Mint Chocolate Mousse

Chocolate-Dipped Strawberries

Mocha Fondue

Dark Chocolate Brownies

Easy Fudge

Spiced Coffee   Chocolate Coffee

Mocha Café au Lait

Menu Prep Plan

1 DAY AHEAD:

- Bake Dark Chocolate Brownies; store in airtight container.
- Prepare Easy Fudge; chill.

4 TO 6 HOURS AHEAD:

- Prepare Mint Chocolate Mousse; chill.
- Prepare Chocolate Dipped Strawberries; do not store in refrigerator.
- Prepare dippers for Mocha Fondue.

1 HOUR AHEAD:

- Prepare fondue; keep warm.
- Prepare Chocolate Coffee, Spiced Coffee, and Mocha Café au Lait, but do not top with whipped cream; keep warm.

LAST MINUTE:

- Transfer Mocha Fondue to fondue pot.
- Arrange brownies and fudge on serving trays.
- Whip cream for coffees and chocolate mousse.
- Top Mint Chocolate Mousse with whipped cream.

Mint Chocolate Mousse

If the buffet will be set up for a long period of time, keep mousse cool by setting glasses or bowl in a container of ice.

Prep: 15 min. Stand: 30 min. Chill: 4 hr.

1½ cups miniature marshmallows*
⅓ cup milk
2 (5.32-oz.) packages mint-filled chocolate squares, unwrapped (see note)
2½ cups whipping cream, divided
2 Tbsp. powdered sugar
Garnish: chocolate shavings

Microwave marshmallows, milk, and chocolate squares in a 4-qt. microwave-safe bowl at HIGH 2 minutes, stirring every 30 seconds or until melted. Let stand 30 minutes or until mixture is cool and begins to thicken.

Beat 2 cups whipping cream at medium speed with an electric mixer until stiff peaks form. Fold whipped cream into chocolate mixture; spoon into shot glasses or a 1½-qt. serving bowl. Cover and chill 4 hours.

Beat remaining ½ cup whipping cream with powdered sugar. Spoon on top of mousse, and garnish, if desired. **Yield:** 8 servings.
*15 large marshmallows may be substituted.

Note: For testing purposes only, we used Ghirardelli Dark Chocolate With White Mint Filling.

Chocolate-Dipped Strawberries

Dip the strawberries in chocolate the day of the event, and let them stand at room temperature until serving. Do not refrigerate, as this will cause the chocolate to break down from condensation. *(pictured on page 74)*

Prep: 25 min. Stand: 45 min.

2 (16-oz.) containers fresh strawberries
2 cups (12 oz.) semisweet chocolate morsels
¼ cup shortening

Rinse strawberries, and pat completely dry with paper towels. (Chocolate will not stick to wet strawberries.) Set aside.

Microwave chocolate morsels and shortening in a 1-qt. microwave-safe bowl at HIGH 1½ minutes, stirring every 30 seconds, until smooth.

Hold strawberries by the stems, and dip all the way into melted chocolate, allowing excess to drip. Place on wax paper, and let stand at least 45 minutes or until chocolate hardens. **Yield:** about 4 dozen.

Mocha Fondue

Choose your favorite dippers, such as pineapple chunks, kiwi slices, and low-fat pound cake cubes, to serve with Mocha Fondue.

Prep: 10 min. Cook: 10 min.

½ cup powdered sugar, sifted
2 Tbsp. all-purpose flour
2 cups fat-free half-and-half
3 Tbsp. coffee liqueur, divided (see note)
2 tsp. vanilla extract
5 (1-oz.) semisweet chocolate baking bars, chopped (about 1 cup)

Combine powdered sugar and flour in a large saucepan. Gradually whisk in half-and-half, 2 Tbsp. coffee liqueur, and vanilla over medium heat. Bring to a simmer; cook, stirring constantly, 5 minutes. Reduce heat to medium-low; cook, stirring constantly, 2 minutes or until mixture is smooth.

Place chopped chocolate in a medium bowl. Pour half-and-half mixture over chocolate, and stir until smooth. Stir in remaining 1 Tbsp. liqueur. Transfer chocolate mixture to a fondue pot, and keep warm over a low flame. **Yield:** 2⅓ cups.

Note: For testing purposes only, we used Kahlúa coffee liqueur.

Dark Chocolate Brownies

These chewy and moist brownies make a blissful ending to any meal. *(pictured on page 74)*

Prep: 15 min. Bake: 40 min.

1 cup butter
1 (8-oz.) package bittersweet baking chocolate squares
2 cups (12 oz.) semisweet chocolate morsels, divided
2 cups sugar
4 large eggs
1 Tbsp. vanilla extract
1½ cups chopped walnuts or pecans, toasted
1 cup all-purpose flour, divided
½ tsp. salt

Microwave butter, bittersweet chocolate, and 1 cup semisweet chocolate morsels in a 4-qt. microwave-safe bowl at HIGH 1½ to 2 minutes or until chocolate is melted, stirring mixture every 30 seconds. Whisk in sugar, eggs, and vanilla.

Toss together walnuts, 1 Tbsp. flour, and remaining 1 cup chocolate morsels. Stir remaining flour and salt into sugar mixture. Stir in walnut mixture. Spread batter into a greased 13- x 9-inch pan.

Bake at 350° for 30 to 40 minutes or until edges begin to pull away from pan. (A wooden pick inserted in center will not come out clean.) Cool on a wire rack. Cut into 1½-inch squares. **Yield:** 4 dozen.

Dark Chocolate Bourbon Brownies: Substitute 1 Tbsp. bourbon for vanilla extract, and proceed as directed.

SET A *table of desserts* FOR YOUR NEXT GET-TOGETHER. SERVE *petite portions* SO GUESTS CAN SAMPLE THEM ALL.

Dark Chocolate Brownies,
Chocolate Coffee (page 79)

Easy Fudge

This is the perfect fudge for beginners because it doesn't require a candy thermometer and takes such a short time to prepare. *(pictured on page 74)*

Prep: 10 min. Cook: 10 min. Cool: 2 hr.

2 cups sugar
1 (5-oz.) can evaporated milk
½ cup butter
12 large marshmallows
¼ tsp. salt
1 cup (6 oz.) semisweet chocolate morsels
1 cup chopped pecans, toasted
1 tsp. vanilla extract

Combine first 5 ingredients in a large heavy saucepan. Cook over medium heat, stirring constantly, until mixture comes to a boil; boil, stirring constantly, 5 minutes. Remove from heat.

Stir chocolate morsels into marshmallow mixture, stirring until chocolate melts. Add pecans and vanilla, stirring until well blended. Spread evenly in a buttered 8-inch square pan. Cool completely (at least 2 hours), and cut into squares. **Yield:** 3 dozen.

Mocha Fudge: Add 1 Tbsp. instant coffee granules with sugar, and proceed as directed.

Spiced Coffee

Spiced Coffee

Prep: 5 min.

10 Tbsp. ground coffee
1 tsp. ground cinnamon
¼ tsp. ground nutmeg
6 cups water
½ cup whipping cream
3 Tbsp. powdered sugar
⅛ tsp. ground nutmeg

Combine coffee, cinnamon, and ¼ tsp. ground nutmeg in a coffee filter. Brew with 6 cups water in a coffeemaker, according to manufacturer's instructions.

Beat cream, powdered sugar, and ⅛ tsp. ground nutmeg at high speed with an electric mixer until soft peaks form.

Pour coffee into mugs, and top with whipped cream. **Yield:** 7 cups.

Chocolate Coffee

(pictured on page 74)

Prep: 10 min. Cook: 10 min.

4 (1-oz.) semisweet chocolate squares, chopped
2 cups half-and-half
4 cups hot brewed coffee
¾ cup coffee liqueur
Sweetened whipped cream (optional)

Cook chocolate and half-and-half in a large saucepan over medium-low heat, whisking constantly, 10 minutes or until melted and smooth; stir in coffee. Remove from heat; stir in liqueur. Serve warm with sweetened whipped cream, if desired. **Yield:** 7¼ cups.

COFFEE BAR

Create a tasting buffet by pouring hot coffee into carafes and offering guests plenty of ways to flavor their java. Fill several small bowls with ground nutmeg, cocoa, and cinnamon, and label each bowl. Heap sugar cubes in glass mugs and bowls. Have a selection of stir-ins, such as chocolate syrup, liqueurs, flavored syrups, and whipped cream. Include tasty swizzle sticks, such as peppermint and cinnamon sticks, for easy stirring.

Right before your get-together, wash your coffee mugs in a dishwasher and push the "warm dry" button so the mugs are nice and toasty when the cycle is over.

Mocha Café au Lait

Prep: 5 min. Cook: 8 min.

2 cups milk
6 oz. milk chocolate candy bars, chopped
1½ tsp. vanilla extract, divided
3 cups freshly brewed coffee
½ cup whipping cream
1 Tbsp. powdered sugar
Garnish: semisweet chocolate shavings

Stir together milk, chocolate, and 1 tsp. vanilla in a medium saucepan over low heat. Cook, stirring constantly, 8 minutes or until mixture begins to bubble around edges and chocolate is melted and smooth. Stir in coffee. Remove from heat; set aside.

Beat cream, sugar, and remaining ½ tsp. vanilla at high speed with an electric mixer until soft peaks form.

Pour hot coffee into mugs. Top with whipped cream, and garnish, if desired. **Yield:** about 6 cups.

Red Bean Chili (page 82),
Herbed Sour Cream (page 82)

NEIGHBORHOOD *Chili Party*

Gather the group for a feast of homemade chilis complete with a variety of toppings.

MENU FOR 16

White Bean Chili

Red Bean Chili

Quick-and-Zesty Salsa corn chips

Herbed Sour Cream

ready-to-bake cornbread

Tart Apple Wassail

Menu Prep Plan

MORNING OF:
- Prepare Herbed Sour Cream; chill.
- Prepare Quick-and-Zesty Salsa; chill.

3 HOURS AHEAD:
- Prepare Red Bean Chili; keep warm.
- Prepare White Bean Chili; keep warm.

1 HOUR AHEAD:
- Prepare Tart Apple Wassail; keep warm.

30 MINUTES AHEAD:
- Reheat chili, if needed.
- Bake cornbread.
- Set out bowls of Herbed Sour Cream, shredded Cheddar cheese, and sliced green onions for chili toppings.

White Bean Chili

Prep: 20 min Cook: 1 hr., 15 min.

1 medium onion, chopped
1 Tbsp. olive oil
2 garlic cloves, minced
6 skinned and boned chicken breasts, cut into bite-size pieces
2½ cups water
1½ tsp. salt
2 tsp. ground cumin
1 tsp. chili powder
1 tsp. freshly ground pepper
4 (15-oz.) cans cannellini or great Northern beans, rinsed, drained, and divided
1 (14½-oz.) can chicken broth, divided
2 (4.5-oz.) cans chopped green chiles
¼ cup lime juice

Sauté onion in hot oil in a large Dutch oven over medium-high heat 7 minutes; add garlic, and sauté 2 minutes.

Stir in chicken; cook, stirring constantly, until chicken is lightly browned. Stir in 2½ cups water and next 4 ingredients. Reduce heat; simmer, stirring often, 10 minutes or until chicken is done.

Process 2 cans of beans and ½ can broth in a blender until smooth, stopping to scrape down sides (see note).

Stir bean puree, remaining 2 cans of beans, remaining broth, and chiles into chicken mixture in Dutch oven; bring to a boil over medium-high heat. Reduce heat, and simmer, stirring often, 30 minutes or until thoroughly heated. Stir in lime juice just before serving. **Yield:** 16 cups.

Note: Use a handheld immersion blender to purée the beans and broth, if desired.

Red Bean Chili

(pictured on page 80)

Prep: 15 min. Cook: 1 hr., 15 min.

4 lb. lean ground beef
2 large onions, chopped
4 (15-oz.) cans light red kidney beans
2 (12-oz.) cans tomato juice
2 (10¾-oz.) cans tomato soup
2 (3.03-oz.) chili kits (see note)
Toppings: Herbed Sour Cream (see recipe below), shredded cheese, sliced green onions (optional)

Cook beef and onion in a large Dutch oven over medium-high heat 12 to 15 minutes, stirring until beef crumbles and is no longer pink. Drain and return beef mixture to Dutch oven.

Stir kidney beans and next 3 ingredients into beef mixture; reduce heat, and simmer, stirring occasionally, 1 hour. Serve with desired toppings. **Yield:** 16 cups.

Note: For testing purposes only, we used Wick Fowler's False Alarm Mild Chili Kit.

make ahead • quick & easy

Quick-and-Zesty Salsa

Prep: 10 min.

2 (10-oz.) cans Mexican diced tomatoes
1 (11-oz.) can whole kernel corn, rinsed and drained
½ small green bell pepper, diced
½ small red onion, diced
½ tsp. salt
¼ tsp. ground cumin
2 Tbsp. lime juice
Corn chips

Stir together tomatoes, corn, bell pepper, onion, salt, cumin, and lime juice. Cover and chill until ready to serve. Serve with corn chips or as a chili topping. **Yield:** about 2 cups.

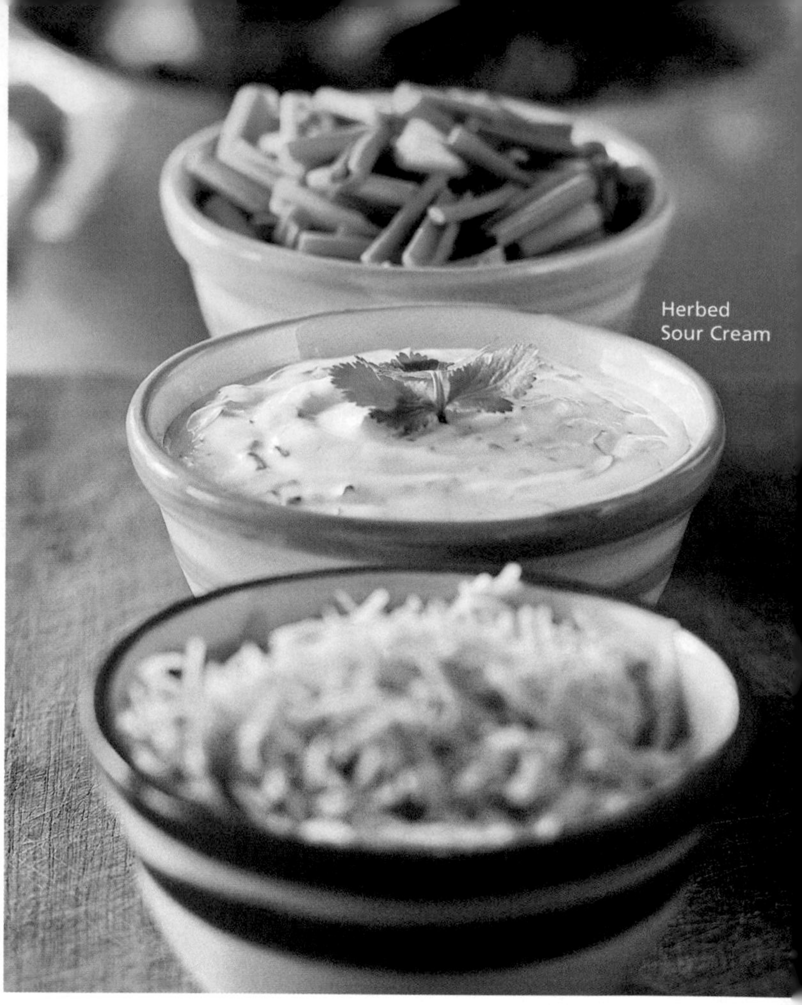

Herbed Sour Cream

make ahead • quick & easy

Herbed Sour Cream

Prep: 10 min.

1 cup sour cream
2 Tbsp. chopped fresh cilantro
2 Tbsp. lime juice
¼ tsp. salt
Garnish: fresh cilantro sprigs

Stir together sour cream, cilantro, lime juice, and salt. Cover and chill until ready to serve. Garnish with fresh cilantro sprigs, if desired. **Yield:** 1 cup.

Quick-and-Zesty Salsa

Tart Apple Wassail

If you'd like your drink to be less tart, reduce the lemon juice to ¼ cup.

Prep: 5 min. Cook: 25 min.

1 (64-oz.) bottle apple juice or cider
1 (12-oz.) can frozen orange juice concentrate, thawed
½ cup lemon juice
4 (3-inch) cinnamon sticks
1 tsp. whole cloves
1 orange, thinly sliced
Garnish: additional orange slices

Bring first 5 ingredients to a boil in a Dutch oven. Reduce heat, and simmer, stirring occasionally, 15 to 20 minutes. Remove cinnamon sticks and cloves. Add orange slices, and garnish, if desired. Serve immediately. **Yield:** about 12 cups.

Note: Keep this drink warm on the stove or in a slow cooker on low heat.

Tart Apple Wassail

Lemon-Vinaigrette Marinated Antipasto, hummus with pita bread chips, Grilled Parsleyed Shrimp and Vegetables (page 86), Pork Tenderloin on Cornmeal Biscuits (page 87)

OPEN HOUSE MENU *for a Crowd*

Host a holiday open house that's classy yet comfortable. The menu and helpful planning tips ensure a hands-down success.

MENU FOR 24

Lemon-Vinaigrette Marinated Antipasto

Grilled Parsleyed Shrimp and Vegetables

Pork Tenderloin on Cornmeal Biscuits

hummus with pita bread chips

Gingerbread Bites With Orange-Cream Cheese Frosting

Menu Prep Plan

1 WEEK AHEAD:
- Bake Gingerbread Bites, but do not frost; freeze in zip-top plastic freezer bags.

1 DAY AHEAD:
- Prepare Grilled Parsleyed Shrimp and Vegetables; chill.
- Prepare Texas Cranberry Chutney for pork tenderloin; chill.
- Trim and cook green beans for antipasto; chill.

MORNING OF:
- Frost Gingerbread Bites; refrigerate.
- Bake Cornmeal Biscuits; store in airtight container.
- Prepare antipasto; chill.

1½ HOURS AHEAD:
- Cook pork tenderloin.

30 MINUTES AHEAD:
- Slice pork tenderloin, and reheat biscuits. Assemble Pork Tenderloin on Cornmeal Biscuits; top with cranberry chutney.

LAST MINUTE:
- Arrange shrimp mixture in serving bowl.
- Transfer antipasto to a serving platter.
- Arrange hummus and pita rounds on serving tray.

Lemon-Vinaigrette Marinated Antipasto

For a party crowd of 24, make two recipes of this dish.

Prep: 25 min. Cook: 5 min. Chill: 2 hr.

1 lb. fresh green beans, trimmed
1 (8-oz.) package feta cheese, cubed
1 (8-oz.) jar pitted kalamata olives, rinsed and drained
1 (6-oz.) jar pitted large Spanish olives, rinsed and drained
1 (16-oz.) jar pickled okra, drained
1 (12-oz.) jar roasted red peppers, drained and cut into thin strips
1 (10.5-oz.) log goat cheese
1½ cups olive oil-and-vinegar dressing (see note)
1 tsp. sugar
¼ tsp. grated fresh lemon rind
¼ cup fresh lemon juice
1 (5-oz.) package sliced hard salami (optional)
Garnish: lemon wedges

Cook green beans in boiling salted water to cover 5 minutes or until crisp-tender; drain. Plunge into ice water to stop the cooking process; drain.

Arrange green beans, feta cheese, and next 5 ingredients in a 13- x 9-inch baking dish, keeping each ingredient separate from the others.

Whisk together dressing and next 3 ingredients. Drizzle evenly over ingredients. Cover and chill 2 hours.

Transfer marinated ingredients to a large serving platter. Add salami to platter, if desired. Garnish platter, if desired. **Yield:** 12 to 14 appetizer servings.

Note: For testing purposes only, we used Newman's Own Olive Oil & Vinegar dressing.

Grilled Parsleyed Shrimp and Vegetables

Grilled Parsleyed Shrimp and Vegetables

Estimate 7 to 8 shrimp per person, and then triple this recipe to serve 24 guests. The lemon halves placed in the bottom of the serving bowl add color and act as a strainer. The shrimp and veggies sit on top, while the marinade settles to the bottom of the bowl. *(also pictured on page 84)*

Prep: 15 min. Grill: 20 min. Chill: 8 hr.

3 lb. unpeeled jumbo raw shrimp (16 to 20 count per lb.)
2 lemons, halved
2 large yellow bell peppers
2 large green bell peppers
2 large red onions
1 cup chopped fresh flat-leaf parsley
1 clove garlic, pressed
1 (16-oz.) bottle olive oil-and-vinegar dressing (see note)
Garnish: fresh flat-leaf parsley sprigs

Peel shrimp, leaving tails on; devein, if desired.

Squeeze juice from lemon halves to measure ¼ cup; set juice aside. Reserve and chill lemon halves for later use.

Grill shrimp, covered with grill lid, over medium-high heat (350° to 400°) 2 to 3 minutes on each side or until shrimp turn pink. Place in a large bowl.

Cut each pepper into 4 large pieces; cut each onion horizontally into 3 large slices.

Grill vegetables, covered with grill lid, over medium-high heat (350° to 400°) 5 to 7 minutes on each side or until bell peppers look blistered and onions are crisp-tender; cut into 2-inch pieces. Add grilled vegetables, chopped parsley, and garlic to shrimp in bowl. Pour dressing and lemon juice over mixture, and stir to coat and combine. Cover and chill 8 hours or overnight.

Arrange reserved lemon halves in bottom of a deep serving bowl. Spoon marinated shrimp and vegetable mixture over top of lemon halves. Garnish, if desired. **Yield:** 6 to 8 appetizer servings.

Note: For testing purposes only, we used Newman's Own Olive Oil & Vinegar dressing.

Pork Tenderloin on Cornmeal Biscuits

Running out of time to assemble sandwiches yourself? Let guests make their own: Serve sliced pork on a platter with chutney and biscuits on the side. (also pictured on page 84)

Prep: 5 min. Broil: 5 min. Bake: 20 min. Stand: 15 min.

4 (¾- to 1-lb.) pork tenderloins
2 tsp. salt
2 tsp. freshly ground pepper
2 Tbsp. olive oil
Cornmeal Biscuits, halved
Texas Cranberry Chutney
Garnish: sliced green onions

Place pork in a lightly greased 15- x 10-inch jelly-roll pan; sprinkle with salt and pepper. Rub evenly with oil.

Broil 5½ inches from heat 5 minutes; reduce oven temperature to 450°, and bake 20 minutes or until a meat thermometer inserted into thickest portion registers 160°. Let stand 15 minutes before slicing. Cut into ¼-inch-thick slices (about 18 slices each).

Place pork slices evenly over Cornmeal Biscuit halves, and top evenly with Texas Cranberry Chutney. Garnish, if desired. **Yield:** 24 servings.

Cornmeal Biscuits:

This recipe is easy but requires some patience to prepare. The butter needs to be cut into the flour evenly and finely, almost until you can't see any bits of butter. Large pieces of butter will melt and leak out of the biscuits.

Prep: 20 min. Bake: 15 min.

4 cups self-rising flour
½ cup yellow cornmeal*
1 cup butter, cut up
2 cups buttermilk
¼ cup milk

Combine flour and cornmeal in a large bowl; cut in butter with a pastry blender or fork until crumbly. Add buttermilk, stirring just until dry ingredients are moistened.

Turn dough out onto a lightly floured surface and knead 2 to 3 times.

Pat or roll dough to a ½-inch thickness, and cut with a 2-inch round cutter. Place on lightly greased baking sheets. Reroll remaining dough, and proceed as directed. Brush tops with milk.

Bake at 425° for 13 to 15 minutes or until golden. **Yield:** about 3 dozen.

*White cornmeal may be substituted.

Pork Tenderloin on Cornmeal Biscuits

Texas Cranberry Chutney:

Prep: 5 min. Cook: 10 min.

2 (8-oz.) cans crushed pineapple
1 (16-oz.) can whole berry cranberry sauce
¼ cup firmly packed brown sugar
½ tsp. ground ginger
¼ tsp. salt
1 to 2 jalapeño peppers, seeded and minced
3 green onions, chopped

Drain pineapple well; pat dry with paper towels.

Stir together pineapple and next 4 ingredients in a small saucepan over medium heat, and bring to a boil. Reduce heat to low, and simmer, stirring often, 5 minutes or until thickened. Remove from heat, and stir in jalapeño and green onions. Cover and chill until ready to serve. **Yield:** 3 cups.

Gingerbread Bites With Orange-Cream Cheese Frosting

editor's favorite • make ahead

Gingerbread Bites With Orange-Cream Cheese Frosting

Use a vegetable peeler to peel carrots and ginger and to make the garnish. Peel a thin layer of rind from 1 orange, and cut into thin strips using a knife. Unfrosted gingerbread muffins may be frozen in zip-top plastic freezer bags up to 1 week. Frost and garnish the morning of the party, and refrigerate until serving time.

Prep: 30 min. Bake: 15 min. per batch

1¾ cups sugar
1½ cups vegetable oil
4 large eggs
2 large carrots, finely grated (about 1 cup)
1 cup minced fresh ginger (about ½ lb.)
2 cups all-purpose flour
2 tsp. baking powder
1½ tsp. baking soda
1½ tsp. ground cinnamon
¾ tsp. salt
½ tsp. ground allspice
¼ tsp. ground cloves
1½ cups chopped pecans, toasted
Orange-Cream Cheese Frosting
Garnishes: small pecan halves, crystallized ginger, orange rind strips

Beat sugar and vegetable oil at medium speed with an electric mixer 3 minutes or until smooth. Add eggs, 1 at a time, beating well after each addition. Beat in grated carrots and fresh ginger.

Combine all-purpose flour and next 6 ingredients; gradually add to egg mixture, beating at low speed until moistened. Stir in 1½ cups chopped toasted pecans.

Pour batter into lightly greased miniature muffin tins, filling two-thirds full.

Bake at 350° for 12 to 15 minutes or until a wooden pick inserted in center comes out clean. Cool in pan on a wire rack 5 minutes. Remove from pan, and cool completely on wire racks. Spread tops evenly with Orange-Cream Cheese Frosting. Store in refrigerator. Garnish, if desired. **Yield:** about 6 dozen.

Orange-Cream Cheese Frosting:

Prep: 5 min.

2 (8-oz.) packages cream cheese, softened
2 Tbsp. orange liqueur*
½ cup powdered sugar

Beat softened cream cheese and orange liqueur at medium speed with an electric mixer until blended. Gradually add powdered sugar, beating until light and fluffy. **Yield:** 2 cups.
*2 Tbsp. orange juice may be substituted

GOOD LUCK AND *Good Cheer*

This menu updates tried-and-true favorites, such as black-eyed peas and collard greens, that tradition says will bring you good luck throughout the year.

MENU FOR 6 TO 8

Spice-Rubbed Pork Tenderloins With Apple-Cherry Salsa

Black-eyed Pea Cornbread Cakes With Jalapeño Sour Cream

Smoky Collard Greens

Sweet Potato Bread Pudding With Bourbon Sauce

Menu Prep Plan

1 DAY AHEAD:

- Bake Super-Moist Cornbread; wrap in plastic wrap.
- Cube French bread for bread pudding.
- Prepare Bourbon Sauce; chill.
- Trim and wash collard greens; refrigerate.
- Chop onion and bell pepper for cornbread cakes; chill.

4 HOURS AHEAD:

- Prepare Sweet Potato Bread Pudding.
- Prepare Jalepeño Sour Cream; cover and chill.
- Thaw cherries for salsa at room temperature.

2½ HOURS AHEAD:

- Mix and shape Black-eyed Pea Cornbread Cakes; chill.
- Cook Smoky Collard Greens; keep warm.
- Prepare Apple-Cherry Salsa; cover and chill.

1½ HOURS AHEAD:

- Prepare Spice-Rubbed Pork Tenderloins; keep warm.
- Cook Black-eyed Pea Cornbread Cakes; keep warm.

LAST MINUTE:

- Slice pork tenderloin.
- Reheat cornbread cakes.

JUST AFTER DINNER:

- Reheat Bourbon Sauce.

Spice-Rubbed Pork Tenderloins With Apple-Cherry Salsa

Prep: 10 min. Stand: 25 min. Bake: 25 min.

⅔ cup firmly packed light brown sugar
1 to 2 Tbsp. ground chipotle chile pepper
1 tsp. salt
1 tsp. ground cumin
3 lb. pork tenderloin
Apple-Cherry Salsa
Garnishes: red onion slices, lime wedges

Stir together first 4 ingredients. Rub tenderloins evenly with sugar mixture. Let stand at room temperature 15 minutes. Place tenderloins on a lightly greased rack in a roasting pan.

Bake at 425° for 20 to 25 minutes or until a meat thermometer registers 155°. Remove from oven, cover loosely with aluminum foil, and let stand 10 minutes or until thermometer registers 160°.

Cut into 1- to 1½-inch-thick slices, and serve with Apple-Cherry Salsa. Garnish, if desired. **Yield:** 6 to 8 servings.

Apple-Cherry Salsa:

Prep: 15 min.

1 cup frozen dark sweet cherries, thawed
1 large Granny Smith apple, coarsely chopped
3 Tbsp. golden raisins
1 to 2 tsp. grated fresh lime rind
¼ cup fresh lime juice (about 2 limes)
3 Tbsp. honey
1 jalapeño pepper, seeded and finely chopped
2 Tbsp. chopped fresh cilantro
1 Tbsp. chopped red onion

Pulse all ingredients in a food processor 5 to 6 times or just until coarsely chopped. Cover and chill until ready to serve. **Yield:** about 2 cups.

Black-eyed Pea
Cornbread Cakes
With Jalapeño Sour Cream

Black-eyed Pea Cornbread Cakes With Jalapeño Sour Cream

This recipe binds cornbread and black-eyed peas into crisp cakes.

Prep: 25 min. Cook: 30 min. Chill: 30 min.

2 (15-oz.) cans seasoned black-eyed peas, drained and divided (see note)
2 Tbsp. butter
1 small sweet onion, finely chopped
1 red bell pepper, finely chopped
2 garlic cloves, minced
1½ cups crumbled Super-Moist Cornbread
¼ cup mayonnaise
1 large egg, lightly beaten
Yellow cornmeal
1 Tbsp. vegetable oil
Jalapeño Sour Cream (opposite page)
Garnish: green onion curls

Process 1 can black-eyed peas in a food processor or blender until smooth. Set aside.

Melt 2 Tbsp. butter in a large nonstick skillet over medium heat; add chopped onion and bell pepper; sauté 7 minutes. Add minced garlic, and sauté 1 minute.

Stir together puréed black-eyed peas, remaining can black-eyed peas, onion mixture, crumbled Super-Moist Cornbread, mayonnaise, and egg until well blended.

Shape black-eyed pea mixture into 12 (3-inch) patties. Dust lightly with cornmeal. Place on a lightly greased baking sheet; cover and chill 30 minutes.

Cook, in batches, in hot oil in a large nonstick skillet over medium-high heat 3 minutes on each side or until golden; drain on paper towels. Serve cakes immediately with Jalapeño Sour Cream. Garnish, if desired. **Yield:** 6 to 8 servings.

Note: For testing purposes only, we used Glory Foods Seasoned Southern Style Blackeye Peas.

Super-Moist Cornbread:

You can bake this cornbread 1 day in advance. Let it cool completely; then wrap tightly in aluminum foil or plastic wrap.

Prep: 10 min. Bake: 35 min.

⅓ cup butter
1 (8-oz.) container sour cream
2 large eggs, lightly beaten
1 (8-oz.) can cream-style corn
1 cup self-rising white cornmeal mix

Heat butter in a 9-inch cast-iron skillet in 400° oven 5 minutes or until butter melts.

Combine sour cream, eggs, and corn in a medium bowl. Whisk in cornmeal mix just until combined. Whisk in melted butter. Pour batter into skillet.

Bake at 400° for 30 minutes or until golden brown. **Yield:** 8 servings.

Jalapeño Sour Cream:

Prep: 5 min.

1 (8-oz.) container sour cream
¼ cup chopped pickled jalapeño pepper slices
Garnish: pickled jalapeño slices

Stir together first 2 ingredients. Cover and chill until ready to serve. Garnish, if desired. **Yield:** 1 cup.

Smoky Collard Greens

Prep: 30 min. Cook: 1 hr., 10 min.

2 (16-oz.) packages fresh collard greens*
1 Tbsp. olive oil
1 qt. water
2 ham bouillon cubes or 4 tsp. ham bouillon granules (see note)
¼ tsp. hickory liquid smoke
2 tsp. sugar
2 tsp. liquid from hot peppers in vinegar

Remove stems and discolored spots from greens. Wash thoroughly, and drain.

Sauté one-fourth of greens in hot oil in a large Dutch oven 2 minutes. Sauté remaining greens in 3 batches, pushing cooked greens to side of Dutch oven. Gradually add 1 qt. water and next 4 ingredients; bring to a boil. Reduce heat; cover and simmer 45 minutes to 1 hour or until greens are tender. **Yield:** 8 servings.
*2 (16-oz.) packages frozen collard greens may be substituted for fresh collard greens. Omit first step; sauté greens as directed, simmering greens 15 to 20 minutes or until tender.

Note: For testing purposes only, we used Knorr Ham Bouillon Cubes.

Sweet Potato Bread Pudding With Bourbon Sauce

Use day-old or lightly toasted fresh French bread for the bread pudding. Also, resist the temptation to use canned sweet potatoes; there's no substitute for the vibrant color and taste of fresh sweet potatoes.

Prep: 35 min. Bake: 1 hr., 50 min.

2 medium-size sweet potatoes (about 2 lb.)
2½ cups half-and-half
6 large eggs, lightly beaten
⅔ cup sugar
1 Tbsp. vanilla extract
½ tsp. ground cinnamon
¼ tsp. ground nutmeg
1 (16-oz.) day-old French bread loaf, cubed
¼ cup butter, cut up and softened
Bourbon Sauce

Pierce potatoes with a fork; place on a baking sheet.

Bake at 400° for 1 hour and 15 minutes or until potatoes are tender. Cool slightly, peel, and cut into quarters.

Process potatoes in food processor with ½ cup half-and-half until smooth, stopping to scrape down sides. Whisk together potato puree, remaining 2 cups half-and-half, lightly beaten eggs, and next 4 ingredients in a large mixing bowl until smooth.

Arrange bread cubes evenly in a lightly greased 13- x 9-inch baking dish. Pour sweet potato mixture evenly over bread cubes. Top evenly with butter.

Bake at 350° for 30 to 35 minutes or until set. Serve with Bourbon Sauce. **Yield:** 8 servings.

Bourbon Sauce:

Prep: 15 min. Cook: 10 min.

3 Tbsp. butter
1½ tsp. all-purpose flour
½ cup sugar
1 cup whipping cream
⅛ tsp. ground nutmeg
1 tsp. vanilla extract
2 Tbsp. bourbon

Melt 3 Tbsp. butter in a small saucepan over medium heat; whisk in flour, and cook, whisking constantly, 3 minutes. Stir in sugar, whipping cream, and ground nutmeg. Bring to a boil over medium heat, stirring constantly. Reduce heat, and simmer 5 minutes or until slightly thickened. Remove from heat; stir in vanilla and bourbon. Serve warm over Sweet Potato Bread Pudding. **Yield:** 1¼ cups.

Champagne Salad With
Pear-Goat Cheese Tarts

TWELFTH NIGHT *Celebration*

Mark the conclusion of the Twelve Days of Christmas with an elegant evening meal. The easy, no-cook appetizer and speedy salad shortcuts streamline the preparation.

MENU FOR 8

Kir Royale

assorted cheeses, crackers, breads, and fruit

Champagne Salad With Pear-Goat Cheese Tarts

Apricot-Ginger Salmon

Citrus Sweet Potatoes

Sautéed Beans and Peppers

Easy Apple Tart With Ol' South Custard

Menu Prep Plan

UP TO 3 DAYS AHEAD:
- Prepare sauce for salmon; chill.
- Prepare Sugared Walnuts and Champagne Vinaigrette; chill in separate containers.
- Prepare custard; chill.

1 DAY AHEAD:
- Chill Champagne.
- Cook green beans; chill.
- Thaw puff pastry sheets for apple tart in refrigerator.

6 HOURS AHEAD:
- Prepare tart shells, and partially bake.
- Cook apples for apple tart.

2 TO 3 HOURS AHEAD:
- Prepare Citrus Sweet Potatoes; keep warm.
- Bake Easy Apple Tart.
- Prepare and bake Pear-Goat Cheese Tarts.

45 MINUTES AHEAD:
- Prepare salmon.
- Prepare beans and peppers.

LAST MINUTE:
- Arrange tray of cheeses, crackers, breads, and fruit.
- Prepare Kir Royale.

quick & easy

Kir Royale

Prep: 10 min.

10 Tbsp. crème de cassis
2 (750-milliliter) bottles Champagne or sparkling white wine

Pour 1 Tbsp. liqueur into each of 10 Champagne flutes; fill with Champagne. **Yield:** 10 servings.

Champagne Salad With Pear-Goat Cheese Tarts

Prep: 10 min.

2 (5-oz.) bags gourmet mixed salad greens
⅓ cup sweetened dried cranberries
Sugared Walnuts
Pear-Goat Cheese Tarts (following page)
Champagne Vinaigrette (following page)

Combine salad greens and cranberries in a large bowl. Arrange mixture on a serving plate. Sprinkle evenly with Sugared Walnuts. Top with 8 Pear-Goat Cheese Tarts. Serve immediately with Champagne Vinaigrette. **Yield:** 8 servings.

Sugared Walnuts:

Prep: 5 min. Cook: 10 min.

1½ cups walnut halves
¾ cup sugar

Stir together walnuts and sugar in a heavy saucepan over medium heat, and cook, stirring constantly, 8 to 10 minutes or until sugar melts and turns golden brown.

Spread mixture in a single layer on lightly greased wax paper; cool. Break into pieces; store in an airtight container up to 3 days. **Yield:** 1½ cups.

Pear-Goat Cheese Tarts:

Leftover tarts are great served for breakfast the next morning.

Prep: 20 min. Bake: 18 min. Cool: 2 min.

1 (15-oz.) package refrigerator piecrusts
2 (4-oz.) packages goat cheese, crumbled
1 to 2 ripe pears, chopped
2 Tbsp. honey
½ tsp. dried thyme

Unfold piecrusts, and cut each in half; cut each half into 3 pieces. Place 1 piece into a lightly greased muffin cup in a muffin pan. Fold and press pastry piece to form a cup shape. Repeat procedure with remaining pastry pieces.

Bake at 375° for 8 minutes or until edges of pastries are lightly browned. Remove pan to a wire rack.

Stir together goat cheese and next 3 ingredients. Spoon evenly into pastry shells.

Bake at 375° for 8 to 10 minutes or until thoroughly heated. Remove to a wire rack, and let cool 2 minutes. **Yield:** 12 tarts.

Champagne Vinaigrette:

Prep: 10 min. Chill: 30 min.

¼ cup extra virgin olive oil
¼ cup Champagne vinegar
2 Tbsp. Dijon mustard
2 tsp. honey
¾ tsp. salt
¼ tsp. freshly ground pepper

Whisk together all ingredients. Cover and chill at least 30 minutes or up to 3 days. **Yield:** about ¾ cup.

Apricot-Ginger Salmon

If you're unsure whether your skillet handle is ovenproof, double-wrap it with heavy-duty aluminum foil.

Prep: 10 min. Cook: 4 min. Bake: 6 min. Stand: 2 min.

8 (6-oz.) salmon fillets
½ tsp. salt
½ tsp. freshly ground pepper
Apricot-Ginger Sauce

Sprinkle fillets evenly with salt and pepper. Cook, skin sides up, in a lightly greased, large, ovenproof nonstick skillet over medium-high heat 2 minutes; turn and cook 2 more minutes. Pour Apricot-Ginger Sauce over salmon.

Bake at 350° for 4 to 6 minutes or until a sharp knife is warm to the touch when inserted into center of fillet and removed. Remove from oven, and let stand 2 minutes. **Yield:** 8 servings.

Apricot-Ginger Sauce:

Prep: 5 min.

½ cup vegetable oil
3 Tbsp. raspberry vinegar
2 Tbsp. apricot preserves
2 Tbsp. honey mustard
1 Tbsp. honey
½ tsp. salt
½ tsp. fresh coarsely ground pepper
½ tsp. ground ginger

Process all ingredients in a blender or food processor until smooth. Cover and refrigerate up to 1 week. **Yield:** 1 cup.

AN EASY NO-COOK APPETIZER

Offer guests Humboldt Fog goat cheese paired with toasted baguette slices and store-bought clementine preserves to start off this elegant menu with ease. The preserves nicely complement the subtle tang of the cheese. Bring the soft and creamy cheese to room temperature before serving.

Apricot-Ginger Salmon,
Sautéed Beans and Peppers (following page),
Citrus Sweet Potatoes (following page)

make ahead

Citrus Sweet Potatoes

For a more intense flavor, bake whole sweet potatoes at 350° for 1 hour and 30 minutes or until tender, instead of boiling them. (pictured on previous page)

Prep: 15 min. Cook: 15 min.

5 to 6 medium-size sweet potatoes (about 3½ lb.)
2 Tbsp. light brown sugar
2 Tbsp. fresh lime juice
2 Tbsp. honey
½ tsp. salt
⅛ tsp. ground nutmeg
⅛ tsp. ground cinnamon

Peel potatoes; cut into 1-inch pieces.

Bring potatoes and water to cover to a boil in a large saucepan, and cook 12 minutes or until tender.

Drain and return potatoes to pan. Add remaining ingredients. Mash with a potato masher or fork until smooth. **Yield:** 8 servings.

Make-Ahead Note: Spoon mashed potato mixture into a large baking dish; cover and keep warm in a 350° oven up to 1 hour.

Sautéed Beans and Peppers

Cook green beans the day before the party. Pat dry with paper towels, and store in a zip-top plastic freezer bag. (pictured on previous page)

Prep: 10 min. Cook: 10 min.

2 lb. fresh green beans
1 red bell pepper, cut into thin strips
1 yellow bell pepper, cut into thin strips
1 to 2 Tbsp. olive oil
1 Tbsp. chopped fresh basil
½ tsp. salt

Cook green beans in boiling salted water to cover in a Dutch oven over medium-high heat 4 to 5 minutes or until crisp-tender. Drain and plunge into ice water to stop the cooking process; drain.

Sauté peppers in hot oil in a Dutch oven over medium-high heat 5 minutes or until tender. Add green beans, basil, and salt. Cook, stirring constantly, until thoroughly heated. Serve immediately. **Yield:** 8 servings.

editor's favorite

Easy Apple Tart With Ol' South Custard

Roll out the puff pastry no more than 10 minutes before apples are done; the pastry needs to stay as cold as possible for maximum puff.

Prep: 20 min. Cook: 30 min. Bake: 12 min. Cool: 15 min.

12 to 14 Rome or Braeburn apples (about 7 lb.)
1½ cups sugar
1 (17.3-oz.) package frozen puff pastry sheets, thawed
Ol' South Custard

Peel and core apples; cut in half lengthwise. Toss together apples and sugar; place in a 12-inch cast-iron or ovenproof skillet.

Cook over medium-high heat, stirring often, 20 to 30 minutes or until apples soften and start to caramelize.

Unfold and stack pastry sheets on top of each other on a lightly floured surface. Roll to a 12-inch square. Place on top of cooked apples, with pastry corners overlapping sides of skillet.

Bake at 450° for 10 to 12 minutes or until dark golden brown.

Cool on a wire rack 10 to 15 minutes. Carefully invert tart onto a serving plate; remove skillet. Cut tart into wedges, and serve with Ol' South Custard. **Yield:** 8 servings.

Ol' South Custard:

Prep: 10 min. Cook: 20 min. Chill: 24 hr.

1 qt. milk
4 large eggs
1 cup sugar
2 tsp. vanilla extract
¼ tsp. salt

Cook milk in a heavy nonaluminum saucepan over medium heat, stirring often, 10 minutes or just until it begins to steam. (Do not boil.) Remove from heat.

Whisk together eggs and next 3 ingredients until blended. Gradually whisk 1 cup hot milk into egg mixture; whisk egg mixture into remaining hot milk, stirring constantly.

Cook over medium heat, stirring constantly, 8 to 10 minutes or until a thermometer registers between 170° and 180°. (Do not boil.)

Remove from heat, and pour mixture through a fine wire-mesh strainer into a bowl. Place heavy-duty plastic wrap directly on warm custard to prevent a film from forming on top, and chill at least 24 hours or up to 3 days. Mixture will thicken as it cools. **Yield:** 5 cups.

Easy Apple Tart
With Ol' South Custard

EASY APPLE TART

Cook sugared apple halves in a 12-inch skillet. As they cook, they'll reduce in size and soften. Place puff pastry directly on top of apples in the skillet.

HOLIDAY *Cooking*

Sausage-Cheese Muffins (page 101)

Brussels Sprouts With Pecans (page 178)

Sugarplum Thumbprints (page 249)

Eggnog Frappé (page 126)

FROM APPETIZERS TO DESSERTS, BROWSE THESE PAGES TO FIND THE PERFECT RECIPE TO SUIT ANY MEAL.

Apricot-Pecan Cinnamon Rolls

TREATS FOR *Early Risers*

Make every day a holiday with this tempting array of scrumptious delights. Your choices range from yummy cinnamon rolls that start with frozen biscuits to individual sausage-and-egg casseroles that are baked in coffee mugs.

editor's favorite

Apricot-Pecan Cinnamon Rolls

To make individual rolls, prepare as directed; place one slice in each of 12 lightly greased 3-inch muffin cups. Bake at 375° for 20 to 25 minutes or until golden brown. Cool slightly, and remove from pan.

Prep: 10 min. Stand: 55 min. Bake: 40 min.

1 (26.4-oz.) package frozen biscuits
1 (6-oz.) package dried apricots
All-purpose flour
¼ cup butter, softened
¾ cup firmly packed brown sugar
1 tsp. ground cinnamon
½ cup chopped pecans, toasted
1 cup powdered sugar
3 Tbsp. milk
½ tsp. vanilla extract

Arrange frozen biscuits, with sides touching, in 3 rows of 4 biscuits on a lightly floured surface. Let stand 30 to 45 minutes or until biscuits are thawed but still cool to the touch.

Pour boiling water to cover over dried apricots, and let stand 10 minutes; drain well. Chop apricots.

Sprinkle thawed biscuits lightly with flour. Press biscuit edges together, and pat to form a 10- x 12-inch rectangle of dough; spread evenly with softened butter. Stir together brown sugar and cinnamon; sprinkle evenly over butter. Sprinkle chopped apricots and pecans evenly over brown sugar mixture.

Roll up, starting at one long end; cut into 12 (about 1-inch-thick) slices. Place rolls into a lightly greased 10-inch cast-iron skillet, 10-inch round pan, or 9-inch square pan.

Bake at 375° for 35 to 40 minutes or until center rolls are golden brown and done; cool slightly.

Stir together 1 cup powdered sugar, 3 Tbsp. milk, and ½ tsp. vanilla; drizzle evenly over rolls. **Yield:** 1 dozen.

Cinnamon-Raisin Rolls: Prepare Apricot-Pecan Cinnamon Rolls as directed, substituting 1 cup golden raisins for 1 (6-oz.) package dried apricots.

Peaches-and-Cream Cinnamon Rolls: Prepare Apricot-Pecan Cinnamon Rolls as directed, substituting ½ (8-oz.) package softened cream cheese for ¼ cup butter and 1 (6-oz.) package dried peaches for 1 (6-oz.) package dried apricots.

Chocolate-Cherry-Cream Cheese Cinnamon Rolls: Prepare Apricot-Pecan Cinnamon Rolls as directed, substituting ½ (8-oz.) package softened cream cheese for ¼ cup butter, 1 (6-oz.) package dried cherries for 1 (6-oz.) package dried apricots, and 1 cup semisweet chocolate morsels for ½ cup pecans.

editor's favorite

Sausage-Cheese Muffins

(pictured on page 99)

Prep: 16 min. Bake: 16 min.

1 (1-lb.) package ground pork sausage
3 cups all-purpose baking mix
1½ cups (6 oz.) shredded Cheddar cheese
1 (10¾-oz.) can condensed cheese soup
½ cup water

Cook sausage in a large skillet, stirring until it crumbles and is no longer pink. Drain and cool.

Combine sausage, baking mix, and shredded cheese in a large bowl; make a well in center of mixture.

Stir together soup and ½ cup water; add to sausage mixture, stirring just until dry ingredients are moistened. Spoon into lightly greased mini muffin pans, filling to top of cups.

Bake at 375° for 16 minutes or until golden. **Yield:** 4 dozen.

Raspberry Crumble Muffins

Raspberry Crumble Muffins

Prep: 25 min. Bake: 28 min.

1½ cups all-purpose flour
2 tsp. baking powder
½ cup granulated sugar
1 large egg
½ cup milk
6 Tbsp. butter, melted and divided
1 cup frozen raspberries
1 Tbsp. flour
¼ cup sliced almonds, chopped
¼ cup firmly packed light brown sugar

Combine first 3 ingredients in a large bowl.

Whisk together egg, milk, and 5 Tbsp. butter. Add to dry ingredients, stirring just until moistened. Gently stir in raspberries.

Spoon batter evenly into a lightly greased muffin pan, filling two-thirds full.

Stir together remaining 1 Tbsp. melted butter, 1 Tbsp. flour, almonds, and brown sugar; sprinkle evenly over batter in muffin pan.

Bake at 350° for 25 to 28 minutes or until golden. **Yield:** 1 dozen.

freezer friendly • make ahead

Basic Buttery Biscuits

Keep a dozen or two of these tasty gems in the freezer for drop-in company.

Prep: 10 min. Bake: 9 min.

2¼ cups all-purpose baking mix (see note)
⅓ cup buttermilk
6 Tbsp. unsalted butter, melted and divided

Stir together baking mix, buttermilk, and 5 Tbsp. melted butter just until blended.

Turn dough out onto a lightly floured surface, and knead 1 to 2 times. Pat to a ½-inch thickness; cut with a 1½-inch round cutter, and place on lightly greased baking sheets.

Bake at 450° for 7 to 9 minutes or until lightly browned. Brush tops evenly with remaining 1 Tbsp. melted butter. **Yield:** about 2 dozen.

Note: For testing purposes only, we used Bisquick all-purpose baking mix.

Make-Ahead Note: Freeze unbaked biscuits on a lightly greased baking sheet 30 minutes or until frozen. Store in a zip-top plastic freezer bag up to 3 months. Bake as directed for 8 to 10 minutes.

Cranberry-Orange-Glazed Biscuits: Decrease baking mix to 2 cups plus 2 Tbsp. Add ½ cup chopped dried cranberries to baking mix. Prepare dough, and bake as directed. Omit 1 Tbsp. butter for brushing biscuits after baking. Stir together 6 Tbsp. powdered sugar, 1 Tbsp. orange juice, and ¼ tsp. grated orange rind. Drizzle evenly over warm biscuits.

Make-Ahead Note: Freeze unbaked biscuits on a lightly greased baking sheet 30 minutes or until frozen. Store in a zip-top plastic freezer bag up to 3 months. Bake as directed for 8 to 10 minutes or until lightly browned. Proceed with recipe as directed.

freezer friendly • great gift

Vanilla Scones

For gift giving, bake these homemade goodies in decorative disposable foil pans, available at the supermarket. Pass along the scones the day you bake them. Or cool completely, place in large zip-top plastic freezer bags, and freeze for up to 1 month.

Prep: 15 min. Bake: 15 min.

2 cups all-purpose flour
⅓ cup sugar
2 tsp. baking powder
⅛ tsp. salt
½ cup butter, cut up
⅔ cup whipping cream
1 large egg
1 Tbsp. vanilla extract
1 egg white
1 tsp. water
2 Tbsp. sparkling sugar (see note)

Combine first 4 ingredients. Cut butter into flour mixture with a pastry blender or fork until crumbly.

Whisk together whipping cream, egg, and vanilla; add to flour mixture, stirring just until dry ingredients are moistened.

Turn dough out onto a lightly floured surface; pat into an 8½-inch circle. Cut into 8 wedges, and place 1 inch apart on a lightly greased baking sheet.

Whisk together egg white and 1 tsp. water; brush over tops of scones. Sprinkle with sparkling sugar.

Bake at 425° for 15 minutes or until golden brown. **Yield:** 8 servings.

Note: We used sparkling sugar, which has larger crystals, to give the scones a festive look. Sparkling sugar is available in stores that carry cake-decorating supplies, gourmet grocery stores, and from Sweet Celebrations at 1-800-328-6722 or www.sweetc.com. Granulated sugar can be substituted for sparkling sugar, if desired.

Chocolate Sprinkle Scones: Prepare Vanilla Scones as directed, stirring 1 finely chopped (4-oz.) semisweet chocolate bar into the flour mixture before adding the wet ingredients.

Vanilla Scones

SPREAD THE HOLIDAY SPIRIT

Box up a batch of Vanilla Scones, and deliver with a festive jar of apricot butter. To make fruit-flavored butters, stir together ½ cup softened butter and ¼ cup of your favorite fruit preserves, such as apricot, strawberry, or blackberry.

Sparkly Cranberry Scones

Prep: 10 min. Bake: 20 min.

2 cups all-purpose flour
½ cup granulated sugar
2 tsp. baking powder
½ tsp. salt
1 cup fresh or frozen cranberries, thawed
½ cup butter, melted
½ cup milk
2 large eggs
1 Tbsp. milk
2 Tbsp. sparkling sugar (see note)

Stir together first 4 ingredients in a large bowl; stir in cranberries.

Whisk together butter, ½ cup milk, and 1 egg; add to flour mixture, stirring just until dry ingredients are moistened and dough forms. Drop dough by ⅓ cupfuls onto a lightly greased baking sheet. Whisk together remaining 1 egg and 1 Tbsp. milk. Brush tops of dough with egg mixture, and sprinkle evenly with sparkling sugar.

Bake at 400° for 20 minutes or until golden brown. **Yield:** 9 scones.

Note: We used sparkling sugar, which has larger crystals, to give the scones a festive look. Sparkling sugar is available in stores that carry cake-decorating supplies, gourmet grocery stores, and online from Sweet Celebrations, 1-800-328-6722 or www.sweetc.com. Granulated sugar can be substituted for sparkling sugar, if desired.

Bananas Foster French Toast

Keep cooked French toast slices warm in a 200° oven while preparing the bananas. This dish doubles as breakfast or dessert.

Prep: 15 min. Cook: 20 min.

1 cup milk
1 cup refrigerated or canned eggnog
4 large eggs, lightly beaten
12 (¾-inch-thick) slices egg bread
10 Tbsp. butter, divided
4 ripe bananas
1 cup firmly packed brown sugar
½ cup bourbon

Whisk together first 3 ingredients. Pour into a large shallow dish. Place bread slices, 1 at a time, into egg mixture, coating both sides of bread.

Melt 1 Tbsp. butter in a large nonstick skillet over medium heat. Add 6 bread slices, and cook 2 to 3 minutes on each side or until golden brown. Repeat procedure with 1 Tbsp. butter and remaining 6 bread slices.

Cut bananas in half; cut each half in half lengthwise.

Melt remaining 8 Tbsp. butter in a large skillet over medium-high heat; add brown sugar, and cook, stirring constantly, 2 minutes. Add bananas to pan, gently stirring to coat with sugar mixture. Remove from heat. Stir in bourbon, and ignite with a long match just above mixture to light the fumes (not mixture itself). Let flames die down.

Return pan to heat, and cook 3 to 4 minutes or until bananas are soft and curl slightly. Remove from heat. Serve immediately over French toast slices. **Yield:** 4 servings.

make ahead

Pecan Pancakes

We like the hearty thickness of these pancakes. If you prefer yours thinner, add up to ⅔ cup additional milk to batter.

Prep: 10 min. Cook: 6 min. per batch

1 cup all-purpose flour
⅓ cup finely chopped pecans or walnuts, toasted
1 tsp. granulated sugar
1 tsp. light brown sugar
½ tsp. baking powder
½ tsp. ground cinnamon
¼ tsp. baking soda
⅛ tsp. salt
1 cup nonfat buttermilk*
2 Tbsp. vegetable oil
1 large egg

Stir together first 8 ingredients until well combined.

Whisk together buttermilk, oil, and egg in a bowl; add to flour mixture, stirring just until dry ingredients are moistened.

Pour about ¼ cup batter for each pancake onto a hot, lightly greased griddle or large skillet. Cook pancakes 2 to 3 minutes or until tops are covered with bubbles and edges look cooked. Turn and cook other sides. Serve immediately. **Yield:** about 10 pancakes.

*½ cup fat-free milk and 1½ tsp. lemon juice can be substituted for buttermilk. Let stand 10 minutes before blending batter.

Make-Ahead Note: Mix up the dry ingredients ahead, and store in an airtight container up to 1 week.

Pecan Pancakes

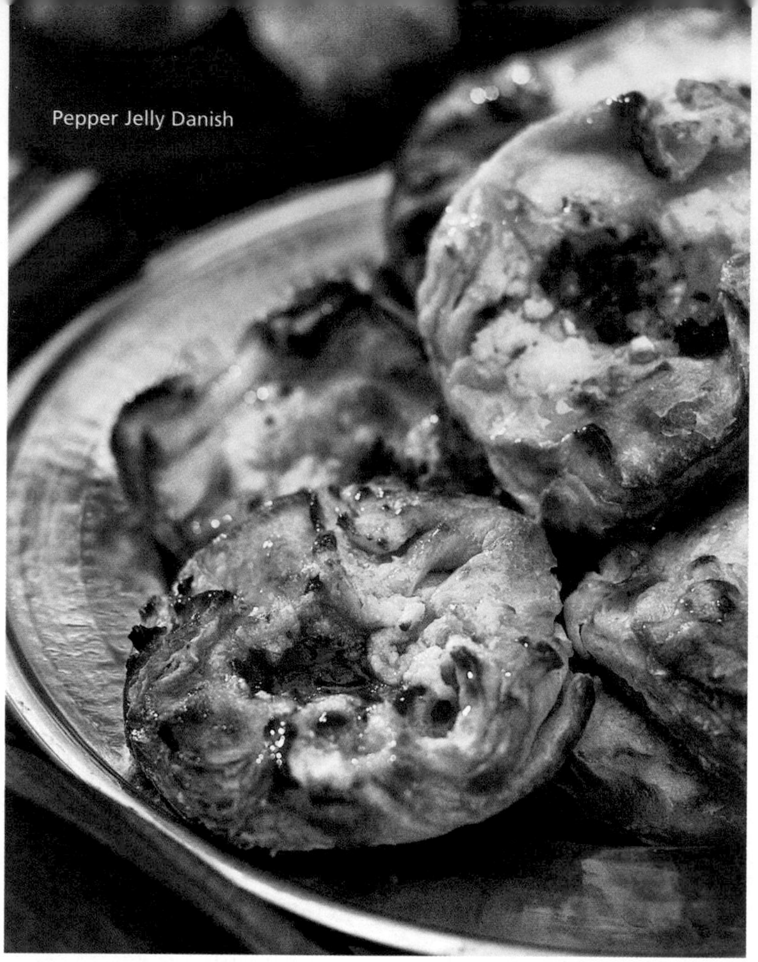

Pepper Jelly Danish

Pepper Jelly Danish

Martha Foose, owner of Mockingbird Bakery in Mississippi, shared this recipe. She uses a locally produced honey-infused pepper jelly; we added honey to regular pepper jelly for a similar taste.

Prep: 25 min. Bake: 18 min. per batch

4 (8-oz.) cans refrigerated crescent rolls
1 (8-oz.) package cream cheese, softened
1 large egg, lightly beaten
⅓ cup pepper jelly
1 Tbsp. honey

Unroll 1 can crescent roll dough onto a lightly floured surface; divide into 2 pieces, separating at center perforation. Press each piece into a 7-inch square. Bring corners to center, partially overlapping each; gently press corners into centers using thumb, making a small indentation. Repeat process with remaining cans of crescent rolls. Transfer to lightly greased baking sheets.

Stir together cream cheese and egg; stir together pepper jelly and honey. Spoon 1 Tbsp. cream cheese mixture into center of each dough circle, and top with 2 tsp. pepper jelly mixture. Bake, in batches, at 375° for 15 to 18 minutes or until golden. **Yield:** 8 servings.

make ahead

Breakfast Enchiladas

Serve this make-ahead casserole with salsa.

Prep: 10 min. Chill: 8 hr. Stand: 40 min. Bake: 39 min.

2 cups diced cooked ham (about ¾ lb.)
½ cup chopped green onions
10 (8-inch) flour tortillas
2 cups (8 oz.) shredded Cheddar cheese, divided
6 large eggs
2 cups half-and-half
½ tsp. salt
¼ tsp. ground red pepper

Sprinkle cooked ham and chopped green onions evenly down the center of each tortilla; top each with 2 Tbsp. shredded cheese. Roll up tortillas, and place, seam sides down, in a lightly greased 13- x 9-inch baking dish.

Whisk together eggs and next 3 ingredients in a large bowl. Pour mixture evenly over tortillas.

Cover and chill at least 8 hours. Remove from refrigerator, and let stand 30 minutes at room temperature before baking.

Bake, covered, at 350° for 20 minutes; uncover and bake 15 minutes. Sprinkle with remaining ¾ cup Cheddar cheese, and bake 3 to 4 more minutes or until cheese melts. Let stand 10 minutes before serving. **Yield:** 8 to 10 servings.

freezer friendly • make ahead

Mini Sausage-and-Egg Casseroles

Use 1 (16-oz.) package of crumbled pork sausage instead of the patties, if desired. Simply cook in a nonstick skillet until browned and crumbled.

Prep: 20 min. Bake: 30 min.

8 (1½-oz.) sourdough bread slices, cut into ½-inch cubes
Vegetable cooking spray
1 (12-oz) package fully cooked pork sausage patties, chopped
2½ cups 2% reduced-fat milk
4 large eggs
1 Tbsp. Dijon mustard
½ cup buttermilk
1 (10¾-oz.) can cream of mushroom soup
1 cup (4 oz.) shredded sharp Cheddar cheese

Divide bread cubes evenly among 10 (8- to 10-oz.) ovenproof coffee mugs coated with cooking spray, placing in bottom of mugs. Top evenly with sausage. Whisk together 2½ cups milk, eggs, and Dijon mustard. Pour evenly over bread mixture in mugs.

Whisk together buttermilk and cream of mushroom soup. Spoon over bread mixture in mugs; sprinkle with Cheddar cheese. Place coffee mugs on a baking sheet.

Bake at 350° for 25 to 30 minutes or until casseroles are set and puffed. Serve immediately. **Yield:** 10 servings.

Make-Ahead Note: Unbaked mugs of casserole can be covered with plastic wrap, then foil, and frozen up to 1 month. Thaw overnight in the refrigerator. Bake as directed.

Sausage-and-Egg Casserole: Omit coffee mugs. Arrange bread in 2 lightly greased 8-inch square baking dishes or 1 lightly greased 13- x 9-inch baking dish. Proceed as directed, increasing bake time to 1 hour or until casserole is set.

Make-Ahead Note: An unbaked casserole can be covered with plastic wrap, then foil, and frozen up to 1 month. Thaw overnight in the refrigerator. Bake as directed.

Golden Egg Casserole

Prep: 30 min. Cook: 10 min. Bake: 30 min.

- 2 Tbsp. butter or margarine
- 1 cup sliced fresh mushrooms
- 1 medium-size green bell pepper, chopped
- 10 large eggs
- ½ cup all-purpose flour
- 1 tsp. baking powder
- ¼ tsp. salt
- 1 (16-oz.) container small-curd cottage cheese
- 2 cups (8 oz.) shredded Monterey Jack cheese
- ½ lb. ground pork sausage, cooked and drained
- 6 bacon slices, cooked and crumbled
- 1 (2¼-oz.) can sliced ripe black olives, drained

Melt butter in a large skillet over medium-high heat; add mushrooms and bell pepper, and sauté 8 minutes or until tender. Remove from heat; cool slightly.

Whisk together eggs and next 3 ingredients in a large bowl until smooth. Stir in mushroom mixture, cottage cheese, and remaining ingredients. Pour mixture into a greased 13- x 9-inch baking dish.

Bake at 400° for 15 minutes. Reduce heat to 350°; bake 15 more minutes or until set and lightly browned. **Yield:** 8 to 10 servings.

Mini Sausage-and-Egg Casserole

Fiesta Dip

PARTY *Starters*

Begin your seasonal celebrations with a selection of sweet and savory snacks, such as Bing Cherry-and-Brie Bites and Cranberry Meatballs. Add to the cheer with one of a dozen festive beverages offered here.

quick & easy

Fiesta Dip

This super-simple dip is a hit at any party. The best part is that it's ready in only 15 minutes.

Prep: 15 min.

1 (10-oz.) can diced tomatoes and green chiles, drained and divided
1 (16-oz.) can refried beans
2 (8-oz.) containers guacamole
2 green onions, sliced
¼ cup sour cream
1 (2¼-oz.) can sliced ripe olives, drained
1 cup (4 oz.) shredded Cheddar cheese
Garnish: lime wedges
Tortilla chips

Reserve ¼ cup diced tomatoes and green chiles.

Stir together refried beans and remaining tomatoes and green chiles. Spoon bean mixture into a large serving bowl, or spoon evenly into 4 (8- to 9-ounce) martini glasses or ramekins. Top bean layer evenly with guacamole, reserved tomatoes and green chiles, green onions, sour cream, olives, and cheese. Garnish, if desired. Serve with tortilla chips. **Yield:** 6 to 8 appetizer servings.

Cheese-and-Bean Salsa

Prep: 10 min.

1 cup salsa
1 (8-oz.) package pasteurized prepared cheese product, cubed
1 (15-oz.) can black beans, drained
Tortilla chips

Stir together first 3 ingredients in a microwave-safe bowl; microwave at HIGH 3 minutes, stirring well after each minute. Serve with tortilla chips. **Yield:** about 3½ cups.

quick & easy

Cranberry Salsa

Serve with sweet potato chips, with assorted crackers, or over cream cheese topped with chopped pecans.

Prep: 10 min. Chill: 1 hr.

1 small navel orange, peeled and quartered
1 (12-oz.) bag frozen cranberries, thawed
1 cup sugar
2 jalapeño peppers, halved lengthwise and seeded
⅛ tsp. salt

Process all ingredients in a food processor until coarsely chopped, stopping once to scrape down sides. Pulse 2 or 3 times until mixture is finely chopped.

Transfer mixture to a bowl; cover, and chill at least 1 hour. **Yield:** about 2½ cups.

quick & easy

Chutney Cheese Ball

Feel free to use ⅓-less-fat cream cheese instead of regular. Just make sure the ball is well chilled before rolling in almonds. We accented ours with artificial flowers and an ornament for a special holiday touch.

Prep: 10 min. Chill: 30 min.

2 (8-oz.) packages cream cheese, softened
1 (9-oz.) jar hot mango chutney
½ tsp. curry powder
½ tsp. dry mustard
⅔ cup slivered almonds
Assorted crackers

Stir together first 4 ingredients until blended. Shape into a ball, and cover and chill at least 30 minutes. Roll in almonds. Serve with assorted crackers. **Yield:** 10 appetizer servings.

Baked Honey-Raisin Brie

Cook this appetizer ahead, cover with nonstick aluminum foil, and take to a party. To prevent browning, toss apple slices (and pear slices, if desired) in lemon juice diluted slightly with water, or cut and serve fruit immediately when you get there.

Prep: 10 min. Stand: 5 min. Cook: 1 min. Bake: 15 min.

¼ cup orange liqueur
1 cup golden raisins
2 (8-oz.) Brie rounds
3 Tbsp. honey
Apple slices
Assorted crackers

Microwave orange liqueur at HIGH 1 minute in microwave-safe bowl; add raisins, and let stand 5 minutes.

Trim rind from top of Brie rounds, leaving a ½-inch border on tops. Place Brie rounds in 9-inch pieplates or ovenproof plates. Spoon raisin mixture onto Brie rounds; drizzle with honey.

Bake at 350° for 12 to 15 minutes or until cheese is melted. Serve immediately with apple slices and assorted crackers. **Yield:** 10 servings.

quick & easy

Baked Pimiento Cheese

Serve this dip warm with crackers or crunchy veggies.

Prep: 15 min. Bake: 20 min.

1½ cups mayonnaise
1 (4-oz.) jar diced pimiento, drained
1 tsp. Worcestershire sauce
1 tsp. finely grated onion
¼ tsp. ground red pepper
1 (8-oz.) block extra-sharp Cheddar cheese, shredded
1 (8-oz.) block sharp Cheddar cheese, shredded
Garnish: chopped parsley

Stir together first 5 ingredients in a large bowl; stir in cheeses. Spoon mixture into a lightly greased 2-quart or 11- x 7-inch baking dish.

Bake at 350° for 20 minutes or until dip is golden and bubbly. Garnish, if desired. **Yield:** 4 cups.

Baked Honey-Raisin Brie

Baked Pimiento Cheese

Baked Spinach-and-Artichoke Dip

make ahead

Baked Spinach-and-Artichoke Dip

For easy entertaining, this dish can be assembled up to a day ahead. Store in an airtight container in the refrigerator, and then bake just before serving.

Prep: 10 min. Cook: 7 min. Bake: 15 min.

2 (6-oz.) packages fresh baby spinach
1 Tbsp. butter
1 (8-oz.) package ⅓-less-fat cream cheese
1 garlic clove, chopped
1 (14-oz.) can artichoke hearts, drained and chopped
½ cup light sour cream
½ cup shredded part-skim mozzarella cheese, divided
Fresh pita wedges or baked pita chips

Microwave spinach in a large, microwave-safe bowl at HIGH 3 minutes or until wilted. Drain spinach well, pressing between paper towels. Chop spinach.

Melt butter in a nonstick skillet over medium-high heat. Add cream cheese and garlic; cook 3 to 4 minutes, stirring constantly, until cream cheese melts. Fold in spinach, artichokes, sour cream, and ¼ cup mozzarella cheese; stir until cheese melts.

Transfer mixture to a 1-qt. shallow baking dish. Sprinkle with remaining ¼ cup mozzarella cheese.

Bake at 350° for 15 minutes or until hot and bubbly. Serve immediately with fresh pita wedges or baked pita chips. **Yield:** 11 servings.

make ahead

Black-eyed Pea-and-Ham Dip

Prep: 20 min. Cook: 13 min.

½ cup diced country ham
2 (15.8-oz.) cans black-eyed peas, rinsed and drained
¾ cup water
1 large tomato, finely chopped
2 green onions, sliced
1 celery rib, finely chopped
¼ cup chopped fresh parsley
2 Tbsp. olive oil
1 to 2 Tbsp. apple cider vinegar
Cornbread crackers

Sauté ham in a lightly greased large nonstick skillet over medium-high heat 3 to 5 minutes or until lightly brown; stir in black-eyed peas and ¾ cup water. Reduce heat to medium, and simmer 8 minutes or until liquid is reduced by three-fourths. Partially mash beans with back of a spoon to desired consistency.

Stir together tomato and next 5 ingredients. Spoon warm bean mixture into a serving dish, and top with tomato mixture. Serve with crackers. **Yield:** 12 appetizer servings.

Make-Ahead Note: Prepare dip 24 hours in advance, if desired; then reheat before serving.

make ahead

Smoky Pecans

Prep: 10 min. Bake: 25 min.

¼ cup butter, melted
2 Tbsp. lite soy sauce
1 Tbsp. Worcestershire sauce
1 Tbsp. hot sauce
3 cups pecan halves

Stir together first 4 ingredients; stir in pecans. Spread in a single layer in a lightly greased 15- x 10-inch jelly-roll pan.

Bake pecan halves at 300° for 25 minutes or until toasted, stirring often. Place in a single layer on wax paper, and let cool completely. **Yield:** 3 cups.

Make-Ahead Note: These pecans can be made ahead and stored in an airtight container for up to 2 weeks or frozen up to 3 months.

Black-eyed Pea-and-Ham Dip

freezer friendly • great gift • make ahead

Praline Pecans

Pralines are best made when the weather is dry—humidity tends to make them grainy. Be sure to use a heavy saucepan, and work quickly when spooning the pecan mixture onto the wax paper.

Prep: 5 min. Cook: 15 min. Stand: 20 min.

1½ cups granulated sugar
¾ cup firmly packed brown sugar
½ cup butter
½ cup milk
2 Tbsp. corn syrup
5 cups toasted pecan halves

Stir together first 5 ingredients in a heavy 3-qt. saucepan. Bring to a boil over medium heat, stirring constantly. Boil, stirring constantly, 7 to 8 minutes or until a candy thermometer registers 234°.

Remove from heat, and vigorously stir in pecans. Spoon pecan mixture onto wax paper, spreading in an even layer. Let stand 20 minutes or until firm. Break praline-coated pecans apart into pieces. Store in an airtight container at room temperature up to 1 week. Freeze in an airtight container or zip-top plastic freezer bag up to 1 month. **Yield:** about 8 cups.

Magi Olives

make ahead

Hip Snack Mix

Roast the cashews in butter in any small baking dish or pan you have, such as a pieplate or an 8- to 9-inch square baking dish. Wasabi peas have a tangy, spicy flavor. The brighter green the pea, the hotter the flavor. Find the pretzel crackers near the deli case.

Prep: 5 min. Bake: 7 min.

1 tsp. butter
1 (9.75-oz.) can whole salted cashews
1 (10-oz.) bag wasabi peas (see note)
1 (6-oz.) bag thin, crispy pretzel crackers (see note)

Melt butter in a 9-inch cake pan in a 350° oven. Stir in nuts, tossing to coat.

Bake at 350° for 7 minutes; remove from oven. Toss roasted nuts with wasabi peas and pretzel crackers. Store in an airtight container up to 1 week. **Yield:** 8 cups.

Note: For testing purposes only, we used Archer Farms Wasabi Peas and The Snack Factory Deli Style Pretzel Crisps.

make ahead

Magi Olives

Martha Foose, owner of Mockingbird Bakery in Mississippi, enjoys serving this recipe when entertaining. She prefers a mix of green and black Spanish olives as well as Greek kalamatas when she makes it, but your favorite olives will work just fine.

Prep: 15 min. Chill: 8 hr. Stand: 30 min.

5 cups assorted pitted olives
½ cup extra virgin olive oil
1 Tbsp. grated fresh lemon rind
1 Tbsp. fresh lemon juice
1 Tbsp. grated fresh orange rind
2 Tbsp. fresh orange juice
1 Tbsp. minced garlic
1 tsp. fennel seeds
½ tsp. dried crushed red pepper
½ tsp. dried oregano

Stir together olives and remaining ingredients in a large bowl.

Cover and chill at least 8 hours or up to 1 week. Let stand 30 minutes at room temperature before serving. Serve olive mixture with a slotted spoon. **Yield:** 5 cups.

Blue Cheese-Bacon Dip

Prep: 20 min. Cook: 11 min. Bake: 15 min.

7 bacon slices, chopped
2 garlic cloves, minced
2 (8-oz.) packages cream cheese, softened
⅓ cup half-and-half
4 oz. crumbled blue cheese
2 Tbsp. chopped fresh chives
3 Tbsp. chopped walnuts, toasted
Grape clusters
Flatbread or assorted crackers

Cook chopped bacon in a skillet over medium-high heat 10 minutes or until crisp. Drain bacon, and set aside. Add minced garlic to skillet, and sauté 1 minute.

Beat cream cheese at medium speed with an electric mixer until smooth. Add half-and-half, beating until combined. Stir in bacon, garlic, blue cheese, and chives. Spoon mixture evenly into 4 (1-cup) individual baking dishes.

Bake at 350° for 15 minutes or until golden and bubbly. Sprinkle evenly with chopped walnuts, and serve with grape clusters and flatbread or assorted crackers. **Yield:** 12 to 15 servings.

Blue Cheese-Bacon Dip

Creamy Tomato Crostini

If you'd rather not have bread, substitute cucumber slices or sturdy crackers. Stir any leftover cheese spread into mashed potatoes to add richness and flavor.

Prep: 15 min. Broil: 2 min.

1 (8-oz.) French baguette, cut diagonally into ¼-inch-thick slices
1 (6.5-oz.) package garlic-and-herb spreadable cheese (see note)
3 plum tomatoes, cut into ¼-inch-thick slices
¼ cup finely chopped fresh parsley
Salt and pepper to taste

Broil bread slices 5 inches from heat 1 minute on each side or until lightly toasted.

Spread cheese evenly on one side of each bread slice; top each with one tomato slice. Sprinkle evenly with parsley, and add salt and pepper to taste. **Yield:** 8 to 10 servings.

Note: For testing purposes only, we used Alouette Garlic et Herbes Gourmet Spreadable Cheese.

Goat Cheese-and-Olive Crostini: Prepare French baguette as directed. Omit spreadable cheese, tomatoes, parsley, salt, and pepper. Spread 1 (4-oz.) log of goat cheese evenly on one side of the toasted bread slices; top each with 1 tsp. prepared olive tapenade (see note).

Note: For testing purposes only, we used Cantaré Traditional Olive Tapénade.

Curried Chicken-and-Chutney Party Sandwiches

Pressing down on the sandwiches so that some of the cream cheese mixture seeps out helps the pecans stick to the edges of the bread.

Prep: 45 min.

1 (8-oz.) package cream cheese, softened
½ cup butter or margarine, softened
¼ cup whipping cream
½ cup mango chutney
2 tsp. curry powder
1 small garlic clove, minced
2 cups pecans, finely chopped, toasted, and divided
2 cups finely chopped cooked chicken
2 (16-oz.) packages very thinly sliced white bread

Beat first 3 ingredients at medium speed with an electric mixer until creamy. Add chutney, curry powder, garlic, and 1 cup pecans, beating until blended. Stir in chicken. Reserve ¼ cup cream cheese mixture.

Trim crusts from bread; spread cream cheese mixture evenly to the edges on half of bread slices. Cover with remaining bread slices, and cut sandwiches in half diagonally. Press sandwiches slightly so that some cream cheese mixture seeps out; spread ¼ cup reserved cream cheese mixture evenly along edges, as necessary. Press edges of sandwich triangles in remaining 1 cup chopped pecans. Serve immediately, or store, covered with damp paper towels, in an airtight container in the refrigerator (see note). **Yield:** 26 appetizer servings.

Note: Sandwiches may be frozen by placing wax paper between them in an airtight container. Thaw in the refrigerator.

quick & easy

Simple Antipasto Platter

If you can open a package or a jar, you can arrange this appetizer. Roll a log of goat cheese in chopped fresh parsley, and then just arrange the other items for an effortless and tasty offering.

Prep: 10 min.

1 (5-oz.) log goat cheese
2 Tbsp. chopped fresh parsley
1 (16-oz.) jar pickled okra, drained
1 (10-oz.) jar pitted kalamata olives, rinsed and drained
1 (7-oz.) jar roasted red bell peppers, drained and cut into strips
1 (4-oz.) package sliced salami
Assorted crackers and breadsticks

Roll goat cheese log in parsley; place on a serving platter. Arrange okra and next 3 ingredients on platter around goat cheese. Serve with crackers and breadsticks. **Yield:** 8 servings.

Simple Antipasto Platter

Crispy Parmesan Crackers

Look for egg roll wrappers in the produce area or refrigerated section of your grocery store.

Prep: 5 min. Bake: 10 min.

¼ cup freshly grated Parmesan cheese
½ tsp. dried parsley flakes
¼ tsp. garlic powder
6 egg roll wrappers
3 Tbsp. butter or margarine, melted
Salt to taste

Combine first 3 ingredients.

Cut each egg roll wrapper into 4 strips lengthwise. Arrange strips on parchment paper-lined baking sheets. Brush strips with melted butter, and sprinkle with cheese mixture.

Bake at 425° for 8 to 10 minutes or until edges are golden brown. Sprinkle with salt to taste. **Yield:** 2 dozen.

Parmesan Breadsticks: Substitute 1 (11-oz.) can refrigerated breadsticks for egg roll wrappers. Roll each piece of dough into a 10-inch rope. Brush with melted butter, and sprinkle with cheese mixture. Bake at 375° for 11 to 13 minutes or until golden. Yield: 1 dozen.

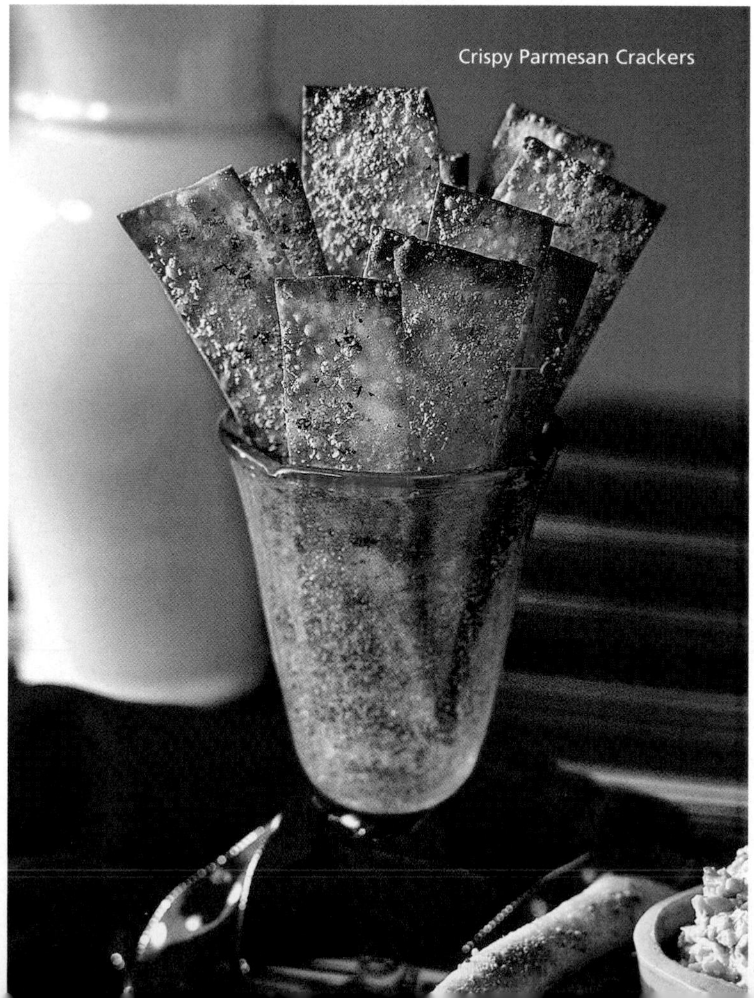
Crispy Parmesan Crackers

Pecan-Cornmeal Shortbreads

Serve these nutty, mildly spiced bites alongside cheese and fresh fruits for a light appetizer.

Prep: 15 min. Chill: 2 hr. Bake: 25 min.

¾ cup butter, softened
1½ cups all-purpose flour
½ cup cornmeal
2 Tbsp. sugar
½ tsp. salt
¼ tsp. ground red pepper
1 large egg, lightly beaten
½ cup chopped pecans
30 pecan halves

Beat butter at medium speed with an electric mixer until creamy. Add flour and next 5 ingredients, beating at low speed until blended. Stir in chopped pecans. Wrap dough with plastic wrap; chill 1 hour.

Shape dough into 2 (9-inch-long) logs. Wrap in plastic wrap, and chill 1 hour.

Cut dough into ½-inch-thick slices. Place rounds on lightly greased baking sheets; top each round with a pecan half.

Bake at 350° for 25 minutes or until lightly browned; remove to wire racks, and let cool completely. **Yield:** 2½ dozen.

Pecan-Havarti Quesadilla With Pear Preserves

This recipe can be easily doubled or tripled to serve more. Try this tasty quesadilla wth your favorite Cabernet Sauvignon for a fresh twist on wine and cheese.

Prep: 5 min. Cook: 4 min.

1 (8-inch) flour tortilla
⅓ cup shredded Havarti cheese
2 Tbsp. chopped pecans, toasted
Vegetable cooking spray
Pear preserves

Sprinkle one side of an 8-inch flour tortilla with ⅓ cup shredded Havarti cheese; top with 2 Tbsp. chopped, toasted pecans. Fold tortilla over filling. Coat a nonstick skillet with vegetable cooking spray, and cook quesadilla over medium-high heat for 2 minutes on each side or until cheese melts. Remove from heat, slice into wedges, and serve with pear preserves. **Yield:** 2 servings.

Pecan-Havarti Quesadilla
With Pear Preserves

Pork Tenderloin Sandwiches With Cranberry-Coriander Conserve

editor's favorite

Pork Tenderloin Sandwiches With Cranberry-Coriander Conserve

Prep: 20 min. Cook: 3 min. Bake: 45 min. Stand: 15 min.

3 (11-oz.) packages frozen dinner rolls (see note)
8 tsp. coriander seeds, divided*
¼ cup olive oil
2 Tbsp. kosher salt
1 tsp. freshly ground black pepper
2 tsp. dried crushed red pepper
1 tsp. ground cumin
4 lb. small boneless pork tenderloins
Melted butter
Poppy or sesame seeds (optional)
Cranberry-Coriander Conserve

Thaw dinner rolls according to package directions.

Preheat oven to 375°.

Cook coriander seeds in a hot skillet over medium-high heat, stirring constantly, 2 to 3 minutes or until seeds are toasted and fragrant.

Pulse coriander seeds in an electric spice or coffee grinder until crushed. (If you don't have a grinder, use a mortar and pestle, or place coriander seeds in a zip-top plastic bag, seal, and pound seeds with a meat mallet or rolling pin until crushed.) Reserve 2 tsp. crushed coriander for Cranberry-Coriander Conserve.

Stir together remaining crushed coriander, olive oil, and next 4 ingredients. Place pork on a lightly greased rack in a broiling pan. Rub all sides of pork with spice mixture.

Place pork in preheated oven. Increase heat to 450°, and bake 25 minutes or until a meat thermometer registers 150°. Remove pork from oven, and reduce heat to 350°. Cover pork loosely with aluminum foil, and let stand 15 minutes or until thermometer registers 160°.

Brush thawed dinner rolls with melted butter; sprinkle evenly with poppy or sesame seeds, if desired.

Bake rolls at 350° for 15 to 20 minutes or until golden.

Cut pork into ¼-inch slices, and serve with Cranberry-Coriander Conserve and dinner rolls. **Yield:** 12 to 15 servings.

*3 tsp. store-bought ground coriander may be substituted. Omit toasting and crushing steps. Reserve ¾ tsp. for Cranberry-Coriander Conserve; use remaining as directed.

Note: For testing purposes only, we used Sister Schubert's Parker House Style frozen yeast rolls.

Cranberry-Coriander Conserve:

Prepare this spiced mixture up to 1 week ahead, and store it in the refrigerator.

Prep: 10 min. Cook: 30 min. Chill: 2 hr.

3 cups fresh cranberries
1½ cups orange juice
⅔ cup apple cider
½ cup granulated sugar
⅓ cup firmly packed brown sugar
2 Tbsp. cider vinegar
2 tsp. reserved crushed coriander or ¾ tsp. ground coriander
1 (3-inch) cinnamon stick
6 fresh mint leaves

Cook all ingredients in a heavy saucepan over medium heat 30 minutes or until mixture thickens. Cool. Remove cinnamon stick. Cover and chill at least 2 hours. **Yield:** 2 cups.

big batch • quick & easy

Bing Cherry-and-Brie Bites

So simple! To toast almonds, place on a baking sheet, and bake at 350° for 7 minutes or until warm to the touch and lightly browned.

Prep: 20 min. Bake: 10 min.

4 (2.1-oz.) packages frozen mini-phyllo pastry shells, thawed
1 (8-oz.) Brie round, rind removed
1 (11½-oz.) jar Bing cherry preserves (see note)
½ cup chopped almonds, toasted

Place pastry shells on ungreased baking sheets. Cut Brie into ½-inch-wide strips. Cut each strip into ½-inch pieces. Fill shells evenly with cheese pieces; top each with ¼ tsp. preserves. Sprinkle evenly with almonds.

Bake at 300° for 10 minutes or until cheese melts. **Yield:** about 5 dozen.

Note: For testing purposes only, we used Dickinson's Pure Bing Cherry Preserves.

Fig-and-Brie Bites: Substitute fig preserves for cherry preserves and pecans for almonds. Proceed with recipe as directed.

editor's favorite

Sausage Quiches

These crispy little pastries laced with sage and sausage mimic the flavor of turkey dressing.

Prep: 15 min. Cook: 8 min. Bake: 15 min.

¼ lb. ground hot pork sausage
¼ cup minced celery
3 Tbsp. minced onion
3 large eggs, lightly beaten
¾ cup half-and-half
½ cup (2 oz.) finely shredded mozzarella cheese
½ tsp. poultry seasoning
¼ tsp. salt
¼ tsp. freshly ground pepper
⅛ tsp. rubbed sage
3 (2.1-oz.) packages mini phyllo shells
Garnish: chopped fresh chives

Cook first 3 ingredients in a skillet over medium-high heat 8 minutes, stirring occasionally, or until sausage is finely crumbled and no longer pink.

Combine sausage mixture, eggs, and next 6 ingredients in a medium bowl; stir well. Spoon mixture evenly into shells.

Bake at 350° for 15 minutes or until set. Garnish, if desired; serve warm. **Yield:** 45 appetizers.

Cranberry Meatballs

freezer friendly • make ahead

Cranberry Meatballs

Prep: 30 min. Cook: 40 min.

2 lb. ground chuck
2 large eggs
⅓ cup dry breadcrumbs
1 tsp. salt
½ tsp. freshly ground pepper
½ tsp. garlic powder
½ tsp. onion powder
½ tsp. thyme
1 (16-oz.) can cranberry sauce
1 (12-oz.) jar chili sauce
¼ cup orange marmalade
¼ cup water
2 Tbsp. soy sauce
2 Tbsp. red wine vinegar
1 tsp. dried red pepper flakes

Combine first 8 ingredients in a large bowl. Shape mixture into about 54 (1-inch) balls.

Cook meatballs, in batches, in a large skillet over medium-high heat until browned (about 5 minutes); remove meatballs from pan, and drain well on paper towels.

Stir together cranberry and chili sauces and next 5 ingredients in a large Dutch oven over medium heat, and cook, whisking occasionally, 5 minutes or until smooth. Add meatballs; reduce heat to low, and cook, stirring occasionally, 15 to 20 minutes or until centers are no longer pink. **Yield:** about 4½ dozen.

Make-Ahead Note: Place cooked meatballs in a zip-top plastic freezer bag, and freeze up to 1 month. Thaw in refrigerator, and cook, stirring occasionally, until thoroughly heated.

AT YOUR SERVICE

Thread fresh cranberries onto short wooden skewers for festive serving picks.

Mini Turkey Sandwiches

Save time by cutting the entire package of rolls at the same time instead of individually; simply remove from the aluminum package, and slice in half horizontally.

Prep: 15 min. Bake: 30 min.

1 (9.25-oz.) package small party rolls
¼ cup mayonnaise
2 Tbsp. mango chutney
¼ tsp. curry powder
¼ tsp. ground red pepper
½ lb. thinly sliced smoked turkey

Cut rolls in half horizontally, using a serrated knife. Return bottom halves of rolls to tray, cut side up.

Stir together mayonnaise, mango chutney, curry powder, and ground red pepper until smooth. Spread mayonnaise mixture on cut sides of top halves of rolls.

Layer turkey on bottom halves of rolls. Cover with tops of rolls, mayonnaise mixture side down.

Bake, covered, at 350° for 20 to 30 minutes or until thoroughly heated. Cut sandwiches apart, using a sharp knife. **Yield:** 2 dozen.

make ahead

Sparkling Holiday Punch

This recipe uses blood oranges, which are available December through May in the produce section of the supermarket. Pomegranate juice may be found in the refrigerated section year-round.

Prep: 5 min. Chill: 2 hr.

3½ cups blood orange juice, chilled*
1 cup pomegranate juice, chilled
1 liter ginger ale, chilled
1 orange, thinly sliced

Stir together blood orange juice and pomegranate juice in a large serving bowl. Chill at least 2 hours or up to 24 hours.

Stir in ginger ale and orange slices. Serve immediately. **Yield:** 7 cups.

*Sweet red grapefruit juice may be substituted.

Pomegranate-Orange Punch: Prepare recipe as directed, omitting ginger ale. Stir in ¾ cup chilled vodka, 1 cup chilled orange liqueur, and orange slices before serving. Yield: 6¾ cups.

STOCK UP FOR EASY ENTERTAINING

During the Christmas season, be sure to keep the following drinks on hand for any impromptu gatherings:

- ginger ale
- cranberry juice cocktail
- club soda
- frozen juice concentrates
- sparkling apple cider
- tea

Sparkling Holiday Punch

make ahead
Brunch Punch

Chill the juices before stirring together to eliminate the need for additional time in the refrigerator.

Prep: 5 min. Chill: 2 hr.

1 (46-oz.) can pineapple juice
3 cups orange juice
2 cups cranberry juice
¾ cup powdered sugar
¼ cup lime juice
Garnishes: fresh mint leaves, lime slices, orange slices, cranberries

Stir together first 5 ingredients. Cover and chill 2 hours. Stir before serving. Garnish, if desired. **Yield:** 12 cups.

Cool Cranberry Tea

Irish Coffee Nog

Prep: 5 min.

2 qt. vanilla ice cream
1 qt. eggnog
2 cups hot brewed coffee
½ cup Irish cream liqueur or flavored syrup
½ cup Irish whiskey (optional)
Garnishes: sweetened whipped cream, ground nutmeg, mint candy sticks

Scoop ice cream into a punch bowl. Add eggnog, coffee, Irish cream liqueur, and, if desired, whiskey, stirring until ice cream melts slightly. Serve in glass mugs. Garnish, if desired. Serve immediately. **Yield:** 12 cups.

Warm Cranberry Tea

Prep: 5 min. Cook: 20 min.

1 (48-oz.) jar cranberry juice cocktail
2 cups sugar
¼ cup lemon juice
4 (3-inch) cinnamon sticks
1 Tbsp. whole allspice
½ gal. unsweetened tea
1 cup orange juice

Bring first 5 ingredients to a boil in a large Dutch oven; reduce heat, and simmer 10 minutes. Remove from heat. Remove cinnamon sticks and allspice; stir in tea and orange juice. **Yield:** 16 cups.

Cool Cranberry Tea: Prepare recipe as directed. Chill tea mixture 2 hours. Stir in 1 liter ginger ale, chilled, just before serving. If desired, garnish with lemon slices, fresh cranberries, and cinnamon sticks. Yield: about 20 cups.

Irish Coffee Nog

Mulled Pomegranate Cider

Sweetness is less pronounced at lower temperatures. If you're serving this over ice, use 2 cups sugar; if serving it hot, use 1½ cups sugar.

Prep: 10 min. Cook: 20 min.

5 (3-inch) cinnamon sticks, halved
1 Tbsp. whole cloves
1½ to 2 cups sugar
2 qt. water
2 (16-oz.) bottles pomegranate juice*
¼ cup fresh lemon juice
1 cup orange juice

Place cinnamon sticks and cloves in center of an 8-inch square of cheesecloth; tie with string.

Bring spice bag, sugar, and next 3 ingredients to a boil in a Dutch oven, stirring occasionally. Reduce heat, and simmer, uncovered, 10 minutes. Remove and discard spice bag; stir in 1 cup orange juice. Serve cider hot or cold. **Yield:** 13 cups.
*1 (32-oz.) bottle cranberry juice cocktail may be substituted. For testing purposes only, we used POM Wonderful Pomegranate Juice, which can be found in the refrigerated produce section of large supermarkets.

Butterscotch Latte

If you have a frothing utensil, this recipe offers a great opportunity to use it.

Prep: 10 min.

4 cups hot brewed coffee*
¾ cup butterscotch Schnapps
2 cups warm milk
2 Tbsp. sugar
Canned whipped dessert topping
Cinnamon sugar

Stir together coffee and Schnapps; pour into 6 mugs.

Combine warm milk and sugar; pour into a blender, and process at HIGH for about 1 minute. (Milk will become frothy.) Divide milk mixture evenly into mugs. Top each serving with whipped dessert topping, and sprinkle with cinnamon sugar. **Yield:** about 6 cups.
*4 cups boiling water and 2 Tbsp. instant coffee granules may be substituted for hot brewed coffee.

Nonalcoholic Latte: Substitute ¾ cup butterscotch ice-cream topping for Schnapps, and proceed as directed.

Mint-Chocolate Cocoa

Prep: 5 min. Cook: 10 min.

2 cups half-and-half
2 cups milk
⅓ cup sugar
¼ cup unsweetened cocoa
1 tsp. peppermint extract
¼ tsp. vanilla extract
Garnishes: miniature marshmallows, candy canes, peppermint candies

Cook first 6 ingredients in a heavy saucepan over medium-low heat, stirring occasionally, 10 minutes or until thoroughly heated. Pour into mugs; garnish, if desired. Serve immediately. **Yield:** about 4 cups.

Creamy Mocha Cocoa: Omit peppermint extract. Add 2 Tbsp. instant coffee granules. Proceed as directed.

Creamy Cocoa: Omit peppermint extract. Proceed as directed.

Hot Fudge Cocoa: Omit sugar and peppermint extract. Add ½ cup bottled hot fudge sauce. Proceed as directed.

quick & easy
Eggnog Frappé

Prep: 5 min.

1 pt. frozen vanilla yogurt
1 cup refrigerated eggnog
⅓ cup bourbon
2 Tbsp. orange liqueur (see note)
Garnish: cinnamon sticks

Process all ingredients in a blender until well combined and frothy. Serve immediately. Garnish, if desired. **Yield:** 3 cups.

Note: For testing purposes only, we used Cointreau for orange liqueur.

Eggnog Frappé

Ambrosia Cocktail

Parson's Ruby Cocktail

Be sure to use 100% cranbery juice for this drink, not cranberry juice cocktail.

Prep: 5 min.

1 Tbsp. orange juice
1 Tbsp. grenadine
Crushed ice
¼ cup cranberry juice
¼ cup ginger ale

Combine orange juice and grenadine in a glass. Add crushed ice, filling three-fourths full. Pour cranberry juice over ice; add ginger ale. **Yield:** 1 cocktail.

Ruby Champagne Cocktail: Place 2 Tbsp. cranberry juice, 1 Tbsp. orange liqueur, and 1 tsp. grenadine in a Champagne flute; add ½ cup dry Champagne.

Ambrosia Cocktail

Martha Foose, owner of Mockingbird Bakery in Mississippi, created this cocktail just for the holidays. She suggests placing turbinado sugar in a saucer rather than a bowl when decorating the glass. The thin layer of sugar will make the rim of the glass more attractive.

Prep: 30 min. Stand: 30 min.

3 navel oranges, peeled and sectioned
1 red grapefruit, peeled and sectioned
½ fresh pineapple, peeled, cored, and cut into cubes
1½ Tbsp. orange liqueur or orange juice
¼ cup turbinado sugar (see note)
1 (750-milliliter) bottle sparkling rosé wine*
½ cup frozen grated coconut, thawed and toasted
8 maraschino cherries

Toss together oranges, grapefruit, and pineapple; set aside.

Pour orange liqueur into a shallow saucer. Dip rims of 8 glasses in liqueur; dip rims in sugar, and let stand 30 minutes to dry completely.

Spoon fruit mixture evenly into glasses. Add rosé wine, filling three-fourths full; top with grated coconut and cherries. Serve immediately. **Yield:** 8 servings.

*Substitute nonalcoholic sparkling rosé for a family-friendly version of this beverage.

Note: For testing purposes only, we used Sugar In The Raw for turbinado sugar.

Wintry White Wine Punch

This cozy punch is spiced for the season with cinnamon, cardamom, and nutmeg.

Prep: 10 min. Cook: 10 min. Steep: 1 hr.

2 (750-milliliter) bottles semidry white wine (see note)
3 (12-oz.) cans pear juice
1 (6-oz.) package dried apricots
1 (5-oz.) package dried apples
1 cup golden raisins
¾ cup sugar
1 orange, sliced
2 tsp. vanilla extract
3 (3-inch) cinnamon sticks
10 cardamom pods
1 whole nutmeg, split

Combine first 8 ingredients in a Dutch oven. Place 3 cinnamon sticks, cardamom pods, and nutmeg on a 6-inch square of cheesecloth; tie with string. Add spice bag to wine mixture.

Bring to a simmer over medium heat, stirring occasionally. Cover, remove from heat, and steep 1 hour.

Pour wine mixture through a wire-mesh strainer into a large bowl, discarding spice bag. Serve warm, let cool to room temperature, or chill and serve over ice. **Yield:** about 10 cups.

Note: For testing purposes only, we used Chenin Blanc for semidry white wine.

Nonalcoholic Punch: Substitute 6 cups white grape juice for the wine, and proceed as directed.

quick & easy

Champagne Shimmers

With less lime juice, this is a sweet beverage; with more, it's sour.

Prep: 5 min.

1 (750-milliliter) bottle sparkling white wine, chilled
1 (11½-oz.) can frozen orange-pineapple-apple juice concentrate, thawed*
¼ to ½ cup fresh lime juice (2 to 4 limes)

Stir together sparkling white wine, juice concentrate, and fresh lime juice. **Yield:** 8 cups.

*1 (11½-oz.) can frozen cranberry juice concentrate, thawed, may be substituted.

Glazed Ham

MAIN *Attractions*

Whether you're cooking for a crowd or a few close friends, menu planning is a breeze when you start with one of the delectable entrées featured on the following pages.

Glazed Ham

Using a utensil called a fat separator is the easiest way to remove unwanted fat from the pan drippings.

Prep: 15 min. Bake: 2 hr., 30 min. Stand: 10 min. Cook: 10 min.

1 (7- to 8-lb.) bone-in smoked shank ham half
1 cup maple syrup
¾ cup firmly packed light brown sugar
¾ cup Dijon mustard
⅓ cup cranberry juice
½ cup sweetened dried cherries
2 red Anjou pears, thinly sliced
Garnish: lettuce leaves, pear slices

Line a 13- x 9-inch pan with heavy-duty aluminum foil; lightly grease foil. Remove skin and excess fat from smoked ham; place ham in prepared pan.

Stir together maple syrup and next 3 ingredients. Pour mixture evenly over ham.

Bake at 350° on lower rack 2 hours and 30 minutes or until a meat thermometer inserted into thickest portion registers 140°, basting every 20 minutes with drippings. (Shield with aluminum foil the last hour of baking to prevent excessive browning.) Let ham stand 10 minutes in pan. Remove from pan, reserving drippings. If desired, cool, cover, and chill ham.

Remove fat from drippings, and discard. Cover and chill drippings, if desired. Stir together drippings, sweetened dried cherries, and pear slices in a saucepan over medium-low heat, and cook, 8 to 10 minutes, stirring occasionally, or until pears are tender. Serve warm sauce with ham. Garnish, if desired. **Yield:** 12 servings.

editor's favorite

Fresh Ham With Garlic and Orange

For a smaller cut of pork, see the instructions below for a 6-lb. Boston butt roast.

Prep: 15 min. Chill: 8 hr. Bake: 7 hr. Stand: 20 min.

1 (15- to 18-lb.) fresh ham (not cured or smoked)
1 Tbsp. salt
½ cup chopped fresh or 1 (4-oz.) jar minced garlic
2 tsp. freshly ground pepper
2 tsp. dried oregano
½ cup fresh lime juice
½ cup fresh orange juice

Place ham in an aluminum foil-lined roasting pan. Cut 4 to 5 (1-inch-deep) slits across top of ham. Sprinkle evenly with salt.

Stir together garlic and next 4 ingredients. Pour mixture evenly over ham, rubbing mixture into slits. Cover and chill 8 hours.

Bake, uncovered, at 350° for 7 hours or until a meat thermometer inserted into thickest portion registers 185°. Let stand 20 minutes before slicing. **Yield:** 18 servings.

Citrus-and-Garlic Pork Roast: Substitute 1 (6-lb.) bone-in pork shoulder roast (Boston butt) for fresh ham. Reduce garlic to 3 Tbsp. Reduce oven temperature to 325°. Proceed as directed, baking for 4½ hours or until meat thermometer inserted into thickest portion registers 175°. Remove from oven, and let stand until thermometer reaches 185°. Yield: 6 to 8 servings.

editor's favorite

Holiday Ham With Cumberland Sauce

For a moist, juicy, herb-infused ham, bake it in an oven bag with rosemary sprigs. The sweet, tart English sauce highlights red currant jelly, citrus, and port wine to spice up each slice of ham.

Prep: 10 min. Bake: 2 hr., 30 min. Stand: 15 min.

1 (7- to 10-lb.) fully cooked spiral-sliced ham half (see note)
8 to 10 fresh rosemary sprigs
1 oven cooking bag
Garnishes: fresh rosemary sprigs, fresh cranberries
Cumberland Sauce

Unwrap ham, and remove plastic disk covering bone. Tuck rosemary sprigs randomly between every 2 or 3 slices of ham. Place ham, cut side down, in an oven cooking bag; place in a 13- x 9-inch baking dish. Close bag with tie. Trim excess plastic to 2 inches. Cut 3 (½-inch) slits in top of bag. Bake at 275° on lowest rack for 2½ hours or until a meat thermometer inserted registers 140°.

Remove ham from oven; let stand in bag with juices 15 minutes. Remove ham from bag, and transfer to a carving board. Separate slices, and arrange on a serving platter. Garnish, if desired. Serve with Cumberland Sauce. **Yield:** 10 servings.

Note: For testing purposes only, we used Smithfield spiral-sliced Honey Ham.

Cumberland Sauce:

Prep: 10 min., Cook: 15 min.

1 Tbsp. butter or margarine
¼ cup minced onion
1 (12-oz.) jar red currant jelly
1 Tbsp. grated fresh orange rind
¼ cup fresh orange juice
1 Tbsp. grated fresh lemon rind
¼ cup fresh lemon juice
1 Tbsp. Dijon mustard
1 cup port wine

Melt butter in a saucepan over medium heat; add onion, and sauté until tender. Add jelly and next 5 ingredients; cook over medium heat, stirring often, until jelly melts. Add wine; simmer, uncovered, 5 to 10 minutes. Serve warm. Cover and store in refrigerator up to 5 days. **Yield:** 2 cups.

editor's favorite

Crown Pork Roast

This roast makes a lot, so if you have some left over, simply cut it into chops, and freeze in zip-top plastic bags up to 3 months. Pull a bag out of the freezer, and thaw in the refrigerator overnight. You can then brown the chops in a skillet to warm them.

Prep: 20 min. Bake: 2 hr., 30 min. Stand: 15 min.

3 Tbsp. dried steak seasoning (see note)
1 (11-rib) crown pork roast, trimmed and tied
1 large apple
1 cup fresh kumquats
Garnishes: fresh thyme sprigs, flat-leaf parsley, apples, pears, and kumquats

Rub steak seasoning evenly over all sides of pork roast. Place roast in a roasting pan; position a large apple in center of roast to help hold its shape.

Bake pork roast at 350° for 2 hours. Top apple with 1 cup kumquats, and bake 30 more minutes or until a meat thermometer inserted between ribs 2 inches into meat registers 160°. Let pork roast stand 15 minutes or until thermometer registers 165° before slicing. Garnish, if desired. **Yield:** 8 to 10 servings.

Note: For testing purposes only, we used McCormick Grill Mates Montreal Steak Seasoning.

CROWN PORK ROAST POINTERS

- An apple inserted in the center of the roast before baking helps the roast keep its shape and lends moisture. Kumquats will be placed on top of the apple during baking for an elegant presentation.
- Placing the meat thermometer at the right spot in the roast is essential to achieving the proper degree of doneness. Insert it 2 inches into the meat between the ribs.

Orange-Glazed Pork Roast

editor's favorite

Orange-Glazed Pork Roast

Prep: 10 min. Bake: 1 hr. Stand: 10 min. Cook: 6 min.

1 (3-lb.) boneless pork loin roast
Vegetable cooking spray
1½ tsp. coarsely ground pepper
½ tsp. salt
1 cup orange marmalade
2 Tbsp. Creole mustard
2 tsp. fresh or dried rosemary
2 Tbsp. all-purpose flour
1 (14½-oz.) can fat-free reduced-sodium chicken broth
Garnish: fresh rosemary sprigs

Place roast on a rack coated with cooking spray in an aluminum foil-lined shallow roasting pan.

Rub roast with pepper and salt.

Heat marmalade in a microwave-safe bowl at HIGH 10 seconds or until melted. Add mustard and rosemary, stirring until blended. Brush mixture over roast.

Bake at 375° for 1 hour or until a meat thermometer inserted into thickest portion registers 155°. Cover with foil; let stand 10 minutes. Remove roast from pan, and cut into slices; cover and keep warm.

Sprinkle roasting pan with flour; place on cooktop, and cook over medium heat, 1 minute, whisking constantly. Add broth, and cook 5 more minutes, whisking constantly or until mixture thickens. Serve with sliced pork. Garnish, if desired. **Yield:** 16 servings.

Dijon Pork Loin

(pictured on following page)

Prep: 10 min. Bake: 1 hr., 15 min. Stand: 15 min.

¼ cup dried steak seasoning (see note)
2 Tbsp. all-purpose flour
¼ cup butter, melted
2 Tbsp. Dijon mustard
1 (3½- to 4-lb.) boneless pork loin roast, trimmed
Garnishes: fresh basil leaves, cherry tomatoes

Combine first 4 ingredients in a small bowl. Rub mustard mixture evenly over roast. Place roast on an aluminum foiled-lined broiler pan.

Bake at 475° for 20 minutes. Reduce heat to 350°, and bake 50 to 55 more minutes or until a meat thermometer inserted in thickest portion registers 155°. Remove from oven, and let stand 15 minutes or until thermometer reaches 160° before slicing. Garnish, if desired. **Yield:** 6 to 8 servings.

Note: For testing purposes only, we used McCormick Grill Mates Montreal Steak Seasoning.

Dijon Pork Loin
(previous page)

editor's favorite

Holiday Pork Chops

Prep: 20 min. Cook: 16 min. Stand: 15 min. Bake: 25 min.

1 Tbsp. butter
½ cup chopped onion
½ cup chopped celery
1 cup fresh breadcrumbs
½ cup sweetened dried cranberries, coarsely chopped
¼ cup chicken broth
1 Tbsp. chopped fresh parsley
1 tsp. grated fresh orange rind
1 tsp. salt
¼ tsp. ground sage
1 (4-lb.) boneless pork loin roast (about 9 inches long), trimmed*
3 Tbsp. dried steak seasoning (see note)
2 Tbsp. olive oil

Melt butter in a large ovenproof skillet over medium-high heat; add onion and celery. Sauté 8 to 10 minutes or until vegetables are tender and liquid evaporates. Remove from heat. Stir in breadcrumbs, cranberries, and next 5 ingredients. Let stand 10 minutes. Spoon breadcrumb mixture into a large zip-top plastic bag; set aside. Wipe skillet clean.

Cut pork loin into 6 (1½-inch-thick) chops. Cut a 1½-inch slit in one side of each chop, cutting to but not through other side (about 1½ to 2 inches), to form a pocket.

Snip one corner of bag, and pipe breadcrumb mixture evenly into slits in pork. Rub both sides of stuffed chops evenly with steak seasoning.

Cook chops in hot oil in ovenproof skillet over medium-high heat 2 to 3 minutes on each side or until chops are browned. Cover skillet with lid or aluminum foil. Bake at 350° for 20 to 25 minutes or until thermometer inserted in pork registers 155°. Remove from oven, and let stand 5 minutes or until thermometer registers 160°. **Yield:** 6 servings.

*Substitute 6 (1½-inch-thick) boneless pork chops for pork loin roast.

Note: For testing purposes only, we used McCormick Grill Mates Montreal Steak Seasoning.

Holiday Pork Chops

HOLIDAY PORK CHOPS STEP-BY-STEP

• To cut boneless pork chops, buy a pork loin roast that is approximately 4 lb., and slice it into 6 (1½ inch) pieces. By cutting your own chops, you get the exact size you need.

• Slice a 1½- to 2-inch slit in the side of each pork chop, cutting to but not through the other side, to form a pocket.

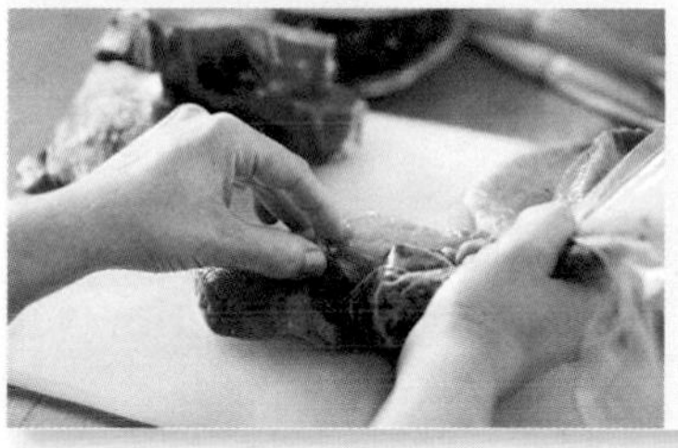

• Spoon the breadcrumb mixture into a large zip-top plastic bag; snip one corner of the bag, and pipe the mixture evenly into the slits in the pork.

Italian-Stuffed Pork Loin Roast

Follow our step-by-step instructions to butterfly the pork roast. Then roll it up with a cornbread stuffing mixture for an impressive effect.

Prep: 30 min. Cook: 15 min. Bake: 1 hr. Stand: 30 min.

⅓ cup finely chopped yellow onion
⅓ cup finely chopped fresh mushrooms
1 garlic clove, minced
3 Tbsp. olive oil, divided
1 cup cornbread stuffing mix (see note)
¼ cup chopped jarred roasted red bell peppers, drained
¾ cup low-sodium fat-free chicken broth
3 Tbsp. chopped fresh flat-leaf parsley
1 (3-lb.) boneless pork loin roast
1 (7-oz.) container olive tapenade (see note)
1 tsp. salt
¼ tsp. freshly ground pepper
2½ cups low-sodium fat-free chicken broth, divided
1 cup Merlot
1 Tbsp. butter
1 Tbsp. flour
½ cup sliced fresh mushrooms
¼ tsp. browning-and-seasoning sauce (optional; see note)
Sautéed Vegetable Garnish (optional; page 138)

Sauté onion, mushrooms, and garlic in 1 Tbsp. hot oil in a large skillet over medium-high heat 5 minutes or until vegetables are tender. Remove from heat. Add cornbread stuffing mix, peppers, ¾ cup chicken broth, and parsley; stir until liquid is absorbed. Let stand 5 minutes.

Butterfly pork loin roast by making a horizontal cut (about one-third down from top) into 1 side of pork, cutting to within ½ inch of other side (photo 1). (Do not cut all the way through roast.) Unfold top cut piece, open, and lay flat. Repeat procedure on opposite side of remaining two-thirds portion of pork loin roast, beginning at top or bottom of inside cut (photos 2 and 3). Place pork between 2 sheets of heavy-duty plastic wrap; flatten to ½-inch thickness using a meat mallet or rolling pin (photo 4).

Spread roast evenly with olive tapenade, leaving a 1-inch border. Spoon stuffing mixture evenly over tapenade. Roll up roast (photo 5), and tie with kitchen string at 1½-inch intervals (photo 6). Place roast, seam side down, in a lightly greased shallow roasting pan. Rub roast with remaining 2 Tbsp. oil; sprinkle evenly with salt and pepper. Pour 1½ cups chicken broth and 1 cup Merlot into pan.

Bake, uncovered, at 375° for 50 minutes to 1 hour or until a meat thermometer inserted into center of roast registers 160°. Remove roast from pan, reserving pan juices. Let roast stand 15 minutes before slicing.

Pour pan juices through a large wire-mesh strainer into a glass measuring cup, discarding solids in strainer. Let pan juices in cup stand 10 minutes; spoon out fat, and discard.

Melt butter in medium saucepan over medium-high heat; whisk in flour until smooth. Cook, whisking constantly, 2 minutes. Whisk in reserved pan drippings, remaining 1 cup chicken broth, and sliced mushrooms; cook over medium-high heat, whisking often, 5 minutes or until thickened. Stir in browning-and-seasoning sauce, if desired. Serve pan dripping sauce with roast. Garnish, if desired. **Yield:** 8 to 10 servings.

Note: For testing purposes only, we used Pepperidge Farm Cornbread Stuffing mix, Cantaré Olive Tapénade, and Kitchen Bouquet Browning & Seasoning Sauce.

ITALIAN-STUFFED PORK LOIN ROAST STEP-BY-STEP

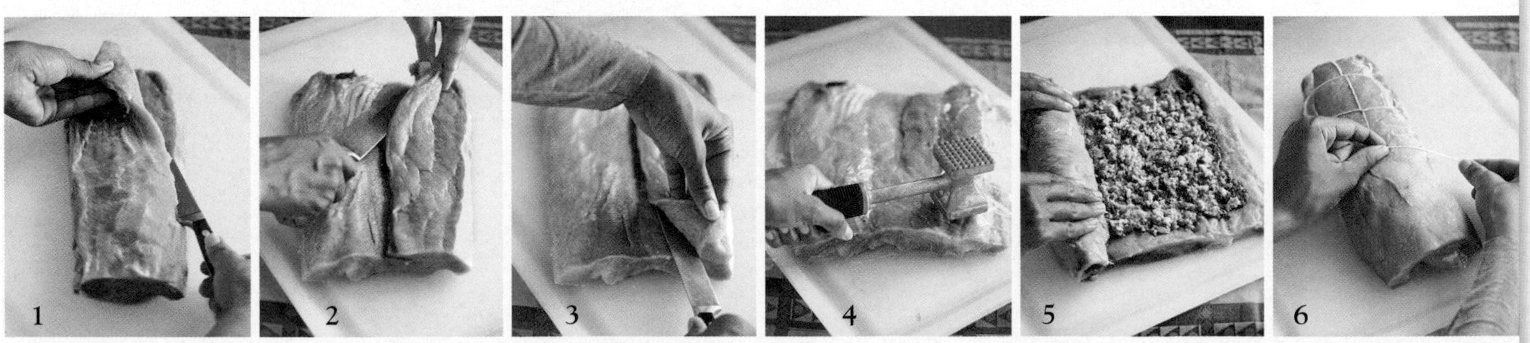

Italian-Stuffed
Pork Loin Roast

Sautéed Vegetable Garnish:

Prep: 8 min. Cook: 8 min.

1 lb. whole fresh mushrooms, halved
1 large red bell pepper, cut into 2-inch strips
1 large onion, cut into 8 wedges
2 Tbsp. olive oil
Salt and pepper to taste (optional)
Fresh flat-leaf parsley sprigs

Sauté first 3 ingredients in hot oil in large nonstick skillet over medium-high heat 8 minutes or just until lightly browned. Add salt and pepper to taste, if desired. Arrange vegetables on platter with Italian-Stuffed Pork Loin Roast. Tuck in fresh flat-leaf parsley sprigs. **Yield:** enough to garnish 1 (15-inch) platter.

editor's favorite

Herbed Roast Beef

The gravy for this recipe calls for a dry red wine. We recommend using either Merlot or Cabernet Sauvignon.

Prep: 10 min. Bake: 3 hr. Stand: 10 min. Cook: 10 min.

¼ cup all-purpose flour
2 Tbsp. dry mustard
1½ Tbsp. chopped fresh rosemary
2 tsp. seasoned salt
2 tsp. seasoned pepper
1 (8-lb.) rolled boneless rib roast
1 cup dry red wine
2 cups beef broth
½ cup water

Combine first 5 ingredients. Reserve 3 Tbsp. flour mixture. Pat remaining flour mixture evenly over roast.

Place roast, fat side up, on a rack in a shallow roasting pan.

Bake, uncovered, at 325° for 3 hours or until meat thermometer registers 135° or until desired degree of doneness. Remove roast from pan, reserving pan drippings. Let stand 10 minutes before serving.

Whisk together reserved 3 Tbsp. flour mixture, ½ cup pan drippings (adding additional water, if necessary, to equal ½ cup), wine, broth, and ½ cup water in a saucepan over medium heat. Cook, stirring occasionally, until thick and bubbly. Serve over roast. **Yield:** 16 servings.

Slow-Cooker Roast and Gravy

Remember, don't lift the slow-cooker lid. Each time you do, heat is lost, and you'll need to cook 20 to 30 more minutes.

Prep: 10 min. Cook: 8 hr.

1 (10¾-oz.) can cream of mushroom with roasted garlic soup
1 (10½-oz.) can condensed beef broth
1 (1-oz.) envelope dry onion-mushroom soup mix
1 (3½- to 4-lb.) eye of round roast, trimmed
2 Tbsp. all-purpose flour
1 tsp. salt
½ tsp. freshly ground pepper
2 Tbsp. vegetable oil

Stir together first 3 ingredients in a 5½-qt. slow cooker.

Sprinkle roast evenly with flour, salt, and pepper. Brown roast on all sides in hot oil in a large Dutch oven over medium-high heat. Transfer roast to slow cooker.

Cover and cook on LOW 8 hours.

Remove roast from slow cooker; slice to serve. Skim fat from gravy in slow cooker, if desired. Whisk gravy; serve over roast. **Yield:** 6 servings.

editor's favorite

Perfect Prime Rib

Top each delicious slice with a dollop of Fluffy Horseradish Sauce.

Prep: 5 min. Bake: 1 hr., 30 min. Stand: 20 min.

1½ tsp. kosher salt
1 tsp. coarsely ground pepper
1 Tbsp. extra virgin olive oil
1 (6-lb.) prime rib roast (about 3 ribs)
Fluffy Horseradish Sauce
Garnish: rosemary sprigs

Combine salt, pepper, and olive oil; rub evenly over roast. Place roast on a wire rack in an aluminum foil-lined roasting pan.

Bake at 450° for 45 minutes; reduce oven temperature to 350°, and bake 45 minutes or until a meat thermometer inserted in thickest portion registers 145° (medium-rare) or to desired degree of doneness. Remove from oven, cover loosely with aluminum foil, and let stand 20 minutes before slicing. Serve with Fluffy Horseradish Sauce. Garnish, if desired. **Yield:** 6 servings.

Perfect Prime Rib

Fluffy Horseradish Sauce:

This robust sauce is inspired by a recipe served with moist and tender beef at Lawry's The Prime Rib restaurants. With just four ingredients, it is easy to whip up while the roast is standing.

Prep: 10 min.

1 cup whipping cream
4 Tbsp. prepared horseradish
1 to 2 Tbsp. chopped fresh parsley
¼ tsp. garlic salt

Beat 1 cup whipping cream at medium-high speed with a heavy-duty stand mixer 1 minute or until stiff peaks form.

Fold in remaining ingredients. Serve immediately, or cover and refrigerate up to 8 hours. **Yield:** about 2 cups.

SLICING A PRIME RIB

Allow the roast to stand 20 minutes before carving. Place the roast on its side on a carving board. Insert a fork into the side, just below the top rib bone. Slice across the roast toward the rib bones.

editor's favorite

Maple-Glazed Lamb Chops With Zesty Horseradish Sauce

This recipe's base of maple syrup and Dijon mustard creates a sweet, slightly tangy crust.

Prep: 10 min. Chill: 8 hr. Broil: 14 min. Stand: 5 min.

⅓ cup maple syrup
¼ cup Dijon mustard
2 Tbsp. balsamic vinegar
2 Tbsp. olive oil
1 shallot, minced
¼ tsp. crushed red pepper
8 (½-inch-thick) lamb loin chops
½ tsp. salt
½ tsp. freshly ground black pepper
Zesty Horseradish Sauce

Combine first 6 ingredients in a shallow dish or large zip-top plastic bag; add lamb chops. Cover or seal, and chill up to 8 hours, turning occasionally.

Remove lamb chops from marinade, discarding marinade. Sprinkle chops evenly with salt and pepper; place chops on a lightly greased rack in a broiler pan.

Broil chops 3 inches from heat 5 to 7 minutes on each side or to desired degree of doneness. Cover with aluminum foil, and let stand 5 minutes. Serve with Zesty Horseradish Sauce. **Yield:** 4 main-dish or 8 appetizer servings.

Zesty Horseradish Sauce:

Leftover horseradish sauce can be refrigerated up to 1 week.

Prep: 5 min.

½ cup sour cream
2 Tbsp. prepared horseradish
2 Tbsp. roughly chopped mint leaves

Stir together all ingredients. Cover and chill until ready to serve. **Yield:** about ½ cup.

Maple-Glazed Lamb Chops With Zesty Horseradish Sauce

Mustard Baked Chicken

editor's favorite

Mustard Baked Chicken

Prep: 10 min. Chill: 30 min. Bake: 50 min. Stand: 15 min.

1 (4-lb.) whole chicken
1 Tbsp. paprika
1½ tsp. dry mustard
1 tsp. salt
1 tsp. freshly ground pepper
2 Tbsp. Worcestershire sauce
1 Tbsp. olive oil

Remove giblets and neck, and rinse chicken with cold water; pat dry. Place chicken in a large zip-top plastic freezer bag. Stir together paprika and next 5 ingredients until well blended; rub over chicken, coating evenly. Seal and chill at least 30 minutes or up to 8 hours, turning occasionally. Remove from marinade, discarding marinade. Place chicken in a roasting pan.

Bake at 425° for 50 minutes or until a meat thermometer inserted in thickest portion registers 170°. Let stand, covered, 15 minutes before slicing. **Yield:** 8 servings.

editor's favorite

Baked Pecan Chicken

Prep: 10 min. Bake: 25 min.

1½ cups finely chopped pecans, toasted
2 Tbsp. chopped parsley
1½ tsp. salt
2 egg whites
4 skinned and boned chicken breasts
Creamy Mushroom-Artichoke Sauce (optional; following page)

Combine first 3 ingredients in a bowl.

Beat egg whites with a fork just until foamy. Dip both sides of chicken in egg; dredge in pecan mixture. Arrange chicken breasts on a lightly greased aluminum foil-lined baking sheet.

Bake at 400° for 20 to 25 minutes or until chicken is done. Serve with Creamy Mushroom-Artichoke Sauce, if desired. **Yield:** 4 servings.

Creamy Mushroom-Artichoke Sauce:

Prep: 15 min. Cook: 12 min.

2 Tbsp. butter
1 Tbsp. vegetable oil
1 (8-oz.) package sliced mushrooms
½ cup chopped onion (about ½ onion)
2 garlic cloves, minced
¾ cup chicken broth
1 (8-oz.) package cream cheese, softened*
1 (14-oz.) can artichoke hearts, drained and coarsely chopped
2 Tbsp. fresh lemon juice
⅛ to ¼ tsp. ground red pepper

Melt butter with oil in a large skillet over medium heat; add mushrooms, onion, and garlic, and sauté 5 to 7 minutes or until tender. Stir in chicken broth and cream cheese, and cook, stirring constantly, 2 to 3 minutes or until cream cheese melts. Stir in artichoke hearts, lemon juice, and red pepper. Reduce heat to low, and cook 2 minutes or until mixture is hot. **Yield:** about 2½ cups.

*1 (8-oz.) package ⅓-less-fat cream cheese may be substituted.

Roasted Chicken Stuffed With Chiles and Cheese

Cut off the tops of several heads of garlic; add the garlic to a roasting pan alongside the chicken. To serve, squeeze the roasted garlic cloves onto a serving dish and spread on crusty bread.

Prep: 50 min. Broil: 10 min. Stand: 20 min. Bake: 1 hr., 5 min.

4 poblano chile peppers, cut in half and seeded
1 cup ricotta cheese
4 oz. goat cheese
¾ cup soft breadcrumbs
½ cup finely chopped green onion
¼ cup chopped fresh cilantro
1 large egg, lightly beaten
1½ tsp. minced garlic
1 tsp. chopped fresh oregano
¾ tsp. salt
½ tsp. ground cumin
¼ tsp. freshly ground pepper
2 (3½-lb.) whole chickens
2 Tbsp. butter, melted
2 Tbsp. olive oil
½ tsp. salt
¼ tsp. freshly ground pepper

Broil poblano peppers, skin side up, on an aluminum foil-lined baking sheet, 5 inches from heat, 5 to 10 minutes or until peppers look blistered. Place pepper halves in a zip-top plastic freezer bag; seal and let stand 10 minutes to loosen skins. Peel and chop pepper halves.

Combine chopped poblano pepper, ricotta cheese, and next 10 ingredients in a large bowl, stirring well.

Split each chicken down the back, open it up, and press down firmly on the breastbone to lay flat. Cut each chicken in half. Carefully loosen skin from chickens at neck area, working down to breast, thigh, and leg area. Stuff cheese mixture evenly under skin. Smooth out skin over cheese mixture.

Combine butter and oil. Brush chicken with oil mixture; sprinkle with ½ tsp. salt and ¼ tsp. pepper. Arrange chickens, skin side up, in a lightly greased roasting pan.

Bake, uncovered, at 350° for 1 hour and 5 minutes or until a meat thermometer inserted in thickest portion of leg reaches 170°. Remove chickens from oven, and let stand 10 minutes before serving. Serve with roasted garlic and pan juices. **Yield:** 8 servings.

STUFFING A WHOLE CHICKEN

- Combine peppers, cheeses, breadcrumbs, and seasonings for the filling.
- Split the chicken down the back using a sharp knife.
- Use a spoon to stuff the cheese mixture evenly under the skin.

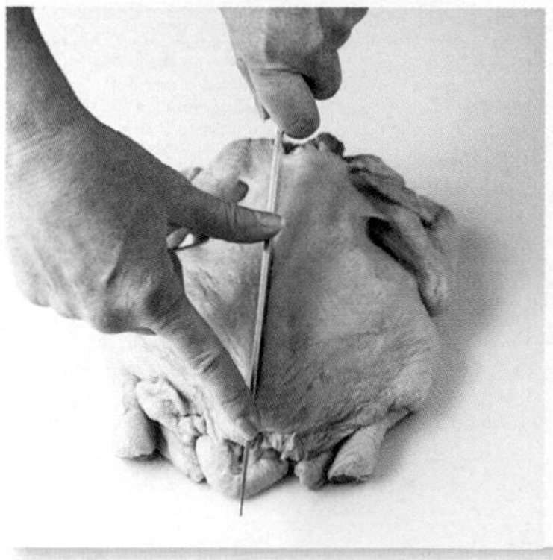

Roasted Chicken Stuffed
With Chiles and Cheese

Apple-Pecan Stuffed Chicken Breasts

Apple-Pecan Stuffed Chicken Breasts

The four-ingredient stuffing is a snap to make and adds loads of texture and flavor. After you quickly brown the chicken in a skillet, place it in the oven to finish cooking.

Prep: 20 min. Cook: 25 min. Bake: 20 min.

1 (4-oz.) package goat cheese, crumbled
½ cup peeled, chopped Granny Smith apple (about 1 apple)
¼ cup chopped pecans, toasted
2 Tbsp. chopped fresh parsley
6 (8-oz.) skinned and boned chicken breasts
½ tsp. salt
½ tsp. freshly ground pepper
3 Tbsp. butter, divided
1 garlic clove, minced
2 Tbsp. all-purpose flour
1 cup chicken broth
⅔ cup dry white wine
1 Tbsp. chopped fresh parsley
⅛ tsp. freshly ground pepper

Combine first 4 ingredients in a small bowl.

Cut a slit (about 2 inches deep and 3 inches long; do not cut in half) in thick side of each chicken breast to form a pocket. Spoon 1 rounded Tbsp. goat cheese mixture into each pocket. Pinch edges to seal; wind 1 or 2 small wooden picks in and out of each chicken breast to secure pocket. Sprinkle chicken evenly with ½ tsp. salt and ½ tsp. pepper.

Melt 2 Tbsp. butter in a large skillet over medium-high heat; add 3 chicken breasts to skillet, and cook 2 to 3 minutes on each side or until lightly browned. Transfer chicken to a lightly greased 13- x 9-inch baking dish. Repeat procedure with remaining chicken.

Bake at 450° for 20 minutes or until chicken is done.

Melt remaining 1 Tbsp. butter in pan drippings in skillet over medium heat; add minced garlic. Whisk in flour, and cook, whisking constantly, 1 minute. Gradually whisk in chicken broth and white wine, and cook, whisking often, 8 to 10 minutes or until thickened and bubbly. Stir in parsley and ⅛ tsp. pepper. Serve sauce over baked chicken. **Yield:** 6 servings.

STUFFING CHICKEN BREASTS

• Use a sharp knife to create a 2-inch-deep, 3-inch-long pocket in each chicken breast.

• Spoon 1 Tbsp. of the stuffing mixture into each chicken breast pocket.

• Use a sturdy wooden pick to secure each chicken breast pocket.

Turkey Cutlets With Avocado-Cranberry Salsa

Prep: 10 min. Cook: 18 min.

¾ cup all-purpose flour
⅓ cup cornstarch
1½ tsp. salt
1 tsp. freshly ground pepper
2 lb. turkey cutlets*
2 Tbsp. vegetable oil
Avocado-Cranberry Salsa
Garnishes: jalapeño pepper strips, halved cranberries

Stir together first 4 ingredients. Dredge cutlets in mixture.

Fry one-third of turkey cutlets in hot oil in a large nonstick skillet over medium-high heat 2 to 3 minutes on each side or until done. Remove from skillet, and keep warm.

Repeat procedure twice, adding more oil, if necessary. Serve cutlets with Avocado-Cranberry Salsa. Garnish, if desired. **Yield:** 6 to 8 servings.

*2 lb. turkey tenderloins may be substituted for cutlets.

Avocado-Cranberry Salsa:

Prep: 20 min.

2 large jalapeño peppers, seeded
½ (12-oz.) package fresh cranberries (1½ cups)
1 large navel orange, peeled and chopped
½ cup sugar
2 Tbsp. balsamic vinegar
2 Tbsp. olive oil
¼ tsp. salt
4 small avocados, peeled and coarsely chopped

Pulse peppers in a food processor 8 to 10 times or until finely chopped. Add cranberries, and pulse 4 to 6 times or until coarsely chopped. Transfer mixture to a bowl; add orange and next 4 ingredients, stirring until sugar dissolves. Chill, if desired. Gently stir in avocados before serving. **Yield:** about 4 cups.

Turkey Cutlets With Avocado-Cranberry Salsa

Hickory-Smoked Bourbon Turkey

editor's favorite

Hickory-Smoked Bourbon Turkey

Prep: 30 min. Chill: 48 hr. Soak: 1 hr. Smoke: 6 hr. Stand: 15 min.

1 (11-lb.) whole turkey, thawed
2 cups maple syrup
1 cup bourbon
1 Tbsp. pickling spice
Hickory wood chips
1 large carrot, halved
1 celery rib, halved
1 medium onion, halved
1 lemon
1 Tbsp. salt
2 tsp. freshly ground pepper
Garnishes: lemon slices, mixed salad greens

Remove giblets and neck from turkey; discard or reserve for later use. Rinse turkey thoroughly with cold water, and pat dry.

Add water to a large stockpot, filling half full; stir in maple syrup, bourbon, and pickling spice. Add turkey and, if needed, additional water to cover. Cover and chill turkey 48 hours.

Soak hickory wood chips in fresh water at least 1 hour. Prepare charcoal fire in smoker; let fire burn 20 to 25 minutes.

Remove turkey from water, discarding water; pat dry. Stuff cavity with carrot, celery, and onion. Pierce lemon with a fork; place in neck cavity. Combine salt and pepper; rub over turkey. Fold wings under, and tie legs together with kitchen twine.

Drain wood chips, and place on coals. Place water pan in smoker, and add water to depth of fill line. Place turkey in center of lower food grate; cover with smoker lid. Smoke 6 hours or until a meat thermometer inserted into thigh registers 170°, adding water, charcoal, and wood chips as needed. Remove turkey from smoker, and let stand 15 minutes before slicing. Garnish, if desired. **Yield:** 12 to 14 servings.

WHAT'S IN THE TURKEY?

The turkey's neck, liver, heart, and gizzard are packed in a bag that's stuffed inside the bird, so cooking a whole turkey requires a brave spirit. Reach into the cavity and remove the bag, but don't throw it away if you plan to make giblet gravy.

editor's favorite

Old-Fashioned Roasted Turkey With Gravy

Prep: 30 min. Bake: 4 hr., 30 min. Cook: 1 hr.

1 (14- to 16-lb.) whole turkey
1½ tsp. mixed-up salt, divided (see note)
1½ tsp. garlic powder, divided
1½ tsp. poultry seasoning, divided
1 tsp. ground sage
1 tsp. freshly ground pepper
5 (14-oz.) cans chicken broth, divided
½ cup butter, melted
2 carrots, sliced
3 celery ribs, sliced
1 medium-size yellow onion, sliced
½ cup chopped fresh parsley
½ cup all-purpose flour
½ cup water

Remove giblets and neck from turkey, and chill for later use. Rinse turkey with cold water; pat dry.

Combine 1 tsp. each of mixed-up salt, garlic powder, poultry seasoning, sage, and pepper; sprinkle cavity and outside of turkey evenly with mixture.

Place turkey, breast side up, in a large roasting pan, tucking wingtips under. Pour 2 cans chicken broth into roasting pan; drizzle melted butter over turkey.

Bake, uncovered, at 450° for 1 hour. Reduce heat to 425°, and shield with aluminum foil to prevent excessive browning. Bake 3½ hours or until a meat thermometer inserted into thigh registers 170°, basting every 45 minutes with pan drippings.

Bring remaining 3 cans broth, neck, giblets, carrots, and next 3 ingredients to a boil in a saucepan. Cover, reduce heat, and simmer 45 minutes or until vegetables are tender.

Remove turkey to a serving platter, reserving drippings in roasting pan. Skim excess fat from drippings in pan, if desired.

Pour giblet mixture through a wire-mesh strainer into drippings in roasting pan; discard solids. Bring to a boil in roasting pan over medium-high heat, stirring to loosen browned bits on bottom of pan.

Stir together flour and ½ cup water until smooth; add to giblet mixture, and cook over medium-high heat, stirring constantly, 10 minutes or until thickened. Stir in remaining ½ tsp. each of mixed-up salt, garlic powder, and poultry seasoning. Serve with turkey. **Yield:** 12 to 15 servings.

Note: For testing purposes only, we used Jane's Krazy Original Mixed-Up Salt.

editor's favorite

Molasses-Coffee Turkey Breast

Roast the turkey with the skin on to lock in the flavors and keep the meat moist and tender. Basting throughout the cooking process also ensures juiciness because it keeps the skin from becoming dry and brittle. Remove the skin before serving for a fantastic low-fat, low-calorie dish.

Prep: 15 min. **Bake:** 2 hr., 30 min. **Stand:** 15 min.

1 (10-oz.) jar apricot spreadable fruit (see note)
¾ cup strong-brewed coffee
¾ cup molasses
2 Tbsp. cider vinegar
1 Tbsp. Dijon mustard
½ tsp. salt
1 (5-lb.) bone-in turkey breast
Vegetable cooking spray

Stir together apricot spreadable fruit and next 5 ingredients until blended. Reserve 1 cup molasses-coffee sauce in a microwave-safe small bowl, and set aside.

Place turkey in an 11- x 7-inch baking dish coated with cooking spray. Pour remaining molasses-coffee sauce evenly over turkey. Cover loosely with aluminum foil.

Bake turkey at 350° for 1 hour; remove aluminum foil, and bake 1 to 1 hour and 30 minutes more or until a meat thermometer inserted into the thickest portion of turkey registers 170°, basting with molasses-coffee sauce every 15 minutes. Remove turkey from oven, and let stand 15 minutes. Remove and discard skin. Serve turkey with 1 cup reserved molasses-coffee sauce heated in the microwave at HIGH 30 seconds or until warm. **Yield:** 12 servings.

Note: For testing purposes only, we used Polaner All Fruit Spreadable Fruit.

editor's favorite

Herbed Turkey Strips With Roasted Peppers and Beans

Be sure to grate the lemon rind before squeezing the juice needed for the recipe. Use the entire 2 Tbsp. of lemon juice in the marinade if you like a tangier flavor.

Prep: 20 min. **Chill:** 30 min. **Cook:** 15 min.

1 (3-lb.) boneless, skinless turkey breast, cut into ½- to ¾-inch-thick slices
1 Tbsp. Italian seasoning
1½ Tbsp. olive oil, divided
1 to 2 Tbsp. fresh lemon juice
2 garlic cloves, minced
1 tsp. salt
½ to 1 tsp. freshly ground pepper
1 (19-oz.) can cannellini beans, rinsed and drained
1 (7-oz.) jar roasted red bell peppers, drained and chopped
2 Tbsp. pine nuts, lightly toasted
1 tsp. grated fresh lemon rind
¼ cup chopped fresh flat-leaf parsley

Pierce turkey slices evenly with a fork.

Stir together Italian seasoning, ½ Tbsp. oil, lemon juice, and next 3 ingredients. Coat turkey slices with oil mixture. Cover and chill 30 minutes.

Cook turkey slices, in batches, in remaining 1 Tbsp. hot oil in a large nonstick skillet over medium heat 3 minutes on each side or until done. Remove turkey from skillet, cover, and keep warm. Add beans and peppers to skillet; cook over medium heat until thoroughly heated, stirring gently.

Cut turkey slices crosswise into ½-inch strips. Arrange on a serving platter. Top with bean mixture. Combine pine nuts, grated lemon rind, and parsley. Sprinkle over beans. Serve immediately. **Yield:** 8 servings.

A *simple main course* MAKES PLANNING YOUR CELEBRATION A SNAP.

editor's favorite

Sticky Ducks With Cornbread Dressing

Purchase ducks in the frozen foods section of your supermarket.

Prep: 30 min. Chill: 8 hr. Bake: 2 hr. Stand: 10 min.

2 (5-lb.) fresh ducks or thawed frozen ducks
1 cup balsamic vinaigrette
2 Tbsp. butter
6 green onions, chopped
½ cup celery, chopped
½ (16-oz.) bag cornbread stuffing (3½ cups)
1 (14-oz.) can chicken broth
½ cup flat-leaf parsley, chopped
½ tsp. freshly ground pepper
¾ cup molasses
2 Tbsp. hot sauce
Garnish: flat-leaf parsley

Remove giblet packages from ducks, and reserve for another use. Rinse ducks, and pat dry; remove excess fat and skin. Place 1 duck and ½ cup balsamic vinaigrette each in 2 large zip-top plastic freezer bags; seal and chill 8 hours, turning occasionally.

Remove ducks from vinaigrette, discarding vinaigrette. Pat ducks dry, and prick legs and thighs with a fork, avoiding the breast area.

Melt butter in a large skillet over medium heat; add chopped green onions and celery, and sauté until tender. Remove from heat. Stir in cornbread stuffing, broth, chopped parsley, and pepper. Stuff each duck with half of mixture, and tie ends of legs together with string; tuck wing tips under. Place ducks, breast sides up, in a roasting pan.

Stir together molasses and hot sauce. Brush ducks evenly with about 3 Tbsp. molasses mixture.

Bake at 350° for 1 hour and 30 minutes, brushing with molasses mixture every 15 minutes. Cover loosely with remaining aluminum foil, and bake 30 more minutes or until a meat thermometer inserted in thickest portion of thigh registers 180° and internal temperature in center of stuffing registers 190°. Let stand 10 minutes. Garnish, if desired. **Yield:** 6 servings.

Sticky Chickens With Cornbread Dressing: Substitute 2 (4-lb.) whole chickens for ducks. Do not prick chickens. Proceed as directed. Bake at 350° for 2 hours or until a meat thermometer inserted in thigh registers 180° and internal temperature in center of stuffing registers 165°.

Sticky Ducks With Cornbread Dressing

Cheesy Vegetable
Chowder

SIMPLE SUPPER *Solutions*

In a hurry and need an easy meal idea? Look no further. Here are over two dozen inspiring recipes that will have supper on the table before you can say "Merry Christmas!"

editor's favorite

Cheesy Vegetable Chowder

Prep: 15 min. Cook: 30 min.

3½ cups chicken broth
8 celery ribs, sliced
4 carrots, sliced
2 medium potatoes, peeled and cubed
1 large onion, chopped
½ tsp. freshly ground pepper
2 cups frozen whole kernel corn, thawed
¼ cup butter or margarine
¼ cup all-purpose flour
2 cups milk
2 cups (8 oz.) shredded sharp Cheddar cheese
Garnish: chopped fresh parsley

Bring first 6 ingredients to a boil in a Dutch oven. Cover, reduce heat to medium, and simmer 15 to 20 minutes or until vegetables are tender. Remove from heat, and stir in corn.

Melt butter in a heavy saucepan over low heat; add flour, whisking until smooth. Cook 1 minute, whisking constantly. Gradually whisk in milk; cook over medium heat, whisking constantly, until mixture is thickened and bubbly. Add cheese, stirring until blended.

Stir cheese mixture gradually into vegetable mixture. Cook over medium heat, stirring constantly, until thoroughly heated. Garnish, if desired. **Yield:** 6 to 8 servings.

Curried Pumpkin Soup

To add an elegant touch to this recipe from Martha Foose at Mockingbird Bakery in Mississippi, top it with cooked shrimp or crabmeat. *(pictured on page 195)*

Prep: 25 min. Cook: 40 min.

1 large sweet onion, chopped
1 Tbsp. olive oil
1 Tbsp. minced garlic
1 Tbsp. minced fresh ginger
1 Tbsp. curry powder
⅛ tsp. ground red pepper
⅛ tsp. ground cumin
2 (15-oz.) cans unsweetened pumpkin
1 cup water
1 (32-oz.) container low-sodium fat-free chicken broth
1 (13.5-oz.) can lite coconut milk
2 Tbsp. fresh lime juice
2½ tsp. salt
Garnishes: sour cream, chopped fresh chives

Sauté onion in hot oil in a Dutch oven over medium-high heat 8 minutes or until tender. Add garlic and next 4 ingredients; sauté 1 minute. Add pumpkin, 1 cup water, and broth; bring to a boil. Reduce heat to medium; add coconut milk, lime juice, and salt, and simmer, stirring often, 25 minutes. Remove from heat; cool.

Process pumpkin mixture, in batches, in a blender or food processor until smooth, stopping to scrape down sides. Return pumpkin mixture to Dutch oven, and cook over medium heat until thoroughly heated. Garnish, if desired. **Yield:** 8 to 10 servings.

Curried Squash-and-Apple Soup With Honey Cream

Prep: 30 min. Bake: 45 min Cook: 50 min. Cool: 10 min.

4 medium acorn squash, halved (about 6 lb.)
¼ cup butter
3 (14½-oz.) cans chicken broth
2 Granny Smith apples, peeled and coarsely chopped
1½ Tbsp. curry powder
½ tsp. ground red pepper
1 tsp. salt
2 cups half-and-half
Honey Cream

Remove and discard seeds from squash. Place squash halves, cut sides down, on an aluminum foil-lined baking sheet.

Bake at 350° for 45 minutes or until tender. Remove from oven, and cool. Scoop out pulp, discarding shells; set pulp aside.

Melt butter in a Dutch oven over medium heat; add chicken broth and next 4 ingredients. Cook, stirring often, 25 to 30 minutes or until apples are tender. Remove apple mixture from heat, and let cool slightly (about 5 to 10 minutes).

Process squash pulp and apple mixture, in batches, in a food processor or blender until smooth, stopping to scrape down sides. Return mixture to Dutch oven.

Gradually stir in half-and-half. Cook, stirring occasionally, over low heat 15 to 20 minutes or until thoroughly heated. Serve with a dollop of Honey Cream. **Yield:** 10 to 12 servings.

Honey Cream:

Prep: 10 min.

1 cup sour cream
2 Tbsp. honey
½ tsp. curry powder

Combine all ingredients, blending well. Cover and chill up to 8 hours, if desired. **Yield:** 1 cup.

Turkey Soup With Green Chile Biscuits

Prep: 15 min. Cook: 30 min.

1 medium onion, diced
1 tsp. vegetable oil
1 garlic clove, minced
3 cups chopped cooked turkey or chicken
1 (15-oz.) can chili beans
3½ cups chicken or turkey broth
1 (11-oz.) can whole kernel corn with red and green peppers, drained
1 (10-oz.) can diced tomatoes and green chiles
½ tsp. chili powder
½ tsp. ground cumin
⅛ tsp. salt
⅛ tsp. freshly ground pepper
Toppings: sour cream, shredded Mexican four-cheese blend
Green Chile Biscuits

Sauté onion in hot oil in a large Dutch oven over medium heat 7 minutes or until tender. Add garlic, and sauté 1 minute. Stir in turkey and next 8 ingredients. Bring to a boil, stirring occasionally; reduce heat, and simmer 15 minutes. Serve with desired toppings and Green Chile Biscuits. **Yield:** 8 servings.

Green Chile Biscuits:

Prep: 5 min. Bake: 12 min.

2 cups all-purpose baking mix (see note)
1 cup (4 oz.) shredded Mexican four-cheese blend
1 (4.5-oz.) can chopped green chiles, drained
⅔ cup milk

Stir together baking mix and remaining ingredients until a soft dough forms. Turn dough onto a lightly floured surface, and knead 3 or 4 times.

Pat or roll dough to a ½-inch thickness; cut with a 2½-inch round cutter, and place on an ungreased baking sheet.

Bake at 450° 10 to 12 minutes or until biscuits are golden brown. **Yield:** 1 dozen.

Note: For testing purposes only, we used Bisquick all-purpose baking mix.

Turkey Soup With Green Chile Biscuits

editor's favorite

Southwestern Chicken-and-Rice Soup With Tortilla Strips

Chopped ripe avocado and crisp tortilla strips are quick additions to finish off this soup with flair.

Prep: 35 min. Cook: 28 min.

1 medium onion, chopped
1 large carrot, peeled and chopped
½ medium-size red bell pepper, chopped
1 Tbsp. vegetable oil
2 garlic cloves, minced
2 cups shredded cooked chicken
¾ cup uncooked white rice*
2 medium plum tomatoes, chopped
1 to 2 Tbsp. chopped pickled jalapeño slices
1 tsp. cumin
¼ tsp. freshly ground pepper
8 cups chicken broth
¼ cup loosely packed cilantro leaves, chopped
Juice of one lime (about 2 Tbsp.)
1 ripe avocado, chopped
Tortilla Strips

Sauté first 3 ingredients in hot oil in a large Dutch oven over medium heat 7 minutes or until vegetables are tender. Add garlic; sauté 1 minute.

Stir in chicken and next 5 ingredients. Stir in chicken broth. Bring to a boil, reduce heat, and simmer 20 minutes or until rice is tender. Stir in cilantro and lime juice. Serve with chopped avocado and Tortilla Strips. **Yield:** about 6 servings.

*¾ cup brown rice may be substituted. Prepare recipe as directed, increasing simmer time to 45 minutes or until rice is tender.

Tortilla Strips:

Prep: 5 min. Bake: 15 min.

6 (6-inch) corn tortillas
Vegetable cooking spray

Cut tortillas into strips; place on a baking sheet coated with vegetable cooking spray. Spray cooking spray over tops of strips. Bake at 400° for 10 to 15 minutes or until crisp, stirring occasionally. **Yield:** about 6 servings.

editor's favorite

Fiesta Chowder

This main dish chowder goes from pantry to table in just 30 minutes. Twist refrigerated breadsticks, and bake for a quick accompaniment.

Prep: 15 min. Cook: 15 min.

3 Tbsp. all-purpose flour
1 (1.4-oz.) package fajita seasoning, divided
4 skinned and boned chicken breasts, cubed
3 Tbsp. vegetable oil
1 medium onion, chopped
1 tsp. minced garlic
1 (15¼-oz.) can whole kernel corn with red and green peppers, drained
1 (15-oz.) can black beans, rinsed and drained
1 (14½-oz.) can Mexican-style stewed tomatoes
1 (4.5-oz.) can chopped green chiles
3 cups water
1 cup uncooked instant brown rice
1 (2¼-oz.) can sliced ripe black olives (optional)
1 (10¾-oz.) can nacho cheese soup
3 Tbsp. chopped fresh cilantro
1 Tbsp. lime juice
Garnish: chopped fresh cilantro
Breadsticks (optional)

Combine flour and 2 Tbsp. fajita seasoning in a zip-top plastic freezer bag; add chicken. Seal and shake to coat.

Cook chicken in hot oil in a large Dutch oven over high heat, stirring often, 4 minutes or until browned. Reduce heat to medium-high; add onion and garlic; sauté 5 minutes. Stir in remaining fajita seasoning, corn, next 5 ingredients, and, if desired, olives. Bring mixture to a boil. Reduce heat to medium-low; cover and simmer 5 minutes. Remove lid, and stir in nacho cheese soup, chopped cilantro, and lime juice. Garnish, if desired, and serve with breadsticks, if desired. **Yield:** 8 to 10 servings.

Fiesta Chowder

editor's favorite

Chicken-Sausage Gumbo

Prep: 20 min. Cook: 25 min.

½ lb. smoked sausage, cut into ½-inch-thick slices (see note)
1 to 3 Tbsp. vegetable oil
5 Tbsp. all-purpose flour
1 cup coarsely chopped onion
1 cup chopped celery
2 large garlic cloves, pressed
1 medium-size green bell pepper, chopped
2 cups chicken broth
1 (28-oz.) can diced tomatoes
1 to 2 tsp. Creole seasoning
4 cups chopped cooked chicken
Hot cooked rice

Cook sausage over high heat in Dutch oven 5 minutes, stirring often. Remove sausage with a slotted spoon. Drain on paper towels.

Add enough oil to drippings in Dutch oven to equal 3 Tbsp., and whisk in flour; cook over medium-high heat, whisking constantly, 5 minutes. Add onion and next 3 ingredients; cook 5 minutes, stirring often. Stir in broth and next 2 ingredients. Bring to a boil; cover, reduce heat, and simmer 5 minutes. Add sausage and chicken; simmer, covered, 5 minutes. Serve over rice. **Yield:** 4 to 6 servings.

Note: For testing purposes only, we used Conecuh Original Smoked Sausage.

Chesapeake Chowder

Prep: 25 min. Cook: 45 min.

½ lb. unpeeled, medium-size raw shrimp
½ lb. fresh crabmeat
1 onion, chopped
3 garlic cloves, minced
2 celery ribs, chopped
1 Tbsp. olive oil
¼ cup all-purpose flour
2½ cups chicken broth
1 cup dry white wine or chicken broth
1 (8-oz.) bottle clam juice
5 red potatoes, peeled and diced
1 Tbsp. Old Bay seasoning
½ cup heavy cream

Peel shrimp; devein, if desired. Drain and flake crabmeat, removing any bits of shell. Set seafood aside.

Sauté onion, garlic, and celery in hot oil in a Dutch oven over medium-high heat 8 minutes or until tender. Stir in flour, and cook, stirring constantly, 1 minute. Stir in broth and next 4 ingredients. Bring to a boil; cover, reduce heat, and simmer, stirring occasionally, 30 minutes or until potatoes are tender.

Stir in shrimp, crabmeat, and heavy cream; cook over low heat 5 minutes or just until shrimp turn pink. **Yield:** 8 cups.

Easy Brunswick Stew

Prep: 20 min. Cook: 40 min.

1 (1 lb., 4-oz.) package refrigerated diced potatoes
3 cups chicken broth
½ tsp. freshly ground pepper
1 (28-oz.) can diced tomatoes, undrained
1 (16-oz.) package frozen shoepeg corn
1 (15-oz.) can lima beans, drained
1 lb. shredded pork barbecue with sauce*

Bring potatoes and broth to a boil in a Dutch oven over medium-high heat; stir in pepper. Reduce heat to medium; boil 5 minutes.

Stir in tomatoes and remaining ingredients; reduce heat to medium-low, and cook, covered, 30 minutes or until heated. **Yield:** 12 cups.

*1 (18-oz.) container refrigerated shredded pork barbecue may be substituted.

Turnip Greens Stew

Frozen seasoning blend is a mixture of diced onion, red and green bell peppers, and celery.

Prep: 5 min. Cook: 35 min.

2 cups chopped cooked ham
1 Tbsp. vegetable oil
3 cups chicken broth
2 (16-oz.) packages frozen chopped turnip greens
1 (10-oz.) package frozen seasoning blend*
1 tsp. sugar
1 tsp. seasoned pepper

Sauté ham in hot oil in a Dutch oven over medium-high heat 5 minutes or until lightly browned. Add broth and remaining ingredients; bring to a boil. Cover, reduce heat to low, and simmer, stirring occasionally, 25 minutes. **Yield:** 6 to 8 servings.

*1 chopped fresh onion, 1 chopped celery stalk, and 1 chopped green bell pepper may be substituted for frozen seasoning blend, if desired. For testing purposes only, we used McKenzie's Seasoning Blend.

Collard Stew: Substitute 1 (16-oz.) package frozen chopped collard greens and 1 (16-oz.) can black-eyed peas, drained, for 2 packages turnip greens. Prepare recipe as directed, adding black-eyed peas during the last 10 minutes of cooking.

Turnip Greens Stew

Taco Soup,
Over-the-Border BLT Wrap

Taco Soup

Prep: 10 min. Cook: 30 min.

1 lb. ground beef
2 (16-oz.) cans pinto beans, rinsed and drained
1 (32-oz.) container low-sodium chicken broth
1 (15-oz.) can black beans, rinsed and drained
1 (14½-oz.) can petite diced tomatoes
1 (11-oz.) can shoepeg corn, drained
1 (10-oz.) can diced tomatoes and green chiles
1 (1.25-oz.) package taco seasoning mix
Toppings: sour cream, shredded Monterey Jack cheese, fresh lime juice, corn chips

Cook ground beef in a large Dutch oven over medium heat, stirring until beef crumbles and is no longer pink; drain and return to Dutch oven.

Stir in pinto beans and next 6 ingredients. Bring to a boil. Reduce heat, and simmer, stirring occasionally, 20 minutes. Serve with desired toppings. **Yield:** 10 servings.

quick & easy

Over-the-Border BLT Wraps

Microwave flour tortillas at HIGH for a few seconds for easier rolling during assembly.

Prep: 20 min.

1 cup mayonnaise
1 Tbsp. chopped fresh cilantro
2 tsp. chopped canned chipotle peppers in adobo sauce
8 (10-inch) flour tortillas
1 lb. bacon slices, cooked
½ head iceberg lettuce, chopped
1 cup grape tomato halves

Stir together first 3 ingredients; spread evenly over 1 side of each tortilla, leaving a ½-inch border. Top evenly with bacon, lettuce, and tomatoes. Roll up tightly; cut in half diagonally, and secure with wooden picks. **Yield:** 8 to 10 servings.

quick & easy

Spicy Coleslaw Reubens

Prep: 15 min. Cook: 13 min.

1 (10-oz.) package finely shredded cabbage
4 green onions, sliced
1 tsp. olive oil
½ cup Thousand Island dressing
3 Tbsp. spicy brown mustard
12 sourdough sandwich bread slices
6 (1-oz.) Monterey Jack cheese with peppers slices
1 lb. thinly sliced corned beef

Sauté cabbage and green onions in hot oil in a large nonstick skillet over medium-high heat 3 to 5 minutes or until cabbage is wilted. Remove from heat, and stir in dressing.

Spread mustard evenly on 1 side of 6 bread slices. Layer evenly with cheese slices, corned beef, and cabbage mixture. Top with remaining bread slices.

Cook sandwiches on a lightly greased nonstick griddle or skillet 3 to 4 minutes on each side or until golden brown. **Yield:** 6 servings.

quick & easy

Cranberry-Turkey Panini

This recipe showcases well-known holiday favorites in a warm Italian-style sandwich. If you don't have a panini press, place the sandwiches in a hot skillet, and press with a smaller heavy pan. Cook until the bread is golden brown; turn and continue to cook until the other side is golden brown and the cheese is melted.

Prep: 10 min. Cook: 3 min.

¼ cup mayonnaise
4 tsp. horseradish-Dijon mustard
4 soft sandwich rolls, cut in half
8 (1-oz.) Swiss or provolone cheese slices
8 oz. roasted, fully cooked turkey slices
1 cup canned whole-berry cranberry sauce
Vegetable cooking spray

Spread mayonnaise and mustard evenly on cut sides of rolls. Layer each bottom roll half with 1 cheese slice, and top evenly with turkey, cranberry sauce, and remaining cheese. Cover with roll tops; spray tops with cooking spray.

Cook in a preheated panini press 2 to 3 minutes or until golden brown. **Yield:** 4 servings.

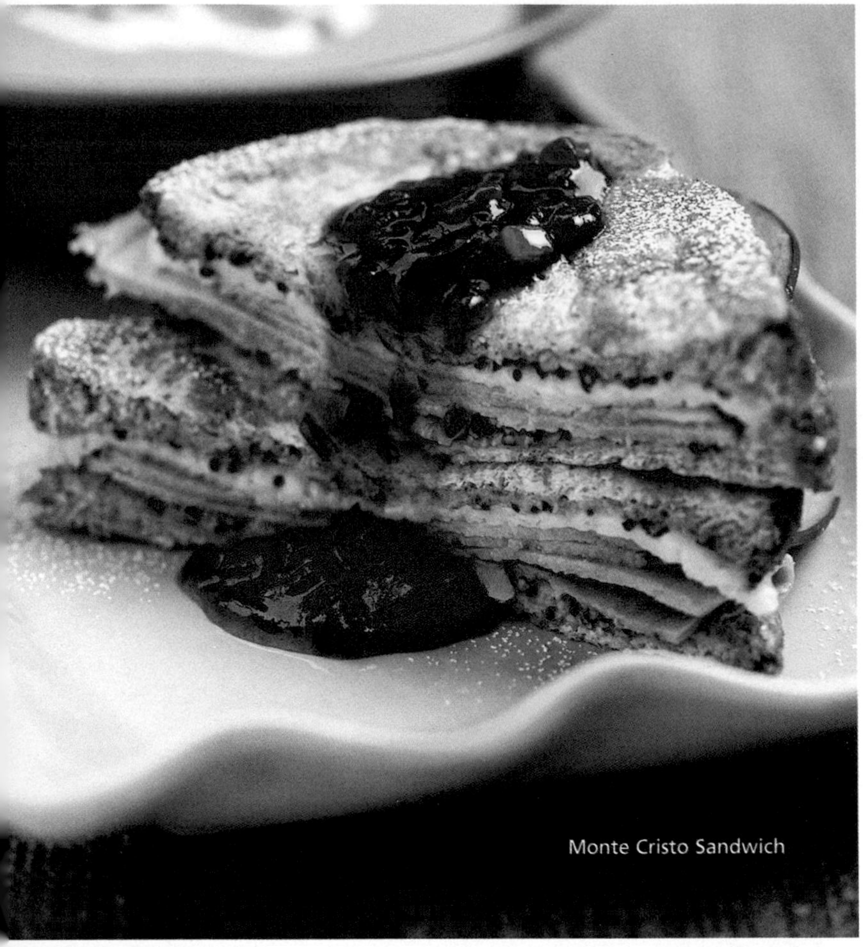

Monte Cristo Sandwich

editor's favorite

Monte Cristo Sandwiches

Prep: 10 min. Cook: 6 min. per batch

3 Tbsp. whole grain mustard
8 (1-oz.) whole wheat bread slices
8 oz. thinly sliced smoked deli ham
4 (1-oz.) reduced-fat Swiss cheese slices
⅓ cup egg substitute
⅓ cup fat-free milk
Vegetable cooking spray
4 Tbsp. tomato chutney
2 Tbsp. powdered sugar (optional)

Spread mustard evenly over 1 side of each bread slice. Layer each of 4 bread slices, mustard sides up, with 2 oz. ham and 1 cheese slice. Top with remaining bread slices, mustard sides down.

Whisk together egg substitute and milk in a shallow dish. Dip both sides of each sandwich into egg mixture.

Cook, in batches, in a large nonstick skillet coated with cooking spray over medium heat 3 minutes on each side or until lightly browned. Top each with 1 Tbsp. chutney, and, if desired, dust with powdered sugar. **Yield:** 4 servings.

Toasted Club Sandwich

Toasted Club Sandwiches

These sandwiches bring heaping layers of good taste to the table.

Prep: 15 min.

¾ cup mayonnaise
2 Tbsp. yellow mustard
12 sourdough bread slices, toasted
8 (1-oz.) slices deli ham
8 (1-oz.) slices deli turkey breast
16 fully cooked bacon slices
8 (¾-oz.) Swiss cheese slices
16 plum tomato slices
4 iceberg lettuce leaves, halved

Stir together mayonnaise and yellow mustard in a small bowl. Spread mayonnaise mixture evenly onto 1 side of toasted bread slices. Layer 4 bread slices, mayonnaise sides up, with 1 slice ham, 1 slice turkey, 2 bacon slices, 1 Swiss cheese slice, 2 tomato slices, and ½ lettuce leaf. Top each with 1 bread slice, mayonnaise side down; layer with remaining ham, turkey, bacon, cheese, and lettuce. Top with remaining 4 bread slices, mayonnaise sides down. Cut each sandwich into quarters, and, if desired, secure with wooden picks. **Yield:** 4 servings.

Sausage Gumbo Pot Pie With Garlic Bread Crust

editor's favorite

Sausage Gumbo Pot Pie With Garlic Bread Crust

Prep: 15 min. Cook: 15 min. Bake: 20 min. Stand: 10 min.

1 lb. smoked sausage, cut into ¼-inch-thick slices
1 medium-size green bell pepper, chopped
1 small onion, chopped
¼ cup instant roux mix (see note)
1 (10-oz.) can diced tomatoes and green chiles
1 (32-oz.) container chicken broth
1 (16-oz.) package frozen okra
1 cup quick-cooking rice, uncooked
½ tsp. Cajun seasoning
½ tsp. dried thyme
3 Tbsp. melted butter
2 garlic cloves, minced
1 (12-oz.) French baguette, cut into ½-inch-thick slices
Garnish: finely chopped fresh parsley

Sauté first 3 ingredients in a Dutch oven over medium-high heat 8 minutes or until browned; stir in roux mix. Cook, stirring constantly, 2 minutes. Stir in tomatoes and next 5 ingredients, and bring to a boil. Remove from heat. Pour into a 13- x 9-inch baking dish.

Stir together butter and garlic; brush on 1 side of bread slices. Top sausage mixture evenly with bread slices, buttered side up.

Bake, covered, at 425° for 10 minutes; uncover and bake 10 minutes more. Let stand 10 minutes. Garnish, if desired. **Yield:** 8 to 10 servings.

Note: For testing purposes only, we used Tony Chachere's Creole Instant Roux Mix.

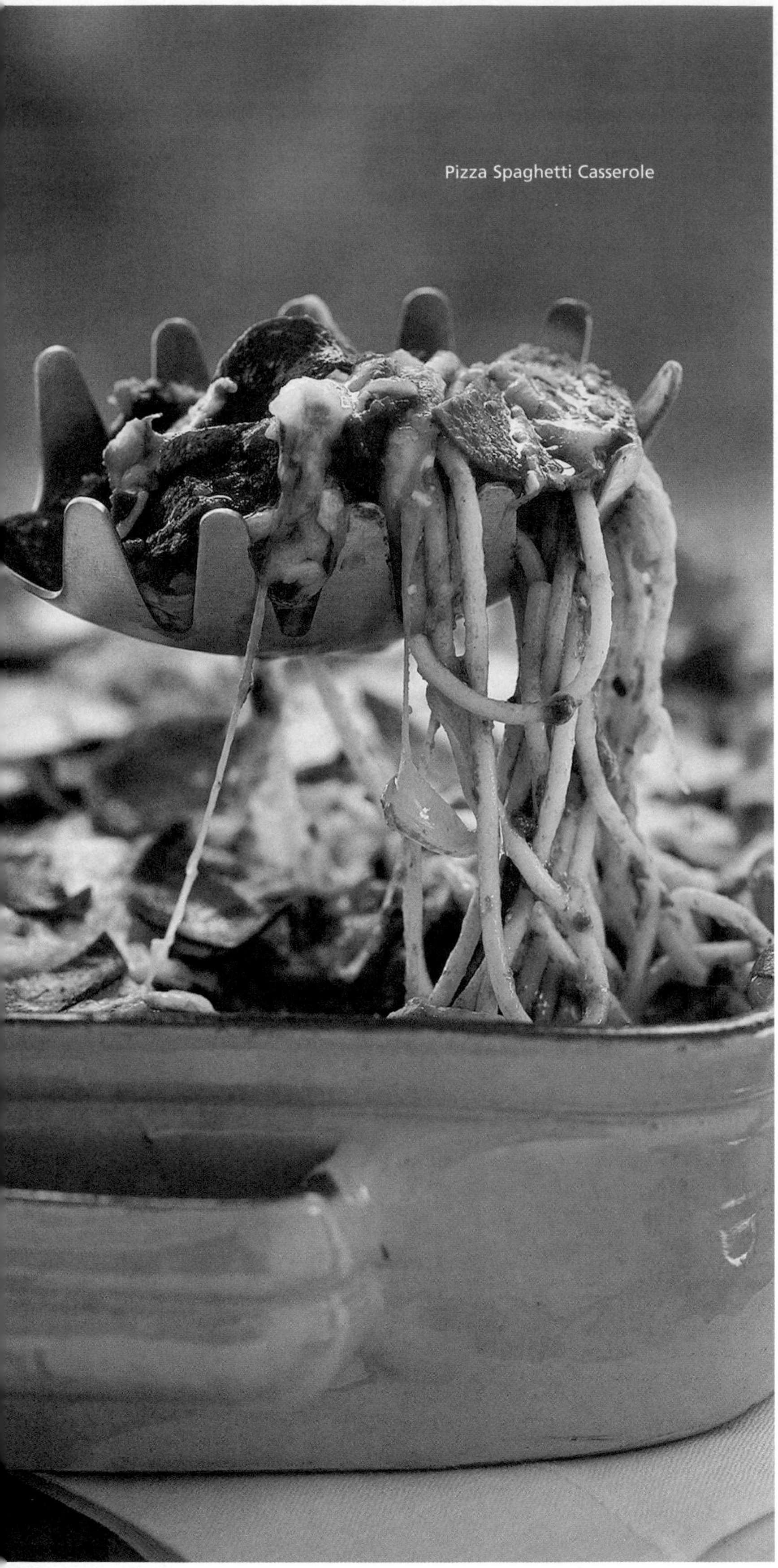

Pizza Spaghetti Casserole

Pizza Spaghetti Casserole

Prep: 15 min. Cook: 15 min. Bake: 40 min.

12 oz. uncooked spaghetti
½ tsp. salt
1 (1-lb.) package mild ground pork sausage
2 oz. turkey pepperoni slices (about 30), cut in half
1 (26-oz.) jar tomato-and-basil pasta sauce
¼ cup grated Parmesan cheese
1 (8-oz.) package shredded Italian three-cheese blend

Cook spaghetti with salt according to package directions. Drain well, and place in a lightly greased 13- x 9-inch baking dish.

Brown sausage in a large skillet over medium-high heat, stirring occasionally, 5 minutes or until meat crumbles and is no longer pink. Drain and set aside. Wipe skillet clean. Add pepperoni, and cook over medium-high heat, stirring occasionally, 4 minutes or until slightly crisp.

Top spaghetti in baking dish with sausage; pour pasta sauce over sausage. Arrange half of pepperoni evenly over pasta sauce. Sprinkle with cheeses. Arrange remaining half of pepperoni over cheese. Cover with nonstick or lightly greased aluminum foil.

Bake at 350° for 30 minutes; remove foil, and bake 10 minutes more or until cheese is melted. **Yield:** 6 servings.

Beef Ravioli in Basil-Cream Sauce

Prep: 10 min. Cook: 15 min.

1 (24-oz.) package frozen beef ravioli
2 Tbsp. butter
1 (8-oz.) package sliced fresh mushrooms
3 green onions, chopped
2 garlic cloves, minced
1 tsp. dried Italian seasoning
1 (10-oz.) can diced mild tomatoes and green chiles, drained
2 Tbsp. chopped fresh basil
1 cup whipping cream
½ cup grated Parmesan cheese
½ tsp. salt

Prepare ravioli in a large Dutch oven according to package directions; drain and keep warm.

Melt butter in Dutch oven over medium-high heat. Add mushrooms and next 3 ingredients; sauté 6 minutes. Stir in tomatoes and green chiles, basil, and cream; bring to a boil. Reduce heat, and simmer, stirring occasionally, 5 minutes. Stir in cheese, salt, and ravioli, tossing to coat. **Yield:** 4 servings.

Beef Ravioli in
Basil-Cream Sauce

Chicken Cobbler Casserole

editor's favorite
Chicken Cobbler Casserole

This quick-and-easy dish combines the robust flavors and cheeesy bread topping of French onion soup with the homey goodness of chicken pot pie. Substitute an equal amount of buttermilk for the wine, if desired. Serve with a green salad tossed with fresh citrus, sliced avocados, toasted pecans, and bottled raspberry vinaigrette.

Prep: 10 min. Cook: 25 min. Bake: 15 min.

6 Tbsp. melted butter, divided
4 cups cubed sourdough rolls
⅓ cup grated Parmesan cheese
2 Tbsp. chopped fresh parsley
2 medium-size sweet onions, sliced
1 (8-oz.) package sliced fresh mushrooms
1 cup white wine
1 (10¾-oz.) can cream of mushroom soup
½ cup drained and chopped jarred roasted red bell peppers
2½ cups shredded cooked chicken

Toss 4 Tbsp. melted butter with next 3 ingredients; set aside.

Sauté onions in remaining 2 Tbsp. butter in a large skillet over medium-high heat 15 minutes or until golden brown. Add mushrooms, and sauté 5 minutes.

Stir in wine and next 3 ingredients; cook, stirring constantly, 5 minutes or until bubbly. Spoon mixture into a lightly greased 9-inch square or 11- x 7-inch baking dish; top evenly with bread mixture.

Bake at 400° for 15 minutes or until casserole is golden brown. **Yield:** 4 servings.

CHOPPED CHICKEN CHOICES

Lots of speedy recipes call for chopped cooked chicken. Here are several ways to achieve that:

- Cooking 1 lb. of boneless chicken breasts yields about 2⅓ cups chopped cooked chicken.
- Cooking 1 (3½-lb.) whole chicken yields about 3 cups chopped cooked chicken.
- Pulling the meat from a deli-roastetd chicken yields about 3 cups chopped cooked chicken.
- Freeze leftover chopped cooked chicken or turkey in 1- or 2-cup amounts for up to 1 month to use as needed.

editor's favorite
Chicken and Dumplings

We used a deli-roasted chicken for this recipe. One chicken yields about 3 cups.

Prep: 15 min. Cook: 25 min.

1 (32-oz.) container low-sodium chicken broth
1 (14½-oz.) can low-sodium chicken broth
3 cups shredded cooked chicken (about 1½ lb.)
1 (10¾-oz.) can reduced-fat cream of celery soup
¼ tsp. poultry seasoning
1 (10.2-oz.) can refrigerated jumbo buttermilk biscuits

Stir together first 5 ingredients in a Dutch oven over medium-high heat; bring to a boil. Reduce heat to low; simmer, stirring occasionally, 15 minutes.

Place biscuits on a lightly floured surface. Roll or pat each biscuit to ⅛-inch thickness; cut into ½-inch-wide strips.

Return broth mixture to a low boil over medium-high heat. Drop strips, 1 at a time, into boiling broth. Reduce heat to low; simmer 10 minutes, stirring occasionally to prevent dumplings from sticking. **Yield:** 4 to 6 servings.

editor's favorite
Cherry-Tarragon Chicken Salad

Look for dried cherries on a hanging rack in the produce department or with the other dried fruit in your grocery store.

Prep: 15 min. Cook: 15 min. Chill: 2 hr.

1 cup fresh orange juice
½ cup dried cherries
4 cups chopped, cooked chicken
⅓ cup mayonnaise
¼ cup sour cream
2 tsp. fresh tarragon
1 tsp. grated fresh orange rind
½ tsp. salt
¼ tsp. freshly ground pepper
Crackers

Bring juice and cherries to a boil in a medium saucepan over medium-high heat. Reduce heat, and simmer, stirring occasionally, 10 to 12 minutes or until liquid is reduced to ¼ cup. Remove from heat, and cool slightly. Pour mixture into a large bowl; stir in chicken and next 6 ingredients, tossing to coat. Cover and chill at least 2 hours. Serve with crackers. **Yield:** 6 to 8 servings.

Holiday Leftovers Casserole

Prep: 30 min. Cook: 7 min. Bake: 15 min.

1 (7-oz.) package spaghetti, broken into 2-inch pieces
2 cups chopped cooked turkey or chicken
¾ cup diced ham
1 (2-oz.) jar diced pimiento, drained*
¼ cup minced green bell pepper
¼ small onion, grated
1 (10¾-oz.) can cream of mushroom soup
½ cup chicken or turkey broth
⅛ tsp. celery salt
⅛ tsp. freshly ground pepper
1½ cups (6 oz.) shredded Cheddar cheese

Prepare spaghetti according to package directions in a large Dutch oven. Drain well, and return spaghetti to pot.

Stir in turkey and next 8 ingredients; cook 7 minutes or until heated through. Remove from heat, and stir in 1 cup cheese. Pour into a lightly greased 8-inch square baking dish. Sprinkle evenly with remaining ½ cup cheese.

Bake at 350° for 15 minutes or until cheese melts. **Yield:** 4 to 6 servings.

*1 jarred roasted red bell pepper, diced, can be substituted.

Turkey à la King

Prep: 15 min. Cook: 16 min.

1 Tbsp. butter or margarine
1 bunch green onions, chopped
1 (10¾-oz.) can cream of celery soup
1 (10¾-oz.) can cream of chicken soup
1 cup milk
½ tsp. chicken bouillon granules
¼ tsp. seasoned pepper
⅛ tsp. white pepper
3 cups chopped cooked turkey or chicken
Split biscuits or toast points

Melt butter in a medium saucepan over medium heat; add green onions, and sauté 8 minutes or until tender. Whisk in cream of celery soup and next 5 ingredients until smooth; cook 5 minutes. Stir in turkey; cook 2 to 3 minutes or until thoroughly heated. Serve over split biscuits or toast points. **Yield:** 4 to 6 servings.

editor's favorite

Raspberry-Turkey Salad

This main-dish salad starts with a simple dressing from raspberry preserves, wine, and mango chutney. You may substitute 1 lb. chicken cutlets for the turkey.

Prep: 15 min. Cook: 24 min.

½ tsp. seasoned salt
½ tsp. garlic powder
½ tsp. onion powder
1 lb. turkey breast cutlets
1 Tbsp. butter
1 Tbsp. olive oil
½ cup seedless raspberry preserves
½ cup chicken broth
½ cup white wine*
½ cup hot mango chutney
1 (7-oz.) package mixed salad greens, thoroughly washed

Stir together first 3 ingredients; rub evenly over turkey cutlets.

Melt butter with oil in a large skillet over medium-high heat; add cutlets, and cook 3 to 4 minutes on each side or until lightly browned. Remove from skillet, and keep warm.

Stir raspberry preserves and next 3 ingredients into skillet over medium-high heat, stirring until preserves melt and to loosen particles from bottom of skillet. Cook, stirring occasionally, 14 to 16 minutes or until mixture is reduced by half.

Toss salad greens with ¼ to ⅓ cup warm preserves mixture in a large salad bowl just until greens are thoroughly warmed and lightly coated with preserve mixture. Arrange on salad plates, and top with turkey cutlets. **Yield:** 4 servings.

*¼ cup chicken broth and ¼ cup fruit juice (such as white grape, orange, or apple) may be substituted.

Shrimp Casserole

Prep: 30 min. Cook: 17 min. Bake: 25 min.

1½ cups uncooked long-grain rice
1½ lb. unpeeled medium-size raw shrimp
½ cup butter
1 green bell pepper, chopped
1 onion, chopped
3 celery ribs, chopped
2 garlic cloves, minced
4 green onions, chopped
2 (10¾-oz.) cans cream of shrimp soup, undiluted*
¼ tsp. salt
¼ tsp. freshly ground pepper
1 cup (4 oz.) shredded Cheddar-colby cheese blend
¼ cup fine, dry breadcrumbs

Prepare rice according to package directions; set aside.

Peel shrimp, and devein, if desired.

Melt butter in a large skillet over medium heat; add bell pepper and next 4 ingredients, and sauté 10 to 12 minutes or until tender. Stir in soup, shrimp, salt, and pepper; cook 3 minutes or just until shrimp turn pink. (Do not overcook.)

Combine shrimp mixture and rice. Pour mixture into a lightly greased 13- x 9-inch baking dish. Sprinkle evenly with 1 cup shredded cheese and ¼ cup breadcrumbs.

Bake at 350° for 25 minutes or until cheese is melted.

Yield: 8 servings.

*2 (10¾-oz.) cans cream of celery soup, undiluted, may be substituted.

Chicken-and-Rice Casserole: Substitute 3 cups chopped cooked chicken for shrimp and 2 (10¾-oz.) cans cream of chicken soup, undiluted, for cream of shrimp soup. Proceed with recipe as directed.

Shrimp Casserole

Easy Cornbread Stuffing

SEASON'S FAVORITE *Dressings*

Holiday meals are not complete without dressing, gravy, and cranberry sauce. Treat your guests to some of these tempting offerings.

freezer friendly • make ahead

Easy Cornbread Stuffing

This savory side dish is created by adding vegetables, pecans, and seasonings to commercial stuffing mix.

Prep: 20 min. Bake: 45 min.

1 (16-oz.) package herb-seasoned stuffing mix (see note)
1 (8-oz.) package cornbread stuffing mix (see note)
4 (14-oz.) cans low-fat chicken broth, divided
2 celery ribs, chopped
½ medium onion, chopped
½ green bell pepper, chopped
½ cup chopped fresh parsley
¼ cup chopped pecans, toasted
½ tsp. poultry seasoning
½ tsp. garlic powder

Combine stuffing mixes, 3 cans chicken broth, chopped celery, and next 6 ingredients. Spoon stuffing mixture evenly into a lightly greased 13- x 9-inch pan or baking dish.

Pour remaining 1 can broth evenly over stuffing in pan. Bake at 350° for 40 to 45 minutes or until golden. **Yield:** 8 to 10 servings.

Note: For testing purposes only, we used Pepperidge Farm stuffing mix.

Make-Ahead Note: Spoon unbaked stuffing mixture into a lightly greased freezer-safe, disposable aluminum pan; cover and freeze up to 1 month. Thaw in refrigerator. Uncover and bake as directed.

Cornbread Dressing

Prep: 20 min. Bake: 1 hr., 25 min. Cook: 6 min.

½ cup butter, divided
1½ cups self-rising white buttermilk cornmeal mix (see note)
½ cup all-purpose flour
5 large eggs, divided
1½ cups buttermilk
1½ cups fresh soft breadcrumbs
1 small sweet onion, diced
2 celery ribs, diced
2 Tbsp. finely chopped fresh sage
2 Tbsp. finely chopped fresh parsley
2 tsp. seasoned pepper
¼ tsp. salt
2 (14-oz.) cans chicken broth

Place ¼ cup butter in an 8-inch cast-iron skillet; heat in a 425° oven 4 minutes.

Stir together cornmeal and flour; whisk in 1 egg and buttermilk. Pour hot butter from skillet into batter, and stir until blended. Pour batter into hot skillet.

Bake at 425° for 30 minutes or until golden brown. Remove from pan, and cool. Crumble cornbread into a large bowl; stir in fresh soft breadcrumbs.

Melt remaining ¼ cup butter in skillet over medium heat; add diced onion and celery, and sauté 5 minutes. Stir in chopped sage and next 3 ingredients; sauté 1 minute. Remove from heat, and stir into cornbread mixture.

Whisk together chicken broth and remaining 4 eggs; stir into cornbread mixture. Pour evenly into a lightly greased 9-inch square pan.

Bake at 400° for 50 to 55 minutes or until golden brown. **Yield:** 8 servings.

Note: For testing purposes only, we used White Lily Self-Rising Buttermilk Cornmeal Mix.

editor's favorite
Grits Dressing

There's no need for gravy here. This unique Southern dressing sports crusty grits croutons and spicy sausage. Make the croutons and brown the sausage 1 day in advance.

Prep: 11 min. Cook: 15 min. Bake: 1 hr., 17 min.

3 (10½-oz.) cans condensed chicken broth, undiluted
1¼ cups uncooked quick-cooking grits (see note)
¾ cup freshly shredded Parmesan cheese
1 lb. ground hot pork sausage
5 celery ribs with leaves, finely chopped
4 garlic cloves, minced (about 1 Tbsp.)
1 large onion, chopped
⅓ cup butter or margarine, melted
1 large egg, lightly beaten
½ cup chopped fresh parsley

Bring broth to a boil in a large saucepan. Stir in grits, and return to a boil. Cover, reduce heat, and simmer 7 minutes or until grits are thickened, stirring twice. Stir in cheese. Remove from heat.

Spoon grits into a greased 13- x 9-inch baking dish. Cover and chill until firm. Unmold onto a large cutting board, sliding knife or spatula under grits to loosen them from dish. Cut grits into ¾-inch cubes. Place in a single layer on a large greased baking sheet or jelly-roll pan. Bake at 450° for 20 minutes; turn grits, and bake 10 to 12 minutes more or until crisp and browned.

Meanwhile, cook sausage in a large skillet, stirring until it crumbles and is no longer pink; drain.

Sauté celery, garlic, and onion in butter 5 minutes or until tender. Stir together onion mixture, sausage, and grits croutons, tossing gently. Drizzle egg over mixture; add parsley, stirring gently. Spoon dressing loosely into a greased 11- x 7-inch baking dish. Bake, uncovered, at 350° for 35 to 45 minutes or until browned. **Yield:** 8 servings.

Note: For testing purposes only, we used Quaker grits.

editor's favorite • make ahead
Hot-and-Spicy Cranberry-Pear Chutney

Try this chutney with baked chicken, Cornish hens, turkey, or pork tenderloin.

Prep: 5 min. Cook: 13 min.

1½ cups fresh cranberries
1 (6-oz.) package sweetened dried cranberries (see note)
⅓ cup sugar
1 cup fresh orange juice
1 Tbsp. grated fresh ginger
2 (10½-oz.) jars pear preserves
1 (10½-oz.) jar hot jalapeño jelly
1 (9-oz.) jar hot mango chutney
1 Tbsp. grated fresh orange rind

Bring first 5 ingredients to a boil in a large saucepan, stirring constantly. Reduce heat, and simmer, stirring constantly, 5 minutes or until cranberry skins split.

Stir in pear preserves and remaining ingredients; simmer, stirring constantly, 5 minutes. Remove from heat, and cool. Pour into hot sterilized jars, and seal. Store in refrigerator up to 1 month. **Yield:** about 8 cups.

Note: For testing purposes only, we used Craisins for sweetened dried cranberries.

editor's favorite
Fresh Cranberry Sauce

Prep: 20 min. Cook: 15 min. Chill: 1 hr.

1 cup sugar
1 cup water
1 (12-oz.) package fresh cranberries
1 Tbsp. grated fresh orange rind
1 Tbsp. orange liqueur
¼ cup chopped pecans or sliced almonds, toasted (optional)

Bring sugar and 1 cup water to a boil in a saucepan, stirring until sugar dissolves. Add cranberries, rind, and liqueur; return to a boil, reduce heat, and simmer 10 minutes. If desired, stir in toasted pecans. Cover and chill 1 hour or until firm. **Yield:** about 2 cups.

editor's favorite

Cinnamon-Scented Cranapple Sauce

This jewel-toned cranberry sauce gets embellished with tart apple, cinnamon pears, and citrus. It's a wonderful match for pork roast or turkey.

Prep: 5 min. Cook: 45 min.

1 (16-oz.) can whole-berry cranberry sauce
1 (15-oz.) can cinnamon-flavored pear halves, drained and chopped (see note)
1 (11-oz.) can mandarin orange segments, drained
1 Granny Smith apple, peeled and chopped
1 cup sugar
½ cup dried fruit mix (see note)

Combine all ingredients in a large saucepan; cook, uncovered, over medium-low heat 45 minutes or until thickened, stirring often. Remove sauce from heat; cover and chill.

Serve as an accompaniment with pork or turkey, or as a topping over vanilla ice cream, pound cake, or pancakes. **Yield:** 3½ cups.

Note: If you can't find cinnamon-flavored pears, use regular canned pear halves, and add ½ tsp. ground cinnamon. For testing purposes only, we used Mariani Harvest Medley dried fruit mix.

A CRANBERRY SIDE DISH IS A *flavorful complement* TO PORK ROAST, CHICKEN, OR TURKEY.

editor's favorite

Make-Ahead Turkey Gravy

This recipe uses a homemade stock. If you prefer pan drippings, substitute the first 7 ingredients with 2 cups pan drippings.

Prep: 15 min. Cook: 1 hr.

2 turkey necks
1 Tbsp. vegetable oil
1 medium onion, coarsely chopped
1 celery rib, coarsely chopped
5 cups low-sodium chicken broth
¼ cup loosely packed fresh flat-leaf parsley
1 fresh thyme sprig
3 Tbsp. butter
¼ cup all-purpose flour
¼ cup white wine
¼ tsp. rubbed sage
Salt and freshly ground pepper to taste

Brown turkey necks in hot oil in a large saucepan over medium-high heat 2 to 3 minutes on each side. Add onion and celery; sauté 5 minutes. Stir in broth, parsley, and thyme. Bring to a boil; reduce heat, and simmer, stirring occasionally, 30 minutes. Pour through a wire-mesh strainer; discard solids.

Melt butter in a large skillet over medium-low heat; whisk in flour until smooth. Cook, whisking constantly, 4 to 5 minutes or until mixture is golden. Gradually whisk in stock (or pan drippings), wine, and sage; bring to a boil over medium heat. Reduce heat; simmer, stirring occasionally, 5 to 10 minutes or until thickened. Stir in salt and pepper to taste. **Yield:** about 2 cups.

MAKE-AHEAD TURKEY GRAVY STEP-BY-STEP

- Avoid lumpy gravy by thickening it with a roux instead of cornstarch.
- Prepare a roux by cooking melted butter and flour until golden brown, whisking constantly with a wire whisk. Slowly whisk the warm stock or pan drippings into the roux to thicken. When cold liquid is added to a roux, it will seize, causing clumps.

Turkey Giblet Gravy

We used egg yolks and flour as thickeners in this luscious recipe. Don't like giblets? Simply skip the step of cooking and chopping them, and substitute 4 cups of chicken broth for the cooking liquid.

Prep: 10 min. Cook: 1 hr., 5 min.

Giblets and neck from 1 turkey
4 cups water
½ cup butter
1 small onion, chopped
1 celery rib, chopped
1 carrot, chopped
¼ cup all-purpose flour
2 egg yolks
½ cup half-and-half
½ tsp. salt
½ tsp. freshly ground pepper
½ tsp. poultry seasoning
Garnish: fresh parsley sprig (optional)

Bring giblets, neck, and 4 cups water to a boil in a medium saucepan over medium heat. Cover, reduce heat, and simmer 45 minutes or until meat is tender. Drain, reserving broth. Chop giblets and neck meat, and set aside.

Melt butter in a large skillet over medium heat (photo 1); add chopped vegetables, and sauté 5 minutes. Add flour, stirring until smooth (photo 2). Add reserved broth; cook, stirring constantly, 10 minutes or until thickened (photo 3). Reduce heat to low. Remove vegetables using a handheld, wire-mesh strainer, and discard, leaving gravy in skillet.

Whisk together egg yolks and ½ cup half-and-half. Gradually stir about one-fourth of hot gravy into yolk mixture; add to remaining hot gravy (photo 4). Add giblets and neck meat; cook, stirring constantly, 4 to 5 minutes or until a thermometer registers 160°. Stir in salt, pepper, and poultry seasoning. Garnish, if desired. Serve immediately. **Yield:** 4 cups.

TURKEY GIBLET GRAVY
STEP-BY-STEP

Turkey Giblet Gravy

Brussels Sprouts With Pecans (page 178)

SIMPLE TO *Spectacular Sides*

Fill the table with a bountiful feast of veggies, fruits, and salads. With over 50 recipes, you're sure to find all your favorites—plus some new ones—to add to the menu.

quick & easy

Asparagus Amandine

Prep: 5 min. Cook: 12 min.

2 lb. fresh asparagus
2 Tbsp. butter
¼ cup sliced almonds
2 Tbsp. diced red bell pepper
1 Tbsp. fresh lemon juice
½ tsp. salt
½ tsp. freshly ground pepper

Snap off tough ends of asparagus. Cook asparagus in boiling salted water to cover in a large skillet 3 minutes or until crisp-tender; drain. Plunge asparagus into ice water to stop the cooking process; drain.

Melt butter in a large skillet over medium heat; add almonds, and sauté 2 to 3 minutes or until golden brown. Add cooked asparagus and bell pepper; cook 3 to 5 minutes. Toss with lemon juice, salt, and pepper; serve immediately. **Yield:** 8 servings.

Broccoli and Parsnips With Horseradish-Butter Sauce

Parsnips are sweet and nutty and complement the other flavors in this dish. If you can't find parsnips, carrots make a terrific substitute.

Prep: 10 min. Cook: 20 min.

1 lb. fresh parsnips, peeled and cut into thin strips
1 lb. fresh broccoli, cut into florets
3 Tbsp. butter
2 Tbsp. prepared horseradish
2 Tbsp. fresh lemon juice
½ tsp. salt
¼ cup chopped walnuts, toasted

Arrange parsnips in a steamer basket over boiling water. Cover and steam 8 minutes. Add broccoli; cover and steam 5 more minutes or until crisp-tender. Place parsnips and broccoli in a large bowl.

Melt butter in a small saucepan over low heat; cook 5 minutes or until lightly browned. Remove from heat. Stir in horseradish, lemon juice, and salt. Pour sauce over vegetables. Sprinkle with walnuts. Serve immediately. **Yield:** 6 servings.

Broccoli and Parsnips With Horseradish-Butter Sauce

Broccoli With Orange Sauce

Broccoli With Orange Sauce

These beautiful florets are a powerful source of vitamins A and C.

Prep: 20 min. Cook: 11 min.

2 oranges
1½ lb. fresh broccoli, cut into florets
1 tsp. butter or margarine
1 small onion, chopped
2 tsp. finely chopped crystallized ginger
1 (8-oz.) container low-fat lemon yogurt

Grate 1 orange to equal 1 tsp. grated rind; set aside. Peel and section oranges, removing seeds; set aside.

Place broccoli florets in a steamer basket over boiling water, and cook 3 to 4 minutes or until crisp-tender.

Melt butter in a nonstick skillet over medium-high heat; add onion and ginger, and sauté until tender. Remove from heat.

Toss together broccoli florets, onion mixture, 1 tsp. orange rind, and orange sections in a large bowl. Stir in yogurt. Serve immediately. **Yield:** 6 servings.

Broccoli-Spinach Casserole

Prep: 15 min. Bake: 45 min.

2 (10-oz.) packages frozen chopped broccoli, thawed
2 (10-oz.) packages frozen chopped spinach, thawed and drained
2 (10¾-oz.) cans cream of mushroom soup
4 large eggs, lightly beaten
1 large sweet onion, diced
2 cups (8 oz.) shredded sharp Cheddar cheese
1 cup mayonnaise
1 tsp. salt
½ tsp. freshly ground pepper
½ tsp. garlic powder
36 round buttery crackers, crushed (see note)

Stir together first 10 ingredients in a large bowl until combined. Spoon mixture into a lightly greased 13- x 9-inch baking dish. Sprinkle evenly with crushed crackers.

Bake at 350° for 40 to 45 minutes or until set. **Yield:** 12 to 16 servings.

Note: For testing purposes only, we used Ritz crackers.

Carrot Soufflé

One bite of this sweet side will leave your taste buds craving another fluffy spoonful.

Prep: 10 min. Cook: 45 min. Bake: 45 min.

1 lb. carrots, peeled and chopped
3 large eggs, lightly beaten
½ cup sugar
½ cup butter or margarine, melted
3 Tbsp. all-purpose flour
1 tsp. baking powder
1 tsp. vanilla extract

Bring carrots and water to cover to a boil in a medium saucepan; cook 45 minutes or until very tender. Drain.

Process carrots in a food processor until smooth.

Stir together carrot puree, eggs, and remaining ingredients. Spoon into a lightly greased 1-qt. baking dish.

Bake at 350° for 45 minutes or until set. **Yield:** 8 servings.

Honey-Glazed Carrots

Prep: 10 min. Cook: 20 min.

1½ qt. water
1 (1-lb.) package whole carrots, diagonally sliced
2 Tbsp. butter
2 Tbsp. honey
½ tsp. grated fresh orange rind
½ tsp. salt
¼ tsp. freshly ground pepper
1 Tbsp. chopped fresh parsley
Garnish: orange rind curls

Bring 1½ qt. water to a boil in a Dutch oven over medium heat. Add carrots, and cook 10 minutes or until tender. Drain well. Return carrots to Dutch oven; add butter and next 4 ingredients. Cook, stirring occasionally, 3 to 5 minutes or until glazed. Stir in parsley. Garnish, if desired, and serve immediately. **Yield:** 6 servings.

Honey-Glazed Carrots

Brussels Sprouts With Pecans

These sprouts take just a brief turn in the pan—slicing them cuts down on their cooking time. The dish's sweet, buttery flavors mellow the bite of the Brussels sprouts. *(pictured on page 174)*

Prep: 20 min. Cook: 11 min.

2 tsp. butter
1 cup chopped onion
4 garlic cloves, thinly sliced
8 cups halved and thinly sliced Brussels sprouts (about 1½ lb.)
½ cup low-sodium fat-free chicken broth
1½ Tbsp. sugar
½ tsp. salt
8 tsp. coarsely chopped pecans, toasted

Melt butter in a large nonstick skillet over medium-high heat. Add onion and garlic; sauté 4 minutes or until lightly browned. Stir in Brussels sprouts; sauté 2 minutes. Add broth and sugar; cook 5 minutes or until liquid almost evaporates, stirring frequently. Stir in salt. Sprinkle with pecans. **Yield:** 8 servings.

Roasted Garlic-and-Chipotle Cauliflower Mash

Prep: 15 min. Bake: 30 min. Stand: 10 min. Cook: 20 min.

1 garlic bulb
1 head cauliflower (about 2½ lb.)
½ cup fat-free sour cream
2 Tbsp. butter
1 to 2 tsp. minced canned chipotle peppers in adobo sauce
1 tsp. salt
¼ tsp. freshly ground pepper

Cut off pointed end of garlic; place garlic on a piece of aluminum foil. Fold foil to seal.

Bake at 425° for 30 minutes; remove from oven, and let stand 10 minutes. Squeeze pulp from garlic into the bowl of a food processor.

Cut cauliflower into florets; arrange in a steamer basket over boiling water. Cover and steam 20 minutes or until cauliflower is tender.

Add cauliflower, sour cream, and remaining ingredients to garlic in food processor. Process until smooth, stopping to scrape down sides. **Yield:** 8 (½-cup) servings.

Make-Ahead Note: To prepare garlic ahead, roast as directed; squeeze pulp into a small bowl. Cover pulp with a thin layer of olive oil; cover with plastic wrap. Store in the refrigerator up to 1 week. One garlic head yields approximately 1 Tbsp. pulp.

editor's favorite

Green Beans With Mushrooms and Bacon

We loved the dash of dried crushed red pepper—it made the flavor lively, not hot.

Prep: 20 min. Cook: 20 min.

2 lb. fresh green beans, trimmed
8 bacon slices
3 cups sliced shiitake mushrooms (about 7 oz.)
¼ cup chopped shallots
⅛ to ¼ tsp. dried crushed red pepper
½ tsp. freshly ground black pepper
¼ tsp. salt

Cook beans in boiling salted water to cover in a Dutch oven over medium-high heat 4 minutes or until crisp-tender; drain. Plunge into ice water to stop the cooking process; drain and set aside.

Cook bacon in a large skillet until crisp; remove bacon, and drain on paper towels, reserving 1½ Tbsp. drippings in skillet. Discard remaining drippings. Crumble bacon.

Sauté mushrooms and shallots in hot drippings over medium-high heat 5 minutes or until tender. Add beans and crushed red pepper; sauté 1 to 2 minutes or until heated. Stir in crumbled bacon, ½ tsp. black pepper, and ¼ tsp. salt. **Yield:** 8 servings.

TECHNIQUES FOR GREEN BEANS WITH MUSHROOMS AND BACON

- Do the first recipe step the day before serving. Pat beans dry with paper towels, and store in a zip-top plastic bag in the refrigerator.
- Use the mushroom caps only; discard the tough stems. Use a soft brush to clean caps. Avoid rinsing them with water; they soak it up like sponges.

Green Beans With
Mushrooms and Bacon

quick & easy

Green Beans With Cranberries, Blue Cheese, and Walnuts

Prep: 10 min. Cook: 10 min.

¾ cup chicken broth
¼ tsp. salt
¼ tsp. freshly ground pepper
1 (16-oz.) package frozen whole green beans
4 oz. blue cheese, crumbled
1 cup walnuts, toasted
½ cup sweetened dried cranberries

Bring first 3 ingredients to a boil in a large skillet over medium heat; add green beans, and cook 5 to 7 minutes or to desired degree of tenderness. Spoon green beans into a serving dish. Sprinkle evenly with blue cheese, walnuts, and cranberries; serve immediately. **Yield:** 4 servings.

Gingered Green Beans

Look for fresh ginger (also called gingerroot) in the specialty produce section of your grocery store. Peel it with a vegetable peeler, and mince with a sharp knife. Leftover ginger can be frozen up to 1 month.

Prep: 15 min. Cook: 15 min.

3 cups low-sodium fat-free chicken broth
1 lb. fresh green beans, trimmed
1 Tbsp. butter
1 small sweet onion, diced
2 garlic cloves, minced
2 Tbsp. peeled and minced fresh ginger
¼ tsp. salt
½ tsp. seasoned pepper

Bring broth to a boil in a large saucepan over medium-high heat. Add green beans, and cook 4 to 6 minutes or until crisp-tender; drain.

Melt butter in a large nonstick skillet over medium-high heat. Add onion, garlic, and ginger; sauté 2 minutes. Add beans, salt, and pepper; sauté 1 minute or until thoroughly heated. **Yield:** 6 servings.

quick & easy

Orange-Ginger Peas

This dish is equally good without ginger, so if you don't have or don't like it, leave it out.

Prep: 5 min. Cook: 7 min.

1 (16-oz.) package frozen green peas
1 cup water
1 Tbsp. grated fresh orange rind
2 Tbsp. honey
¼ to ½ tsp. salt
¼ tsp. ground red pepper
1 (1-inch) piece fresh ginger, peeled (optional)

Combine first 6 ingredients and ginger, if desired, in a large saucepan over medium-high heat. Bring to a boil; reduce heat, and simmer 3 minutes. Remove and discard ginger. Serve with a slotted spoon. **Yield:** 6 servings.

Country Cornbread With Black-eyed Pea Topping

Prep: 10 min. Cook: 10 min. Bake: 20 min.

5 bacon slices
4 green onions, finely chopped
½ red bell pepper, finely chopped
½ green bell pepper, finely chopped
2 (15-oz.) cans black-eyed peas, undrained
1 tsp. hot sauce
1 (6-oz.) package cornbread mix
⅔ cup milk
Toppings: salsa, sour cream

Cook bacon in a 10-inch skillet over medium heat until crisp; remove bacon, and drain on paper towels, reserving 2 Tbsp. drippings in skillet. Crumble bacon, and set aside.

Sauté green onions and bell peppers in hot drippings in skillet 5 to 7 minutes or until tender. Add black-eyed peas and hot sauce, and cook until thoroughly heated.

Prepare cornbread mix according to package directions using ⅔ cup milk. Bake as directed. Cut into wedges. Top cornbread with black-eyed pea mixture, and sprinkle evenly with crumbled bacon. Serve with desired toppings. **Yield:** 6 servings.

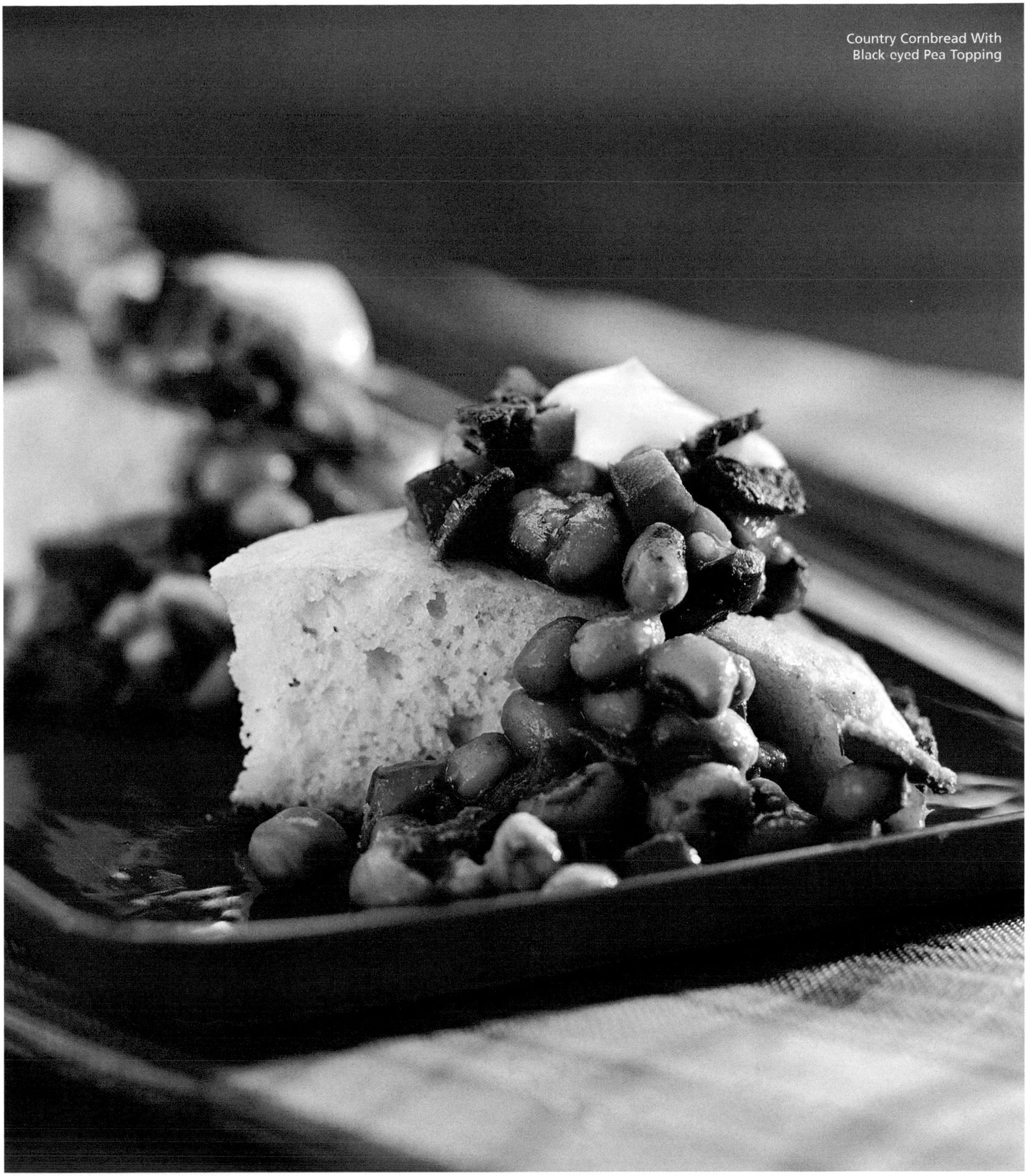

Country Cornbread With Black-eyed Pea Topping

editor's favorite

Buttermilk Mashed Potatoes

Prep: 25 min. Cook: 30 min.

3 garlic cloves, minced
1 Tbsp. olive oil
2 cups low-sodium chicken broth
3½ lb. Yukon gold potatoes, peeled and cubed
1¼ tsp. salt, divided
1½ cups warm buttermilk
⅓ cup butter, melted
¾ tsp. pepper
4 Tbsp. chopped fresh chives

Sauté garlic in hot oil in a Dutch oven over medium heat 3 minutes. Add 8 cups water, chicken broth, potatoes, and ¼ tsp. salt; bring to a boil. Cover, reduce heat, and cook 15 to 20 minutes or until potatoes are tender.

Drain potatoes, and return to Dutch oven. Add buttermilk, butter, pepper, and remaining 1 tsp. salt. Mash potatoes with a large fork or potato masher to desired consistency. Sprinkle evenly with chives; serve immediately. **Yield:** 6 servings.

make ahead

Potato-and-Caramelized Onion Casserole

To cut down the cook time, start the potatoes while the onions cook. The eggs create a puffy look and add texture to the potatoes. Sweet onion varieties are 'Vidalia,' '1015 Supersweet,' 'Maui,' or 'Walla Walla.' Dress up this dish with a sprinkle of cracked black pepper, chopped parsley, or paprika right before serving.

Prep: 45 min. Cook: 1 hr., 15 min. Bake: 35 min.

¾ cup butter, divided
¼ cup olive oil
5 lb. sweet onions, diced
1 Tbsp. sugar
4 lb. baking potatoes, peeled and cubed
4 cups chicken broth
1 cup fat-free half-and-half
1 cup light sour cream
4 large eggs, lightly beaten
½ tsp. salt

Melt ¼ cup butter in a large skillet over medium heat. Add olive oil, onions, and sugar. Cook, stirring often, 45 to 50 minutes or until onions are caramel-colored (a deep golden brown). Remove from heat, and set aside.

Bring potatoes and chicken broth to a boil in a Dutch oven; cook 20 minutes or until tender. Drain.

Add remaining ½ cup butter to potatoes, and mash with a potato masher until smooth. Whisk together half-and-half and next 3 ingredients; add to potato mixture, stirring until blended.

Spoon half of potato mixture into a lightly greased 13- x 9-inch baking dish. Spoon caramelized onions evenly over potatoes in dish. Spoon remaining potatoes evenly over onions. (Cover and chill up to 2 days, if desired. Remove casserole from refrigerator, and let stand 30 minutes before baking.)

Bake casserole, uncovered, at 350° for 30 to 35 minutes or until golden. (If casserole was chilled, bake about 15 minutes more.) **Yield:** 10 to 12 servings.

Bourbon-Sweet Potato Stacks

Prep: 20 min. Cook: 50 min. Bake: 25 min.

6 medium-size sweet potatoes
½ cup chopped pecans
6 Tbsp. butter, melted
½ cup firmly packed brown sugar
½ cup fresh orange juice
½ cup bourbon
½ tsp. ground cinnamon
¼ tsp. ground cloves
¼ tsp. ground nutmeg
Garnish: pecan halves

Bring sweet potatoes and water to cover to a boil in a large Dutch oven over high heat. Reduce heat, and cook 30 to 45 minutes or just until potatoes are tender. Drain and let cool to touch; peel. Cut ends off, and discard. Cut remaining potato into 1-inch-thick rounds. Arrange slices evenly into 12 stacks in a lightly greased 13- x 9-inch baking dish. Sprinkle evenly with chopped pecans.

Combine butter and next 6 ingredients; pour evenly over potatoes and pecans.

Bake at 350° for 25 minutes or until thoroughly heated. Garnish, if desired. **Yield:** 10 to 12 servings.

Spicy Roasted Sweet Potato Fries

Prep: 15 min. Bake: 30 min.

1 Tbsp. olive oil, divided
2 large sweet potatoes (about 1¼ lb.)
¼ tsp. salt
¼ tsp. chili powder
1 tsp. brown sugar

Brush an aluminum foil-lined jelly-roll pan with 2 tsp. olive oil. Heat pan in a 425° oven 5 minutes.

Peel sweet potatoes, and cut into 3- x ½-inch strips. Combine strips, salt, chili powder, brown sugar, and remaining 1 tsp. oil in a large zip-top plastic freezer bag, tossing to coat.

Place strips in a single layer in prepared pan.

Bake at 425° for 30 minutes or until crisp, stirring every 10 minutes. **Yield:** 4 servings.

Stuffed Sweet Potatoes

Use the pumpkin pie spice blend for a quick and cost-effective way to enjoy the flavors of cinnamon, cardamom, ginger, allspice, and nutmeg.

Prep: 15 min. Bake: 1 hr., 10 min. Cool: 5 min.

4 small sweet potatoes (about 8 oz. each)
¼ cup firmly packed light brown sugar
3 Tbsp. light sour cream
1 tsp. grated fresh orange rind
1 Tbsp. fresh orange juice
2 tsp. butter
1 tsp. pumpkin pie spice
2 Tbsp. chopped toasted pecans (optional)

Pierce sweet potatoes several times with a fork. Place on an aluminum foil-lined jelly-roll pan.

Bake at 350° for 1 hour or until tender; cool 5 minutes.

Cut a 1½-inch-wide strip from top of each baked potato. Carefully scoop out pulp into a medium bowl, leaving potato shells intact.

Mash together pulp, brown sugar, and next 5 ingredients. Spoon mixture evenly into shells. Place shells on jelly-roll pan.

Bake at 350° for 10 minutes or until thoroughly heated. Top potatoes evenly with 2 Tbsp. chopped toasted pecans, if desired. **Yield:** 4 servings.

Streusel-Topped Sweet Potatoes

Using canned sweet potatoes makes this dish so easy to prepare.

Prep: 15 min. Bake: 30 min.

3 (29-oz.) cans sweet potatoes, drained
⅓ cup granulated sugar
2 egg yolks
1 tsp. grated fresh orange rind
1 Tbsp. fresh orange juice
1½ tsp. pumpkin pie spice
1 tsp. salt
3 egg whites
Vegetable cooking spray
½ cup chopped pecans, toasted
½ cup firmly packed brown sugar
¼ cup all-purpose flour
3 Tbsp. butter, melted
¼ tsp. pumpkin pie spice

Stir together first 7 ingredients in a large bowl. Mash well with a potato masher until blended and smooth. Beat egg whites in a small bowl at high speed with an electric mixer until soft peaks form. Gently fold beaten egg whites into sweet potato mixture. Spoon mixture into a 13- x 9-inch or shallow 3-qt. baking dish coated with cooking spray.

Stir together pecans and next 4 ingredients. Sprinkle over sweet potato mixture.

Bake at 400° for 30 minutes or until topping is lightly browned. **Yield:** 12 servings.

SWEET POTATO TIME-SAVING TIP

Canned sweet potatoes may be substituted for fresh. Three medium-size sweet potatoes are roughly equivalent to 1 (16-oz.) can sweet potatoes or 2 cups cooked and mashed.

Smashed Rutabagas and Turnips
With Parmesan Cheese

Smashed Rutabagas and Turnips With Parmesan Cheese

Using a very sharp knife, cut a small slice off one side of the rutabaga. Rest the rutabaga on the sliced side for stability. Holding the rutabaga firmly with a dish towel, cut several slices using a rocking motion with the rutabaga and knife. Peel slices using a potato peeler or sharp paring knife. Chop to the desired size.

Prep: 15 min. Cook: 50 min.

1 lb. rutabagas, peeled and chopped
1 tsp. salt
6 cups water
1½ lb. turnips, peeled and chopped
¼ cup grated Parmesan cheese
6 Tbsp. butter
½ cup whipping cream
¾ tsp. salt
¼ tsp. freshly ground pepper
2 Tbsp. bourbon (optional)
Garnishes: flat-leaf or curly parsley, majoram leaves

Combine rutabagas, 1 tsp. salt, and 6 cups water in a large Dutch oven; bring to a boil, and cook 25 minutes. Add turnips, and cook 20 more minutes or until vegetables are tender; drain.

Combine vegetables, cheese, and next 4 ingredients in a large mixing bowl; mash with a potato masher (or beat at medium speed with an electric mixer) to desired consistency. Stir in bourbon, if desired. Garnish, if desired. **Yield:** 6 servings.

Roasted Root Vegetables

A close cousin of carrots, cream-colored parsnips have a delicate, sweet flavor that pairs well with other root vegetables. The vegetables in this dish are cooked on 2 baking sheets on separate racks in the oven. You may need to swap the placement of the baking sheets after 15 to 20 minutes to ensure even cooking.

Prep: 15 min. Bake: 45 min.

1 (1-lb.) bag parsnips
2 large sweet potatoes
1 large rutabaga
Vegetable cooking spray
¾ tsp. salt
¾ tsp. freshly ground pepper
¼ cup butter, melted
¼ cup chopped fresh chives

Peel first 3 ingredients, and cut vegetables into large pieces.

Coat 2 aluminum foil-lined baking sheets with cooking spray. Arrange vegetables in a single layer on prepared baking sheets; lightly coat vegetables with cooking spray, and sprinkle evenly with salt and pepper.

Bake vegetables at 425°, stirring occasionally, 35 to 45 minutes or until tender.

Toss vegetables with butter and chives. **Yield:** 8 servings.

OVEN MAGIC

Our recipe for Roasted Root Vegetables calls for a combination of parsnips, sweet potatoes, and rutabaga, but many other fall and winter vegetables, such as butternut squash, beets, or onions, would be equally delicious. Just follow these tips:

- Trim and cut vegetables into uniform pieces. Most vegetables can be prepared up to a day ahead and stored, covered with water, in the refrigerator. Drain and dry thoroughly before roasting.
- Choose a rimmed baking sheet or heavy roasting pan, and line with aluminum foil for easy cleanup. For extra crispness, try roasting vegetables in a cast-iron skillet.
- Don't overload the pan; use more than one, if necessary. Arrange the vegetables in a single layer so each piece will crisp and caramelize to a golden brown rather than steam.
- Before roasting, season cut vegetables with salt and pepper, and drizzle with olive oil or lightly coat with vegetable cooking spray.
- Vegetables are best roasted at a high temperature (400° to 450°). Bake times can vary, depending on the size and type of vegetable, but use our recipe for Roasted Root Vegetables above as a guide. When the outer edges begin to brown, check for tenderness by piercing the veggies with a fork.

Apple-Cranberry Compote

editor's favorite

Apple-Cranberry Compote

Look for cranberry-orange sauce near the applesauce in the canned fruit aisle of your supermarket. If you can't find it, 1 (16-oz.) can whole-berry cranberry sauce will also work.

Prep: 20 min. Cook: 5 min. Bake: 50 min.

1 (12-oz.) container whole cranberry-orange sauce
2 Tbsp. brown sugar
2 Tbsp. fresh lemon juice
2 tsp. grated fresh ginger
¼ tsp. salt
6 Granny Smith apples, peeled, cored, and quartered
Vegetable cooking spray
¼ cup chopped pecans
Garnishes: orange rind strips, fresh rosemary sprigs

Bring cranberry-orange sauce and next 4 ingredients to a boil in a medium saucepan over medium-high heat, stirring constantly. Remove from heat.

Arrange apple quarters in a round baking dish coated with cooking spray; pour cranberry mixture over apples.

Bake at 350° for 45 minutes or until apples are tender. Sprinkle evenly with chopped pecans. Bake 5 minutes more. Garnish, if desired. **Yield:** 12 servings.

make ahead

Pineapple-Apple Ambrosia

Prep: 30 min. Chill: 2 hr. Bake: 4 min.

4 medium oranges, peeled
2 Fuji or Braeburn apples, cubed
2 cups fresh pineapple chunks*
1 cup seedless red grapes, halved
1 cup unsweetened pineapple juice
⅓ cup sugar
½ tsp. ground ginger
¼ tsp. vanilla extract
⅛ tsp. almond extract (optional)
½ cup sweetened flaked coconut

Cut oranges into ¼-inch-thick slices. Cut orange slices into quarters, and place in a large bowl. Add apples, pineapple chunks, and grape halves.

Stir together pineapple juice, next 3 ingredients, and if desired, almond extract. Pour over fruit, and toss. Cover and chill 2 hours.

Bake coconut in a shallow pan at 350°, stirring once, 4 minutes or until lightly toasted. Sprinkle coconut over fruit mixture, and serve immediately. **Yield:** 10 cups.

*2 cups unsweetened canned pineapple chunks may be substituted for fresh.

Pineapple-Apple Ambrosia

Rosemary Baked Vegetables

The recipe calls for an entire bulb of garlic. Remove any loose paper-like skin before cutting off the top. Once cooked, you squeeze the bulb, releasing the individual cloves of just-cooked garlic. Left whole, the cooked cloves will have a milder flavor than if pressed or chopped.

Prep: 15 min. Bake: 45 min.

3 red potatoes, cut into 1-inch pieces (about 1 lb.)
12 baby carrots
1 medium-size sweet potato, peeled and cut into 1-inch pieces
1 large or 2 small zucchini, cut into 1-inch pieces
1 onion, quartered
1 garlic bulb, pointed end cut off
¼ cup olive oil
1 tsp. crushed dried rosemary
½ tsp. salt

Toss together all ingredients; place in a single layer in a 15- x 10-inch jelly-roll pan.

Bake at 400° for 45 minutes or until tender. Carefully squeeze pulp from garlic bulb; discard husk. Stir together garlic and vegetables. **Yield:** 4 servings.

Creamed Spinach

This is one of the best lightened creamed spinach recipes that we've ever tasted.

Prep: 5 min. Cook: 15 min.

2 (6-oz.) packages fresh baby spinach
⅓ cup minced white onion
1 Tbsp. butter
2 tsp. all-purpose flour
½ tsp. salt
Pinch of ground nutmeg
½ cup fat-free milk
½ (8-oz.) package ⅓-less-fat cream cheese, softened

Cook spinach, a handful at a time, in a lightly greased large Dutch oven over medium-high heat until wilted. Drain spinach well, pressing between paper towels.

Sauté onion in melted butter in large Dutch oven over medium-high heat 2 minutes. Stir in flour, salt, and nutmeg; cook 30 seconds. Stir in ½ cup milk and cream cheese; cook, stirring constantly, until smooth and mixture is thickened. Add spinach, and cook, stirring constantly, 2 minutes or until thoroughly heated. Serve immediately. **Yield:** 4 servings.

make ahead

Maple Butternut Squash

Prep: 10 min. Cook: 12 min. Stand: 5 min.

2 butternut squash, cut in half (about 3½ lb.)
2 Tbsp. butter
¼ cup maple syrup
¼ tsp. salt
¼ tsp. freshly ground pepper
3 bacon slices, cooked and crumbled

Remove seeds and strings from squash. Cover with plastic wrap. Microwave at HIGH 10 to 12 minutes or until tender. Let stand 5 minutes.

Carefully scoop cooked squash into a large bowl. Add butter, and mash with a potato masher or fork until smooth; stir in next 3 ingredients. Transfer to a serving dish, and sprinkle evenly with bacon. Serve immediately. **Yield:** 6 servings.

Make-Ahead Note: Prepare squash as directed, omitting bacon. Cover and chill up to 2 days. When ready to serve, stir well, and microwave at HIGH 2 to 3 minutes or until thoroughly heated, stirring at 1-minute intervals. Sprinkle evenly with bacon.

Squash Casserole

Prep: 20 min. Cook: 20 min. Bake: 35 min.

3 lb. yellow squash, sliced
5 Tbsp. butter, divided
1 small onion, chopped (about ½ cup)
1 cup (4 oz.) shredded sharp Cheddar cheese
2 large eggs, lightly beaten
¼ cup mayonnaise
2 tsp. sugar
1 tsp. salt
20 round buttery crackers, crushed (about ¾ cup)

Cook squash in boiling water to cover in a large skillet 8 to 10 minutes or just until tender. Drain well, and gently press between paper towels.

Melt 4 Tbsp. butter in skillet over medium-high heat; add onion, and sauté 5 minutes or until tender. Remove skillet from heat; stir in squash, cheese, and next 4 ingredients. Spoon mixture into a lightly greased 11- x 7-inch baking dish.

Melt remaining 1 Tbsp. butter. Stir together melted butter and crushed crackers; sprinkle evenly over top of casserole.

Bake at 350° for 30 to 35 minutes or until set. **Yield:** 8 servings.

Maple Butternut Squash

PREPARING BUTTERNUT SQUASH

• After cutting squash in half lengthwise and removing seeds and strings, wrap each half securely in plastic wrap before cooking. Microwave according to the recipe directions.

• Allow the squash to stand 5 minutes. Hold the squash with a towel or pot holder as it will be very hot. Carefully scoop soft, cooked squash into a large bowl; add butter, and mash with a potato masher or fork.

Grand Oranges and Strawberries

Grand Oranges and Strawberries

This elegant compote is also a wonderful accompaniment to egg dishes and ham biscuits.

Prep: 30 min. Cook: 5 min. Chill: 8 hr.

½ cup orange marmalade
1½ cups sparkling white grape juice, chilled
¼ cup orange liqueur (see note)
10 to 12 large navel oranges, peeled and sectioned
2 cups sliced fresh strawberries
Garnish: fresh mint sprigs

Melt marmalade in a small saucepan over low heat, stirring constantly; remove from heat, and let cool slightly.

Stir together marmalade, white grape juice, and orange liqueur in a large serving dish or bowl until blended. Add orange sections, and gently stir. Cover and chill 8 hours.

Add strawberries to oranges in bowl, and gently toss to coat. Serve with a slotted spoon. Garnish, if desired. **Yield:** 10 to 12 servings.

Note: For testing purposes only, we used Grand Marnier for orange liqueur.

make ahead

Spiced Fruit Bake

Prep: 10 min. Cook: 5 min. Bake: 30 min.

2 (15-oz.) cans sliced pears in syrup, undrained
1 (29-oz.) can sliced peaches in syrup, undrained
1 (20-oz.) can pineapple chunks in juice, undrained
1 (15.25-oz.) can apricot halves in syrup, undrained
1 (14.5-oz.) can pitted red tart cherries in water, drained*
¼ cup firmly packed brown sugar
1 Tbsp. cornstarch
½ tsp. ground cinnamon
¼ to ½ tsp. ground ginger
¼ cup butter
¼ cup bourbon (optional)

Drain first 4 ingredients, reserving syrups and juice in a bowl. Combine fruit in a separate large bowl, and set aside.

Stir syrups and juice until blended; reserve ¾ cup syrup mixture. (Reserve an additional ¼ cup syrup mixture if omitting bourbon.)

Add drained cherries to fruit in large bowl.

Combine brown sugar and next 3 ingredients in a heavy saucepan; gradually stir in reserved ¾ cup syrup mixture. Add butter, and cook over medium heat, stirring constantly, 5 minutes or until butter is melted and mixture is thickened and bubbly. Remove from heat; stir in bourbon if desired, or omit bourbon and stir in reserved ¼ cup syrup mixture. Pour sauce over fruit mixture in a lightly greased 3-qt. round baking dish.

Bake at 350° for 30 minutes or until thoroughly heated. **Yield:** 8 to 10 servings.

*1 (15-oz.) can Royal Ann cherries in heavy syrup, drained, may be substituted.

Make-Ahead Note: Prepare fruit mixture as directed. Do not bake. Cover and refrigerate overnight. Uncover; let stand 10 minutes at room temperature. Bake as directed.

Fruited Rice Pilaf

This scrumptious dish can easily be doubled to serve a large crowd.

Prep: 15 min. Cook: 30 min.

1 Tbsp. butter or margarine
1 Tbsp. olive oil
½ small onion, diced
2 garlic cloves, minced
¼ cup pine nuts, toasted
1 cup golden raisins
1 cup uncooked long-grain rice
2¼ cups water
½ tsp. salt
2 Tbsp. chopped fresh parsley

Melt butter with olive oil in a large saucepan over medium heat; add onion, and sauté 4 to 5 minutes or until tender. Add garlic and next 3 ingredients; cook, stirring constantly, 3 to 4 minutes.

Add 2¼ cups water and ½ tsp. salt. Bring to a boil; reduce heat to low, cover, and simmer 17 to 20 minutes or until liquid is absorbed and rice is tender. Stir in parsley. **Yield:** 6 to 8 servings.

Pecan Pilaf

Prep: 10 min. Cook: 10 min. Bake: 40 min.

3 Tbsp. butter
1 (8-oz.) package sliced fresh mushrooms
½ cup sliced green onions
1 garlic clove, minced
2 cups uncooked long-grain rice
1 tsp. salt
½ tsp. ground thyme
¼ tsp. freshly ground pepper
4 cups vegetable broth
¾ cup chopped pecans, toasted

Melt butter in an ovenproof Dutch oven over medium heat. Add mushrooms, green onions, and garlic; cook, stirring often, 5 minutes or until tender. Add rice, and cook 2 minutes, stirring constantly. Stir in salt, thyme, and pepper. Stir in broth; bring to a boil. Cover and remove from heat.

Bake at 325° for 40 minutes or until rice is tender. Stir in toasted pecans. **Yield:** 8 servings.

Roasted Garlic-and-Cheese Risotto

Arborio rice is a short-grain, starchy rice traditionally used for risotto. Long-grain rice will not work in this recipe.

Prep: 15 min. Bake: 30 min. Cook: 50 min.

1 garlic bulb
7 shiitake mushrooms
1 tsp. butter
1 tsp. olive oil
1 medium onion, chopped
1½ cups uncooked Arborio rice
½ cup frozen corn kernels
½ cup dry white wine
7 to 8 cups fat-free reduced-sodium chicken broth, heated
1½ tsp. minced fresh or ½ tsp. dried thyme
½ tsp. salt
½ tsp. freshly ground pepper
¼ tsp. rubbed sage
½ (8-oz.) package ⅓-less-fat cream cheese, softened

Cut off pointed end of garlic; place garlic on a piece of aluminum foil. Fold foil to seal.

Bake at 425° for 30 minutes; cool. Squeeze pulp from garlic cloves, and chop. Set aside.

Remove stems from mushrooms, and discard. Thinly slice mushroom caps.

Melt butter with oil in a 2-qt. saucepan over medium-high heat. Add onion and mushrooms, and sauté 2 to 3 minutes. Add rice; sauté 1 minute. Stir in corn and wine; reduce heat to medium, and simmer, stirring constantly, until wine is reduced by half. Add ½ cup hot broth, and cook, stirring constantly, until liquid is absorbed. Repeat procedure with remaining hot broth, ½ cup at a time, until rice is tender. (Total cooking time is about 35 to 45 minutes.)

Stir in thyme and next 3 ingredients. Add cream cheese and chopped roasted garlic, stirring until blended. Serve immediately. **Yield:** 8 servings.

Green Rice Timbales

To make the carrot garnish, blanch baby carrots in boiling water 2 to 3 minutes. Cut 4 slits lengthwise into each carrot—without cutting through—and then fan.

Prep: 20 min. Cook: 5 min. Bake: 30 min. Cool: 5 min.

3 cups cooked rice
3 cups (12 oz.) shredded fontina cheese
3 cups half-and-half
4 large eggs
1½ tsp. salt
1 tsp. freshly ground pepper
2 Tbsp. butter or margarine
½ cup minced green onions
4 garlic cloves, minced
1 (10-oz.) package fresh spinach, coarsely chopped
½ cup chopped fresh parsley
Garnishes: baby carrot fans, fresh parsley sprigs

Combine first 6 ingredients in a large bowl.

Melt butter in a large skillet; add green onions and garlic, and sauté 2 to 3 minutes or until tender. Add spinach; cook, stirring constantly, 1 minute or just until wilted. Stir in parsley, and add to rice mixture. Spoon into 12 lightly greased 10-oz. custard cups or individual soufflé dishes, and place in 2 (13- x 9-inch) pans. Add hot water to pans to depth of 1 inch.

Bake at 350° for 30 minutes or until set. Remove from water; cool on wire racks 5 minutes. Loosen edges with a knife; unmold onto a serving platter. Garnish, if desired. **Yield:** 12 servings.

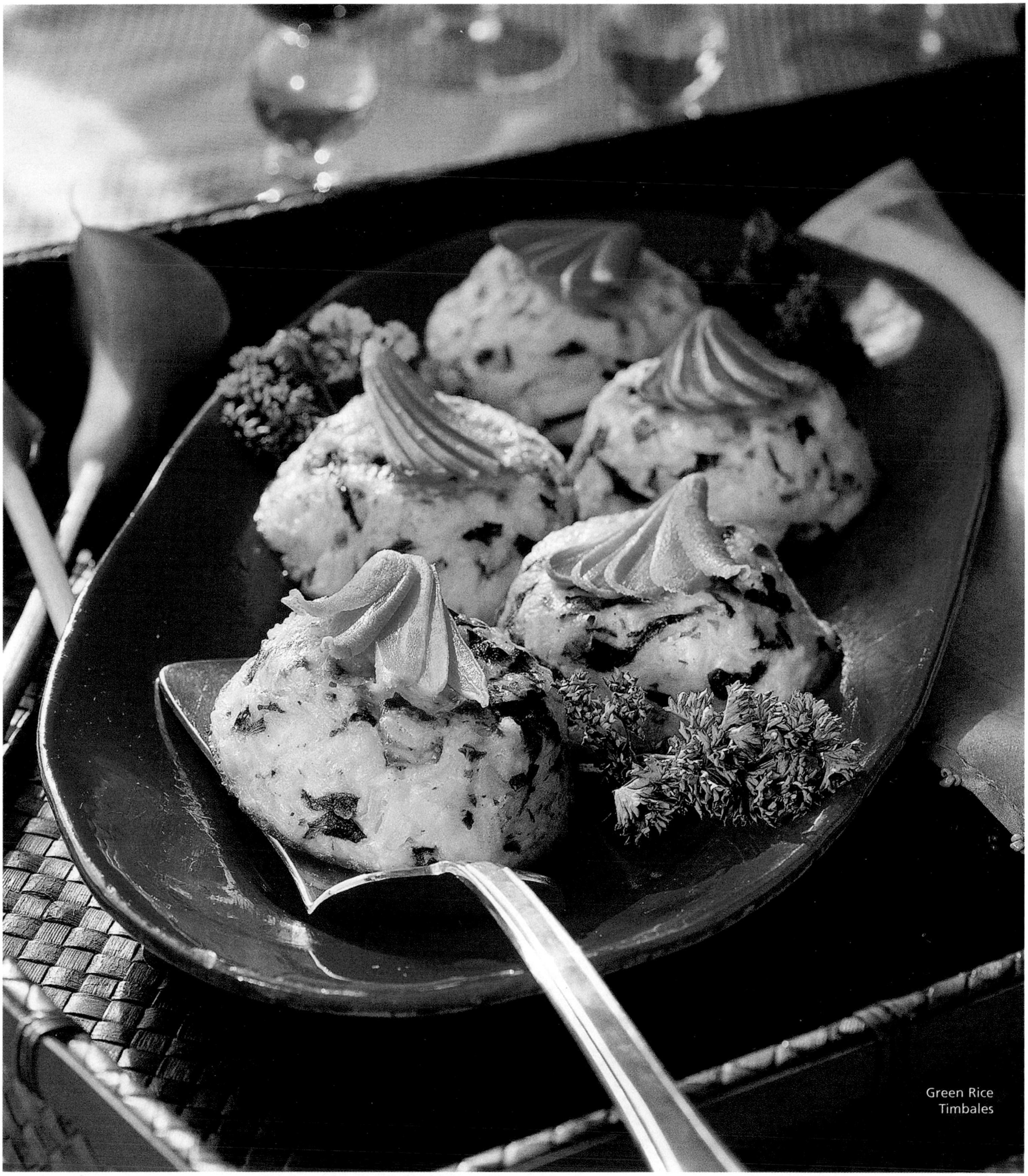

Green Rice Timbales

Cranberry-Almond Wild Rice

Prep: 5 min. Cook: 20 min.

1 (6-oz.) package long-grain and wild rice mix
1 (3.5-oz.) bag quick-cooking brown rice
¾ cup sweetened dried cranberries
⅓ cup toasted slivered almonds

Cook wild rice mix according to package directions. Cook brown rice according to package directions. Stir together wild rice mix, brown rice, cranberries, and almonds. **Yield:** 4 to 6 servings.

make ahead
Sausage-and-Wild Rice Casserole

You can assemble this dish through Step 4 (do not add broth) the night before, and then refrigerate. Stir in broth just before baking.

Prep: 20 min. Cook: 30 min. Bake: 1 hr. Stand: 5 min.

½ cup chopped pecans
1 (1-lb.) package sage ground pork sausage
1 Tbsp. butter
1 large onion, chopped
1 cup chopped celery
2 (6-oz.) packages long-grain and wild rice mix
2 Tbsp. chopped flat-leaf parsley
1 Tbsp. chopped fresh or 1 tsp. dried rubbed sage
½ tsp. freshly ground pepper
3½ cups low-sodium chicken broth

Heat ½ cup chopped pecans in a large nonstick skillet over medium-low heat, stirring often, 5 minutes or until toasted. Remove toasted pecans from skillet.

Brown sausage in same skillet over medium-high heat, stirring often, 10 minutes or until meat crumbles and is no longer pink. Remove sausage from skillet using a slotted spoon; reserve drippings in skillet.

Melt butter in hot drippings over medium heat. Add onion and celery, and sauté 10 to 15 minutes or until celery is tender.

Remove 1 seasoning packet from rice mixes; reserve for another use. Combine sausage, vegetable mixture, remaining seasoning packet, rice, and next 3 ingredients in a lightly greased 13- x 9-inch baking dish. Stir in chicken broth until well blended.

Bake, covered, at 325° for 1 hour or until liquid is almost absorbed. Let stand 5 minutes. Sprinkle chopped pecans on top. **Yield:** 8 to 10 servings.

Creamy Apple-and-Pecan Salad

This recipe from Martha Foose, owner of Mockingbird Bakery in Mississippi, can be used as a side at a sit-down lunch or as a stuffing for pitas at a more casual gathering.

Prep: 25 min. Stand: 10 min.

1 cup water
½ cup dried cranberries
¼ cup golden raisins
½ cup mayonnaise
3 Tbsp. plain yogurt
2 Tbsp. sugar
2 tsp. grated fresh lemon rind
1 Tbsp. fresh lemon juice
4 apples (1 Granny Smith and 3 Gala apples), cored and chopped
1 cup diced celery
½ cup chopped pecans, toasted

Bring 1 cup water to a boil in a medium saucepan. Remove from heat, and stir in dried cranberries and raisins. Let stand 10 minutes, and drain.

Stir together mayonnaise and next 4 ingredients in a large bowl. Stir in apples, celery, cranberries, and raisins. Cover and chill. Sprinkle apple mixture with pecans just before serving. **Yield:** 8 servings.

Creamy Apple-and-Pecan Salad Pita Pockets: Cut 1 regular pita round in half. Stuff pita halves evenly with ¼ cup mixed salad greens and ½ cup Creamy Apple-and-Pecan Salad. Yield: 2 servings.

PAIR A *hearty soup* AND *flavorful salad* FOR A HEALTHY, NO-FUSS MEAL.

Creamy Apple-and-Pecan Salad Pita Pocket,
Curried Pumpkin Soup (page 151)

Spiced Peach Congealed Salad

make ahead

Spiced Peach Congealed Salad

A traditional Southern table wouldn't be complete without a congealed salad. Spiced fruits add seasonal flavor.

Prep: 10 min. Cook: 5 min. Chill: 8 hr.

2 (15-oz.) cans harvest spice sliced peaches*
1 (3-oz.) package lemon-flavored gelatin
½ cup orange juice
1 (15-oz.) can pitted Royal Ann cherries in heavy syrup, drained
1 cup chopped pecans
Bibb lettuce leaves (optional)
1 cup whipping cream
1 Tbsp. mayonnaise
Garnish: fresh cranberries

Drain peaches, reserving 1 cup liquid in a saucepan. Coarsely chop peaches.

Bring reserved 1 cup peach liquid to a boil; remove from heat. Stir in gelatin, stirring 2 minutes or until gelatin dissolves. Stir in orange juice, chopped peaches, cherries, and pecans.

Spoon mixture into a lightly greased 5½-cup ring mold. Cover and chill 8 hours or until firm. Unmold salad onto Bibb lettuce leaves, if desired, on a platter or serving dish.

Beat whipping cream at high speed with an electric mixer until soft peaks form, and fold in mayonnaise. Serve salad with whipped cream mixture. Garnish, if desired. **Yield:** 6 to 8 servings.

*1 (25.5-oz.) jar spiced pickled peaches may be substituted for canned harvest spice peaches. Proceed as directed, using a 4½-cup ring mold.

SALAD KNOW-HOW

Follow these tips for perfectly shaped congealed salads:

- Lightly spray the inside of a mold with vegetable cooking spray before filling with the salad mixture.
- Be sure the gelatin is firm before unmolding the salad. Gently press the top with your finger; it should spring back or jiggle.
- Before unmolding, gently run a small knife around the outer edge to break the seal.
- Dip the bottom of the mold in warm water for about 15 seconds before unmolding (photo 1). Be careful not to get any water in the mold.
- You may also wrap the outside of the mold with a warm, damp tea towel. Wet the towel with hot water, and wring it out. Wrap the towel around the bottom and partially up the sides of the mold. Let stand 1 to 2 minutes.
- If the salad sticks to the mold, return the mold to the warm water for 5 more seconds and try again.
- To serve on a bed of crisp lettuce leaves, place the greens facedown on the salad in the mold. Top with the platter, and turn over (photo 2). If omitting the lettuce leaves, moisten the platter with a little water before inverting the mold to help the gelatin adhere to the surface.
- If your congealed salad breaks and the broken piece is small, put it back into place. All it takes is a tiny bit of water to seal the edges of the seam. For larger accidents, cut away and discard the messed-up part; then preslice a few servings (like a pound cake). Or cube the entire congealed salad, and serve it in a large bowl.

1

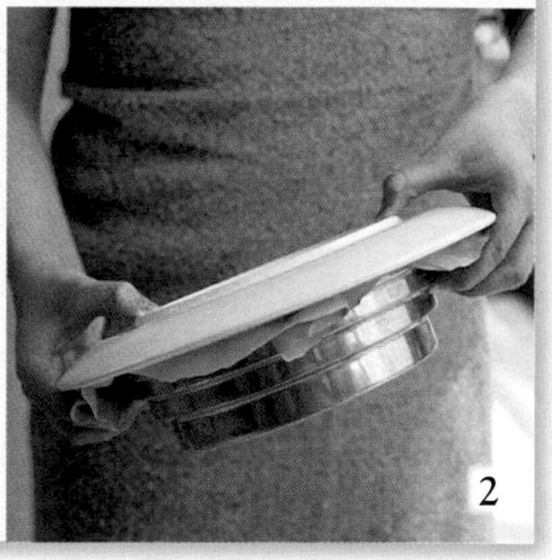

2

make ahead

Holiday Broccoli Salad

Prep: 30 min.

1½ lb. fresh broccoli
1 cup mayonnaise
2 Tbsp. sugar
¼ cup red wine vinegar
¼ tsp. salt
½ tsp. freshly ground pepper
1 (6-oz.) package dried mixed fruit
1 (2.25-oz.) package slivered almonds, toasted
½ small red onion, diced (about ¼ cup)
4 bacon slices, cooked and crumbled

Cut florets from broccoli, reserving stalks. Chop florets, and dice stalks.

Whisk together mayonnaise and next 4 ingredients in a large bowl. Add florets, stalks, dried fruit, almonds, and onion, tossing to coat. Serve immediately, or chill up to 6 hours. Sprinkle evenly with bacon just before serving. **Yield:** 10 to 12 servings.

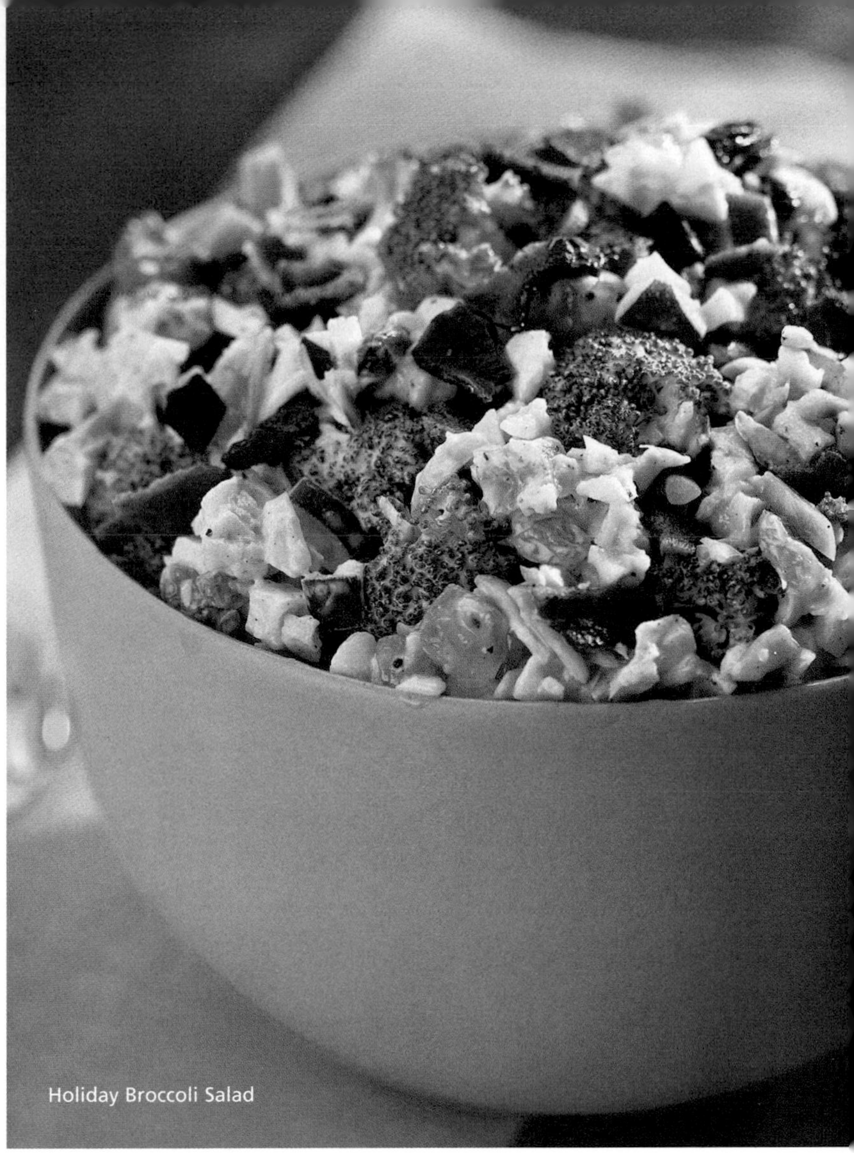

Holiday Broccoli Salad

Roasted Sweet Potato Salad

Prep: 30 min. Bake: 45 min.

1½ lb. sweet potatoes
2 large onions
2 garlic cloves, crushed
2 Tbsp. olive oil
½ tsp. salt
½ tsp. freshly ground pepper
1 (6-oz.) bag baby spinach
Warm Bacon Dressing
Garnish: cooked, crumbled bacon

Peel sweet potatoes, and cut into 1-inch cubes. Cut onions into quarters, and cut each quarter in half.

Toss together sweet potatoes, onions, crushed garlic, and 2 Tbsp. olive oil; place on a lightly greased aluminum foil-lined 15- x 11-inch jelly-roll pan. Sprinkle evenly with salt and pepper.

Bake, stirring occasionally, at 400° for 45 minutes or until tender and lightly brown. Serve over spinach, and drizzle with Warm Bacon Dressing. Garnish, if desired. **Yield:** 6 to 8 servings.

Warm Bacon Dressing:

Prep: 10 min. Cook: 10 min.

4 bacon slices
⅓ cup red wine vinegar
3 Tbsp. orange juice
2 Tbsp. honey
¼ tsp. salt
⅛ tsp. freshly ground pepper

Cook bacon slices in a large skillet until crisp. Remove bacon, and drain on paper towels, reserving 1 Tbsp. drippings in skillet. Crumble bacon.

Stir vinegar and next 4 ingredients into hot drippings in skillet; cook over medium heat, stirring until thoroughly heated. Stir in bacon. **Yield:** ½ cup.

Roasted Potato-
and-Bacon Salad

Roasted Potato-and-Bacon Salad

We cut out some of the extra calories and fat in this warm spinach salad by using less oil and switching to turkey bacon. The results were incredible, and this updated, flavorful dish is now a favorite in our Test Kitchens.

Prep: 20 min. **Bake: 50 min.** **Cook: 10 min.**

2 lb. new potatoes, quartered
2 tsp. olive oil
2 Tbsp. chopped fresh rosemary
1 tsp. salt, divided
1 tsp. freshly ground pepper, divided
Vegetable cooking spray
8 turkey bacon slices
¼ cup red wine vinegar
3 Tbsp. olive oil
1 Tbsp. sugar
2 garlic cloves, pressed
1 (6-oz.) package fresh spinach
1 (5-oz.) package mixed salad greens
¼ cup freshly shredded Parmesan cheese

Combine potatoes, oil, rosemary, ½ tsp. salt, and ½ tsp. pepper, tossing gently, and spread in a 15- x 10-inch jelly-roll pan coated with cooking spray.

Bake at 400° for 40 to 50 minutes or until potatoes are tender and lightly browned. Sprinkle evenly with ¼ tsp. salt and ¼ tsp. pepper; keep warm.

Cook bacon in a large skillet until crisp; remove bacon, and drain on paper towels, reserving drippings in skillet. Crumble bacon, and set aside.

Whisk vinegar, next 3 ingredients, remaining ¼ tsp. salt, and remaining ¼ tsp. pepper into skillet; cook over medium heat, whisking occasionally, 3 to 4 minutes or until thoroughly heated.

Combine spinach and mixed greens; drizzle with warm dressing, tossing to coat. Top with potatoes, bacon, and Parmesan cheese; serve immediately. **Yield:** 8 servings.

Spinach Salad With Cider Dressing

Prep: 10 min.

2 (6-oz.) packages fresh baby spinach
6 bacon slices, cooked and crumbled
3 hard-cooked eggs, chopped
Cider Dressing

Toss together first 3 ingredients in a large bowl; drizzle with Cider Dressing, and toss gently to coat. **Yield:** 6 to 8 servings

Cider Dressing:

Prep: 5 min. **Chill: 30 min.**

½ cup vegetable oil
⅓ cup sugar
1 green onion, chopped
3 Tbsp. cider vinegar
2 Tbsp. prepared mustard
½ tsp. celery seeds

Process all ingredients in a blender or food processor until smooth, stopping to scrape down sides. Cover and chill 30 minutes. **Yield:** about 1 cup.

PREWASHED AND
BAGGED SALAD GREENS
simplify supper.

Autumn Salad With
Maple-Cider Vinaigrette

make ahead
Autumn Salad With Maple-Cider Vinaigrette

Place the pear in a paper sack to speed ripening. The dressing and nuts can be prepared ahead.

Prep: 10 min.

1 (10-oz.) bag baby spinach
1 ripe Bartlett pear, cored and thinly sliced
1 small red onion, thinly sliced
1 (4-oz.) package crumbled blue cheese
Sugared Curried Walnuts
Maple-Cider Vinaigrette

Combine first 5 ingredients in a large bowl. Drizzle with Maple-Cider Vinaigrette, gently tossing to coat. **Yield:** 8 servings.

Sugared Curried Walnuts:

Prep: 5 min. Bake: 10 min.

1 (6-oz.) package walnut halves*
2 Tbsp. butter, melted
3 Tbsp. sugar
¼ tsp. ground ginger
⅛ tsp. curry powder
⅛ tsp. kosher salt
⅛ tsp. ground red pepper

Toss walnuts in melted butter. Stir together sugar and next 4 ingredients in a medium bowl; sprinkle over walnuts, tossing to coat. Spread in a single layer on a nonstick aluminum foil-lined pan.

Bake at 350° for 10 minutes. Cool in pan on a wire rack; separate walnuts with a fork. Store in an airtight container for up to 1 week. **Yield:** 1½ cups.

*Pecan halves may be substituted.

Maple-Cider Vinaigrette:

Prep: 5 min.

⅓ cup cider vinegar
2 Tbsp. pure maple syrup
1 Tbsp. Dijon mustard
¼ tsp. salt
¼ tsp. freshly ground pepper
⅔ cup olive oil

Whisk together first 5 ingredients. Gradually whisk in oil until completely blended. Cover and refrigerate up to 3 days. **Yield:** 1⅓ cups.

quick & easy
Apple-Pear Salad With Lemon-Poppy Seed Dressing

If desired, an equal amount of shredded Swiss cheese may be substituted for shaved.

Prep: 10 min.

1 (16-oz.) package romaine lettuce, thoroughly washed
1 (6-oz.) block Swiss cheese, shaved
1 cup roasted, salted cashews
½ cup sweetened dried cranberries
1 large apple, thinly sliced
1 large pear, thinly sliced
Lemon-Poppy Seed Dressing

Toss together first 6 ingredients in a large bowl. Drizzle with Lemon-Poppy Seed Dressing, tossing gently to coat. **Yield:** 6 to 8 servings

Lemon-Poppy Seed Dressing

Prep: 10 min.

⅔ cup light olive oil
½ cup sugar
⅓ cup fresh lemon juice
1½ Tbsp. poppy seeds
2 tsp. finely chopped onion
1 tsp. Dijon mustard
½ tsp. salt

Process all ingredients in a blender until smooth. Store in an airtight container in the refrigerator up to 1 week; serve at room temperature. **Yield:** 1¼ cups

Mixed Greens With Toasted Almonds and Apple-Cider Vinaigrette

Prep: 10 min. Chill: 2 hr.

1 large cucumber, thinly sliced
⅓ cup Apple-Cider Vinaigrette
8 cups mixed salad greens
2 plum tomatoes, finely chopped
1 cup fresh blueberries
⅓ cup sliced almonds, toasted
½ cup (2 oz.) crumbled goat cheese

Combine cucumber and Apple-Cider Vinaigrette; cover and chill 2 hours, stirring once. Remove and reserve cucumbers using a slotted spoon; reserve Apple-Cider Vinaigrette.

Toss together salad greens, tomatoes, and blueberries. Sprinkle salad evenly with almonds and goat cheese before serving. Add reserved marinated cucumber slices, and toss gently. Serve with reserved Apple-Cider Vinaigrette. **Yield:** 8 servings.

Apple-Cider Vinaigrette:

Prep: 10 min.

½ cup extra-virgin olive oil
¼ cup cider vinegar
4 tsp. granulated sugar
1 Tbsp. brown sugar
1 Tbsp. balsamic vinegar
1 tsp. Worcestershire sauce
½ tsp. salt

Whisk together all ingredients until well combined. **Yield:** 1 cup.

Spinach-Endive Salad With Warm Vinaigrette

This is one time when combining Belgian endive with spinach is definitely worth the splurge. Look for tight, oblong-shaped heads with creamy white leaves. When combined with the baby spinach, the endive adds a subtle bitterness that contrasts with the rich and tangy sweetness of the warm vinaigrette.

Prep: 15 min. Cook: 12 min.

4 apple-smoked bacon slices
¼ cup balsamic vinegar
4 tsp. Dijon mustard
½ cup crumbled blue cheese (optional)
¼ medium-size red onion, thinly sliced
2 tsp. chopped fresh parsley
½ tsp. salt
½ tsp. freshly ground pepper
1 (10-oz.) package fresh baby spinach
1 head Belgian endive, cut into 8 slices lengthwise*
Crumbled blue cheese (optional)

Cook bacon in a large skillet until crisp; remove bacon, and drain on paper towels, reserving ¼ cup drippings in skillet. Crumble bacon, and set aside.

Combine vinegar, mustard, and, if desired, ½ cup crumbled blue cheese, stirring until mixture is smooth.

Add vinegar mixture and onion to hot bacon drippings in skillet over medium heat, stirring to coat. Add bacon, parsley, salt, and pepper. Add spinach and endive; toss in skillet just until combined. Serve immediately. Top with additional crumbled blue cheese, if desired. **Yield:** 6 servings.

*½ (10-oz.) package fresh baby spinach may be substituted.

Spinach-Endive Salad With Warm Vinaigrette

Cinnamon-Almond
Coffee Cake (page 214)

BAKESHOP *Bounty*

Turn your kitchen into a holiday bakery with this taste-tempting selection of biscuits, rolls, breads, and coffee cakes. Treat your family, and then wrap up extras as special surprises for neighbors and friends.

Easy Cheddar Biscuits

Pair these cheesy little biscuits with thinly sliced ham and spicy brown mustard.

Prep: 10 min. Bake: 10 min.

1½ cups all-purpose flour
1 Tbsp. baking powder
1 Tbsp. sugar
½ tsp. salt
1 cup (4 oz.) shredded sharp Cheddar cheese
⅓ cup shortening
½ cup milk

Pulse first 4 ingredients in a food processor 4 or 5 times or until thoroughly combined.

Add shredded cheese and shortening, and pulse 4 or 5 times or until mixture is crumbly. With processor running, gradually add milk through food chute, and process until dough forms a ball and leaves sides of bowl.

Turn biscuit dough out onto a lightly floured surface, and shape into a ball.

Pat or roll dough to ½-inch thickness. Cut with a 2-inch round cutter, and place on lightly greased baking sheets.

Bake at 425° for 10 minutes or until golden brown. **Yield:** 1½ dozen.

Simple Sweet Potato Biscuits

Prep: 15 min. Bake: 10 min.

⅓ cup light butter
2¾ cups reduced-fat all-purpose baking mix
1 cup mashed sweet potato
½ cup 2% reduced-fat milk

Cut butter into baking mix with a pastry blender or 2 forks until mixture is crumbly. Whisk together sweet potato and milk; add to butter mixture, stirring with a fork just until dry ingredients are moistened.

Turn dough out onto a lightly floured surface; knead gently 4 or 5 times. (Dough will be moist.) Pat or roll dough to ½-inch thickness; cut with a 2-inch round cutter. Place biscuits on lightly greased baking sheets.

Bake at 450° for 10 minutes or until biscuits are golden brown. **Yield:** 2 dozen.

Simple Sweet Potato Biscuits

Butter Rolls

editor's favorite • make ahead

Butter Rolls

Prep: 15 min. Stand: 5 min. Rise: 1 hr. Bake: 20 min.

1 (¼-oz.) package active dry yeast
¼ cup warm water (105° to 115°)
2½ cups all-purpose flour
¼ cup sugar
1¼ tsp. salt
2 large eggs, divided
¼ cup milk
¼ cup butter, softened
1 Tbsp. water
Sesame or poppy seeds

Preheat oven to 200°. Stir together yeast and ¼ cup water in a 1-cup measuring cup; let stand 5 minutes.

Combine flour, sugar, and salt in bowl of heavy-duty stand mixer. Add yeast mixture, 1 egg, milk, and butter. Using dough hook attachment, beat at low speed 1 minute; then beat at medium speed 4 minutes.

Place dough in a well-greased glass bowl, turning to grease top. Turn off oven.

Cover dough loosely with plastic wrap; let rise in warm oven 30 to 40 minutes or until doubled in bulk. Remove and discard plastic wrap. Punch dough down, and divide into fourths; shape each portion into 6 (1-inch) balls. Place balls in a lightly greased 13- x 9-inch pan. Cover loosely with plastic wrap. Let rise in warm oven 20 minutes or until doubled in bulk. Remove from oven; increase heat to 375°. Remove and discard plastic wrap.

Whisk together remaining egg and 1 Tbsp. water; brush evenly over rolls, and sprinkle with sesame seeds.

Bake at 375° for 15 to 20 minutes or until golden brown. **Yield:** 2 dozen.

Make-Ahead Note: Freeze baked rolls in large zip-top plastic freezer bags up to 3 months. To reheat, thaw rolls in zip-top bags at room temperature; remove from bags, and place on baking sheets. Bake at 300° for 5 to 10 minutes or until warm.

make ahead

So-Easy Sesame Rolls

Don't overtoast the sesame seeds; they will brown more when the rolls are baked.

Prep: 15 min. Bake: 12 min.

2 (10-oz.) bottles sesame seeds
2 (8-oz.) cans refrigerated crescent rolls
¼ cup butter, melted

Cook sesame seeds in a medium skillet over medium-low heat, stirring constantly, until light golden brown. Cool completely.

Unroll crescent rolls, and separate each triangle. Cut each triangle in half; roll each half into a ball. Coat balls in sesame seeds, rolling balls a second time in palm of hands to press seeds into dough.

Place 2 inches apart on lightly greased baking sheets. Spoon melted butter evenly over rolls.

Bake at 375° for 11 to 12 minutes or until golden. **Yield:** 32 rolls.

quick & easy

Cranberry-Stuffed Crescents

Prep: 25 min. Bake: 17 min.

1 (8-oz.) package cream cheese, softened
1 cup powdered sugar
1 egg yolk
4 (8-oz.) cans refrigerated crescent rolls
1 (16-oz.) can whole-berry cranberry sauce
½ cup finely chopped walnuts, toasted

Beat cream cheese at medium speed with an electric mixer until smooth. Gradually add sugar, beating until combined. Add egg yolk, beating until blended.

Separate crescent rolls into 32 triangles. Spoon 1 tsp. cream cheese mixture onto short end of each triangle. Top with 1 tsp. cranberry sauce, and sprinkle evenly with walnuts. Fold long ends over filling, tucking edges under. Place on lightly greased baking sheets.

Bake at 350° for 15 to 17 minutes or until golden. Serve warm. **Yield:** 32 rolls.

Orange-Almond Stuffed Crescents: Stir 1½ tsp. grated fresh orange rind into cranberry sauce. Substitute ½ cup toasted sliced almonds for walnuts. Prepare and assemble crescents as directed. Stir together 1 egg and 1 tsp. water; brush over unbaked crescents. Sprinkle with additional sliced almonds, if desired. Bake as directed. Stir together 1 cup powdered sugar and 2 Tbsp. orange juice; drizzle over baked crescents. Serve warm.

editor's favorite

Sticky Crescent Rolls

Prep: 20 min. Bake: 15 min.

¼ cup granulated sugar
1 tsp. ground cinnamon
16 large marshmallows
3 Tbsp. butter, melted
2 (8-oz.) cans refrigerated crescent rolls
1 cup powdered sugar
2 Tbsp. milk
¼ cup pecans, toasted and chopped (optional)

Combine granulated sugar and cinnamon in a small bowl.

Dip marshmallows in melted butter, and roll in cinnamon mixture.

Separate crescent rolls into 16 triangles. Wrap 1 marshmallow with 1 triangle, pinching edges to seal. Repeat with remaining marshmallows and triangles. Place each roll in a lightly greased muffin pan cup.

Bake at 375° for 10 to 15 minutes or until golden.

Stir together powdered sugar and milk to form a smooth glaze. Drizzle over warm rolls; sprinkle with pecans, if desired. **Yield:** 16 rolls.

Sunny Cornsticks

Prep: 15 min. Bake: 20 min.

2 Tbsp. butter or margarine
1 cup frozen cream-style corn, thawed
1 (4.5-oz.) can chopped green chiles
½ small onion, diced
1 cup all-purpose flour
1 cup yellow cornmeal
2 Tbsp. sugar
1½ tsp. baking powder
1 tsp. salt
½ tsp. baking soda
1 cup buttermilk
1 large egg
¼ cup butter or margarine, melted
1 cup (4 oz.) shredded Cheddar cheese

Melt 2 Tbsp. butter in a large skillet over medium-high heat; add corn, chiles, and onion, and sauté until tender. Set aside.

Combine flour and next 5 ingredients in a large bowl; make a well in center of mixture.

Whisk together buttermilk, egg, and ¼ cup melted butter; add to dry ingredients, stirring just until moistened. Stir in corn mixture and cheese.

Spoon batter into lightly greased cast-iron stick molds, filling three-fourths full.

Bake at 375° for 18 to 20 minutes or until golden. Remove from pans; cool on wire racks. **Yield:** 18 sticks.

Sweet Potato Cornbread

Be sure to use self-rising cornmeal mix so your cornbread will be light and tender.

Prep: 5 min. Bake: 25 min.

2 cups self-rising cornmeal mix (see note)
¼ cup sugar
1 tsp. ground cinnamon
1½ cups milk
1 cup mashed cooked sweet potato
¼ cup butter, melted
1 large egg, beaten

Whisk together all ingredients, whisking just until dry ingredients are moistened. Spoon batter into a greased 8-inch cast-iron skillet or baking pan.

Bake at 425° for 20 to 25 minutes or until a wooden pick inserted in center comes out clean. **Yield:** 6 servings.

Note: For testing purposes only, we used White Lily Self-Rising Buttermilk Cornmeal Mix.

Orange-Poppy Seed Bread

Prep: 15 min. Bake: 1 hr.

3 cups all-purpose flour
2½ cups sugar
1½ cups milk
1½ cups vegetable oil
3 large eggs
1½ Tbsp. poppy seeds
1 Tbsp. grated fresh orange rind
1½ tsp. baking powder
1½ tsp. salt
2 tsp. vanilla extract

Beat all ingredients at medium speed with an electric mixer until creamy. Pour batter evenly into 2 greased and floured 8- x 4-inch loafpans.

Bake at 350° for 1 hour or until a wooden pick inserted in center comes out clean. Cool completely in pans on wire racks. **Yield:** 2 loaves.

Peppery Cheese Bread

For easy unmolding from the pan, run a knife between the bread and the pan.

Prep: 15 min. Bake: 50 min. Cool: 1 hr., 10 min.

2½ cups all-purpose flour
1 Tbsp. sugar
2 tsp. cracked black pepper
1 tsp. baking powder
¾ tsp. salt
½ tsp. baking soda
2 eggs, lightly beaten
1 (8-oz.) container plain low-fat yogurt
1 cup (4 oz.) shredded Cheddar cheese
½ cup vegetable oil
¼ cup thinly sliced green onions
¼ cup milk
1 Tbsp. spicy brown mustard

Combine first 6 ingredients in a large bowl; make a well in center of mixture. Stir together eggs and next 6 ingredients; add to dry ingredients, stirring just until moistened.

Lightly grease bottom of a 9- x 5-inch loafpan; pour batter into loafpan.

Bake at 350° for 45 to 50 minutes or until a wooden pick inserted in center comes out clean. Cool in pan on a wire rack 10 minutes; remove bread from pan, and let cool 1 hour on wire rack. **Yield:** 1 loaf.

Garlic Bread

Prep: 10 min. Bake: 20 min. Stand: 3 min.

½ cup butter or margarine, softened
2½ tsp. garlic powder
¾ tsp. Italian seasoning
½ tsp. dried oregano
¼ tsp. freshly ground pepper
1 cup (4 oz.) shredded Italian three-cheese blend
1 (16-oz.) loaf French bread, split

Combine first 5 ingredients and ⅓ cup cheese; spread mixture evenly on cut sides of bread. Sprinkle evenly with remaining ⅔ cup cheese. Place on a baking sheet.

Bake at 375° for 15 to 20 minutes or until cheese is melted and golden. Let stand for 2 to 3 minutes before serving. **Yield:** 8 servings.

Peppery Cheese Bread

Nut Bread

Bake this bread in coffee cans for 2 nicely rounded loaves, or use a traditional loaf pan for 1 loaf.

Prep: 15 min. Bake: 1 hr., 15 min. Cool: 2 hr., 10 min.

3 cups all-purpose flour
1 cup sugar
4 tsp. baking powder
2 tsp. salt
1½ cups milk
1 egg, lightly beaten
¼ cup shortening, melted
1 tsp. vanilla extract
1½ cups chopped walnuts or pecans
½ cup sweetened dried cranberries (optional, see note)

Sift flour and next 3 ingredients into a large bowl; stir to combine. Add milk and next 3 ingredients, stirring just until moistened. Stir in nuts, and, if desired, cranberries.

Pour batter evenly into 2 greased (13-oz.) coffee cans (see note) or into 1 greased and floured 9- x 5-inch loafpan. Bake at 350° for 1 hour and 10 minutes to 1 hour and 15 minutes or until a long wooden pick inserted in center comes out clean. Cool in pan on a wire rack 10 minutes; remove from pan, and cool on wire rack 2 hours or until completely cool. **Yield:** 1 loaf.

Note: For testing purposes only, we used Ocean Spray Craisins for dried cranberries. To remove coffee odor from coffee cans, rinse cans well with soap and water, removing all coffee grounds. Sprinkle 1 to 2 Tbsp. baking soda onto bottom of each can; add 1 tsp. water, and mix, forming a paste. Scrub paste onto entire interior of coffee can; let stand 15 minutes. Rinse well, and dry.

Nut Bread

freezer friendly • great gift • make ahead

Mini Banana-Cranberry-Nut Bread Loaves

Prep: 20 min. Bake: 28 min. Cool: 20 min.

¾ cup butter, softened
1 (8-oz.) package cream cheese, softened
2 cups sugar
2 large eggs
3 cups all-purpose flour
½ tsp. baking powder
½ tsp. baking soda
½ tsp. salt
1½ cups mashed ripe bananas
¾ cup chopped toasted pecans
¾ cup chopped fresh cranberries
½ tsp. vanilla extract
Orange Glaze

Beat butter and cream cheese at medium speed with an electric mixer until creamy. Gradually add sugar, beating until light and fluffy. Add eggs, 1 at a time, beating just until blended after each addition.

Combine flour and next 3 ingredients; gradually add to butter mixture, beating at low speed just until blended. Stir in bananas and next 3 ingredients. Spoon about ⅓ cup batter into 18 greased and floured 2½- x 3¾-inch mini-loaf pans.

Bake at 350° for 26 to 28 minutes or until a wooden pick inserted in center comes out clean and sides pull away from pans. Cool in pans 10 minutes. Remove loaves to wire racks; drizzle Orange Glaze evenly over warm bread loaves, and cool 10 minutes. **Yield:** 18 mini-loaves.

Make-Ahead Note: Freeze baked, unglazed loaves in large zip-top plastic freezer bags. To serve, thaw loaves, warm in a 300° oven 10 to 12 minutes, and drizzle with Orange Glaze.

Orange Glaze:

Prep: 5 min.

1 cup powdered sugar
1 tsp. grated fresh orange rind
3 Tbsp. fresh orange juice

Stir together all ingredients until blended. **Yield:** ½ cup.

Banana Breakfast Bread

This recipe can be doubled easily, so make two loaves and give one as a gift. Try toasting slices and serving with cream cheese or peanut butter.

Prep: 15 min. Bake: 1 hr., 10 min. Cool: 2 hr., 10 min.

½ cup chopped pecans
1½ cups whole wheat flour
1 tsp. baking powder
1 tsp. baking soda
½ tsp. ground cinnamon
½ cup sugar
2 Tbsp. butter, melted
4 medium-size ripe bananas, mashed
1 egg, lightly beaten
1 (7-oz.) package dried fruit bits
Vegetable cooking spray

Place pecans in a single layer in a jelly-roll pan.

Bake at 350° for 8 to 10 minutes or until lightly browned.

Combine flour and next 3 ingredients in a large bowl. Combine sugar and next 3 ingredients in a small bowl; add to flour mixture, stirring just until dry ingredients are moistened. Stir in pecans and fruit bits. Pour mixture into an 8½- x 4½-inch loaf pan coated with cooking spray.

Bake at 350° for 55 to 60 minutes or until a wooden pick inserted in center of bread comes out clean. Cool in pan on wire rack 10 minutes; remove from pan, and cool on wire rack 2 hours or until completely cool. **Yield:** 1 loaf.

FESTIVE PACKAGING

Use disposable foil containers as handy gift packaging for baked treats. Here are some easy ideas:

- Tie an inexpensive, colorful kitchen towel around each container. Tuck in a sprig of berries for the final touch.
- Use your computer to print holiday labels, and secure to the appropriate lids.
- Use scraps of wrapping paper to create a band around each package. Secure the ends with double-sided tape.

Pecan-Pumpkin Bread

great gift

Pecan-Pumpkin Bread With Orange Marmalade-Cream Cheese Spread

Instead of purchasing a lot of separate jars of spices, keep a few versatile seasoning blends, such as pumpkin pie spice, on hand for holiday baking. If you'd like to make your own pumpkin pie spice blend, stir together 2 Tbsp. ground cinnamon, 1 Tbsp. ground ginger, and 1½ tsp. each of ground nutmeg and allspice.

Prep: 20 min. Bake: 1 hr., 15 min. Cool: 2 hr., 10 min.

3 cups sugar
1 cup vegetable oil
4 large eggs
1 (15-oz.) can unsweetened pumpkin
3½ cups all-purpose flour
1 Tbsp. pumpkin pie spice
1 tsp. baking soda
1 tsp. salt
⅔ cup water
1½ cups chopped pecans, toasted
Orange Marmalade-Cream Cheese Spread

Beat first 8 ingredients at low speed with an electric mixer 3 minutes or until blended. Add ⅔ cup water, beating until blended. Stir in pecans. Pour batter into 2 greased and floured 9- x 5-inch loaf pans.

Bake at 350° for 1 hour and 15 minutes or until a long wooden pick inserted in center of bread comes out clean. Cool in pans on a wire rack 10 minutes; remove bread from pans, and cool on wire rack 2 hours or until completely cool. Serve with Orange Marmalade-Cream Cheese Spread. **Yield:** 2 (9-inch) loaves.

Orange Marmalade-Cream Cheese Spread:

Prep: 5 min.

1 (8-oz.) package cream cheese, softened
½ cup orange marmalade
1 tsp. grated fresh orange rind

Stir together all ingredients until blended. **Yield:** about 1½ cups.

editor's favorite

Sour Cream Coffee Cake

If you prefer the creamy flavor of traditional glaze, substitute milk for the orange juice.

Prep: 30 min. Bake: 50 min. Cool: 1 hr., 10 min.

Cooking spray for baking
1 cup coarsely chopped pecans, toasted
1 cup firmly packed light brown sugar
1 Tbsp. ground cinnamon
3 cups all-purpose flour
1½ tsp. baking soda
1½ tsp. baking powder
¾ tsp. salt
¼ cup butter, softened
1 (8-oz.) package ⅓-less-fat cream cheese, softened
1½ cups granulated sugar
1 large egg
½ cup egg substitute
2 tsp. vanilla extract
1 (16-oz.) container light sour cream
1 cup powdered sugar
1 Tbsp. orange juice
Garnish: cinnamon sticks

Coat a 12-cup Bundt pan with cooking spray. Combine pecans, brown sugar, and cinnamon; set aside.

Combine flour, baking soda, baking powder, and salt.

Beat butter, cream cheese, and granulated sugar at medium speed with an electric mixer until creamy. Add egg, and beat until blended. Add egg substitute and vanilla, beating until blended. Add flour mixture to butter mixture alternately with sour cream, beating at low speed just until blended, beginning and ending with flour mixture. Beat on high 1 minute.

Pour one-third of batter into prepared pan. Sprinkle batter with half of pecan mixture. Repeat layers. Top with remaining one-third batter.

Bake at 350° for 50 minutes or until a wooden pick inserted in center comes out clean. Cool in pan on a wire rack 10 minutes. Run a knife around edges to loosen sides. Gently turn cake out onto a rack. Cool 1 hour. Transfer to a serving plate.

Whisk together powdered sugar and orange juice. Drizzle over cake. Garnish, if desired. **Yield:** 10 to 12 servings.

Cinnamon-Almond Coffee Cake

(pictured on page 204)

Prep: 15 min. Bake: 40 min. Cool: 15 min.

1¾ cups all-purpose flour
2 tsp. baking powder
1 tsp. baking soda
½ tsp. salt
¾ cup granulated sugar
3 Tbsp. butter, softened
1 (8-oz.) container light sour cream
3 large egg whites
1¼ tsp. vanilla extract, divided
⅓ cup firmly packed light brown sugar
¼ cup sliced almonds, toasted
1 tsp. ground cinnamon
Vegetable cooking spray
¼ cup powdered sugar
2 tsp. 1% low-fat milk

Combine first 4 ingredients in a small bowl. Beat sugar and butter in a large bowl at medium speed with an electric mixer until well blended. Add sour cream, egg whites, and 1 tsp. vanilla; beat well 1 minute. Add flour mixture to butter mixture, beating just until dry ingredients are moistened. Set batter aside.

Combine brown sugar, almonds, and ground cinnamon in a small bowl.

Spoon half of batter into an 8-inch square baking pan coated with cooking spray. Sprinkle evenly with half of brown sugar mixture. Spread remaining batter over brown sugar mixture in pan. Sprinkle with remaining brown sugar mixture.

Bake at 350° for 35 to 40 minutes or until a wooden pick inserted in center comes out clean. Let cool 15 minutes in pan on a wire rack.

Stir together powdered sugar, milk, and remaining ¼ tsp. vanilla in a small bowl until smooth. Drizzle over coffee cake. **Yield:** 9 servings.

Triple-Chocolate Coffee Cake

Prep: 15 min. Bake: 30 min.

1 (18.25-oz.) package devil's food cake mix
1 (3.9-oz.) package chocolate instant pudding mix
2 cups sour cream
1 cup butter or margarine, softened
5 large eggs
1 tsp. vanilla extract
3 cups semisweet chocolate morsels, divided
1 cup white chocolate morsels
1 cup chopped pecans, toasted

Beat first 6 ingredients at low speed with an electric mixer 30 seconds or just until moistened; beat at medium speed 2 minutes. Stir in 2 cups semisweet chocolate morsels; pour batter evenly into 2 greased and floured 9-inch square cake pans.

Bake at 350° for 25 to 30 minutes or until a wooden pick inserted in center comes out clean. Cool in pans on wire racks.

Microwave white chocolate morsels in a glass bowl at HIGH 30 to 60 seconds or until morsels melt, stirring at 30-second intervals until smooth. Drizzle evenly over cakes; repeat procedure with remaining cup of semisweet morsels. Sprinkle cakes evenly with pecans. **Yield:** 2 (9-inch) coffee cakes.

Orange-Pecan Ring

Prep: 20 min. Chill: 8 hr. Bake: 40 min. Cool: 10 min.

¾ cup orange marmalade
½ cup chopped pecans, toasted
¾ cup firmly packed brown sugar
½ tsp. ground cinnamon
1 (25-oz.) package frozen yeast rolls (see note)
⅔ cup butter, melted

Spread marmalade in bottom of a lightly greased 10-inch Bundt pan; sprinkle evenly with pecans.

Stir together brown sugar and cinnamon in a small bowl. Dip each roll in melted butter, and roll in sugar mixture. Layer rolls in pan. Pour remaining butter evenly over rolls; sprinkle with remaining sugar mixture. Cover and chill 8 hours.

Bake at 350° for 40 minutes or until golden. Cool in pan 10 minutes. Invert onto a serving plate, and serve immediately. **Yield:** 8 servings.

Note: For testing purposes only, we used Bridgford Parkerhouse Yeast Rolls.

Orange-Pecan Ring

Caramel Cream Cake

SWEET *Endings*

A splendid assortment of sweets awaits you on the following pages. There are cakes, pies, pastries, and so many cookies that you'll be faced with the delicious decision of what to bake first.

editor's favorite

Caramel Cream Cake

Prep: 20 min. Bake: 25 min. Cool: 10 min.

1 cup finely chopped sweetened flaked coconut
Pecan Pie Cake Batter
Pecan Pie Filling
Cream Cheese Frosting
1 cup finely chopped pecans, toasted
1 cup sweetened flaked coconut, toasted
Garnishes: raspberries, fresh mint sprig

Stir 1 cup finely chopped coconut into cake batter; spoon into 3 greased and floured 9-inch cake pans.

Bake at 350° for 25 minutes or until a wooden pick inserted in center comes out clean. Cool in pans on wire racks 10 minutes; remove from pans, and cool completely on wire racks.

Spread filling between layers. Spread frosting on top and sides of cake. Sprinkle top and sides with toasted pecans and toasted coconut. Garnish, if desired. **Yield:** 12 servings.

Pecan Pie Cake Batter:

Prep: 20 min.

½ cup butter, softened
½ cup shortening
2 cups sugar
5 large eggs, separated
1 Tbsp. vanilla extract
2 cups all-purpose flour
1 tsp. baking soda
1 cup buttermilk
1 cup finely chopped pecans, toasted

Beat ½ cup butter and shortening at medium speed until fluffy; gradually add sugar, beating well until blended. Add egg yolks, 1 at a time, beating just until blended. Stir in vanilla.

Combine flour and baking soda; add to butter mixture alternately with buttermilk. Beat at low speed until blended after each addition. Stir in pecans.

Beat egg whites at medium speed until stiff peaks form; fold one-third of egg whites into batter. Gently fold in remaining egg whites just until blended. Use immediately. **Yield:** about 6 cups.

Pecan Pie Filling:

Prep: 7 min. Cook: 7 min. Chill: 4 hr.

½ cup firmly packed dark brown sugar
¾ cup dark corn syrup
⅓ cup cornstarch
4 egg yolks
1½ cups half-and-half
⅛ tsp. salt
3 Tbsp. butter
1 tsp. vanilla extract

Whisk together first 6 ingredients in a heavy 3-qt. saucepan until smooth. Bring mixture to a boil over medium heat, whisking constantly; boil 1 minute or until thickened. Remove from heat; whisk in butter and vanilla. Place a sheet of wax paper directly on surface of mixture to prevent a film from forming, and chill 4 hours. **Yield:** about 3 cups.

Cream Cheese Frosting:

Prep: 10 min.

½ cup butter, softened
1 (8-oz.) package cream cheese, softened
1 (16-oz.) package powdered sugar
1 tsp. vanilla extract

Beat butter and cream cheese at medium speed with an electric mixer until creamy. Gradually add powdered sugar, beating at low speed until blended; stir in vanilla. **Yield:** about 3 cups.

editor's favorite

Lemon-Coconut Cake

Prep: 30 min. Bake: 20 min. Cool: 10 min.

1 cup butter, softened
2 cups sugar
4 large eggs, separated
3 cups all-purpose flour
1 Tbsp. baking powder
1 cup milk
1 tsp. vanilla extract
Lemon Filling
Cream Cheese Frosting
2 cups sweetened flaked coconut
Garnishes: fresh rosemary sprigs, gumdrops

Beat butter at medium speed with an electric mixer until fluffy; gradually add sugar, beating well. Add egg yolks, 1 at a time, beating until blended after each addition.

Combine flour and baking powder; add to butter mixture alternately with milk, beginning and ending with flour mixture. Beat at low speed until blended after each addition. Stir in vanilla.

Beat egg whites at high speed with electric mixer until stiff peaks form; fold one-third of egg whites into batter. Gently fold in remaining beaten egg whites just until blended. Spoon batter into 3 greased and floured 9-inch round cake pans.

Bake at 350° for 18 to 20 minutes or until a wooden pick inserted in center comes out clean. Cool in pans on wire racks 10 minutes. Remove from pans; cool completely on wire racks.

Spread Lemon Filling between layers. Spread Cream Cheese Frosting on top and sides of cake. Sprinkle top and sides with coconut. Garnish, if desired. **Yield:** 12 servings.

Lemon Filling:

A Microplane grater, available in kitchen shops for about $12, makes grating the lemon rind super easy. It takes only a minute to squeeze fresh lemon juice, and the taste is worth it.

Prep: 10 min. Cook: 5 min.

1 cup sugar
¼ cup cornstarch
1 cup boiling water
4 egg yolks, lightly beaten
2 tsp. grated fresh lemon rind
⅓ cup fresh lemon juice
2 Tbsp. butter

Combine sugar and cornstarch in a medium saucepan; whisk in 1 cup boiling water. Cook over medium heat, whisking constantly, until sugar and cornstarch dissolve (about 2 minutes). Gradually whisk about one-fourth of hot sugar mixture into egg yolks; add to remaining hot sugar mixture in pan, whisking constantly. Whisk in lemon rind and juice.

Cook, whisking constantly, until mixture is thickened (about 2 to 3 minutes). Remove from heat. Whisk in butter; let cool completely, stirring occasionally. **Yield:** about 1⅔ cups.

Cream Cheese Frosting:

Prep: 10 min.

½ cup butter, softened
1 (8-oz.) package cream cheese, softened
1 (16-oz.) package powdered sugar
1 tsp. vanilla extract

Beat butter and cream cheese at medium speed with an electric mixer until creamy. Gradually add powdered sugar, beating at low speed until blended; stir in vanilla. **Yield:** about 3 cups.

LEMON FILLING COOK'S NOTES

Consider these options for even more uses for Lemon Filling:

- For a quick teatime treat, serve it over cream cheese alongside a basketful of vanilla wafers and gingersnaps. Spoon into small tart shells, spread on warm biscuits and scones, or dress up a pan of gingerbread.
- You can make Lemon Filling up to 2 days ahead; simply cover and refrigerate. Don't stir after refrigerating; just spoon onto cake layers, and spread. Once chilled and set, fillings made with cornstarch will break down and liquefy if stirred.

Lemon-Coconut Cake

Chocolate-Mint Cake

editor's favorite

Chocolate-Mint Cake

Adding hot water to the batter helps to create an exceptionally moist and tender cake.

Prep: 25 min. Bake: 30 min. Cool: 10 min.

1½ cups semisweet chocolate morsels
½ cup butter, softened
1 (16-oz.) package light brown sugar
3 large eggs
2 cups all-purpose flour
1 tsp. baking soda
½ tsp. salt
1 (8-oz.) container sour cream
1 cup hot water
2 tsp. vanilla extract
Peppermint Frosting
Chocolate Ganache

Melt chocolate morsels in a microwave-safe bowl at HIGH for 30-second intervals until melted (about 1½ minutes). Stir until smooth.

Beat softened butter and brown sugar at medium speed with an electric mixer about 5 minutes or until well blended. Add eggs, 1 at a time, beating just until blended after each addition. Add melted chocolate, beating just until blended.

Sift together flour, baking soda, and salt. Gradually add to chocolate mixture alternately with sour cream, beginning and ending with flour mixture. Beat at low speed just until blended after each addition. Gradually add 1 cup hot water in a slow, steady stream, beating at low speed just until blended. Stir in vanilla. Spoon batter evenly into 2 greased and floured 10-inch round cake pans.

Bake at 350° for 30 minutes or until a wooden pick inserted in center comes out clean. Cool in pans on wire racks 10 minutes; remove from pans, and let cool completely on wire racks. Spread Peppermint Frosting evenly between cake layers. Spread Chocolate Ganache evenly on top and sides of cake. **Yield:** 16 servings.

Peppermint Frosting:

Peppermint oil, available from cake-supply stores, has an intense, highly concentrated flavor, like that found in the chocolate-covered peppermint patties we used to garnish our cake.

Prep: 10 min.

½ cup butter, softened
1 (16-oz.) package powdered sugar
⅓ cup milk
¼ tsp. peppermint oil

Beat butter at medium speed with an electric mixer until creamy; gradually add powdered sugar alternately with milk, beginning and ending with powdered sugar. Beat at low speed just until blended after each addition. Stir in peppermint oil. **Yield:** about 3 cups.

Chocolate Ganache:

Prep: 10 min. Stand: 20 min.

1 (12-oz.) package semisweet chocolate morsels
1½ cups whipping cream
3 Tbsp. butter

Microwave semisweet chocolate morsels and whipping cream in a 2-qt. microwave-safe bowl at MEDIUM (50% power) 2½ to 3 minutes or until chocolate begins to melt. Whisk until chocolate melts and mixture is smooth. Whisk in butter, and let stand 20 minutes.

Beat at medium speed with an electric mixer 3 to 4 minutes or until soft peaks form. **Yield:** about 2 cups.

CHOCOLATE GANACHE COOK'S NOTES

- Ganache is a rich frosting made with melted chocolate and whipping cream. The mixture, which thickens as it cools, should be warm enough to pour yet thick enough to spread and coat the cake. Pour the ganache onto the center of the cake; spread quickly, using a spatula to push the frosting down the sides of the cake.
- Ganache can also be used as a filling for cakes, cookies, and tarts. After chilling for several hours, it becomes firm enough to shape into truffles.
- Coarsely chopped chocolate-covered peppermint patties add a simple but striking garnish to Chocolate-Mint Cake. For quick, clean cuts, partially freeze the candy before chopping.

editor's favorite

Mama Dip's Carrot Cake

This recipe from Chapel Hill restauranteur Mildred "Mama Dip" Council is one of the best carrot cakes we've tested.

Prep: 30 min. Bake: 35 min. Cool: 10 min.

2¼ cups self-rising flour
1 tsp. baking soda
1½ tsp. ground cinnamon
2 cups sugar
1 cup vegetable oil
4 large eggs
3 cups grated carrots
1½ cups chopped walnuts, toasted and divided
Cream Cheese Frosting

Sift together first 3 ingredients. Set aside.

Line 3 lightly greased 9-inch round cake pans with parchment paper; lightly grease parchment paper.

Beat sugar and oil at medium speed with an electric mixer until smooth. Add eggs, 1 at a time, beating until blended after each addition. Add flour mixture, beating at low speed just until blended and stopping to scrape down sides. Fold in carrots and 1 cup walnuts. Spoon batter evenly into prepared pans.

Bake at 350° for 30 to 35 minutes or until a wooden pick inserted in center comes out clean. Cool in pans on wire racks 10 minutes; remove from pans, and cool completely on wire racks.

Spread Cream Cheese Frosting between layers and on top and sides of cake. Arrange remaining ½ cup walnuts around outer edge on top of cake. Cut with a serrated knife. **Yield:** 12 servings.

Cream Cheese Frosting:

Prep: 10 min.

2 (8-oz.) packages cream cheese, softened
½ cup butter, softened
1 (16-oz.) box powdered sugar
1 tsp. vanilla extract

Beat cream cheese and butter at medium speed with an electric mixer until fluffy; gradually add powdered sugar, beating well. Stir in vanilla. **Yield:** 4 cups.

Praline-Pumpkin Torte

Prep: 20 min. Cook: 5 min. Bake: 35 min. Cool: 5 min.

¾ cup firmly packed brown sugar
⅓ cup butter
3 Tbsp. whipping cream
¾ cup chopped pecans
4 large eggs
1⅔ cups granulated sugar
1 cup vegetable oil
1 (15-oz.) canned unsweetened pumpkin
¼ tsp. vanilla extract
2 cups all-purpose flour
2 tsp. baking powder
2 tsp. pumpkin pie spice
1 tsp. baking soda
1 tsp. salt
Whipped Cream Topping
½ cup chopped pecans, toasted

Cook first 3 ingredients in medium saucepan over low heat, stirring until brown sugar dissolves. Pour brown sugar mixture into 2 (9-inch) greased round cake pans; sprinkle evenly with ¾ cup chopped pecans. Cool to room temperature.

Beat eggs, granulated sugar, and oil at medium speed with an electric mixer. Add pumpkin and vanilla, beating until well blended.

Combine flour and next 4 ingredients; add to pumpkin mixture, beating until blended. Spoon batter evenly into prepared cake pans.

Bake at 350° for 30 to 35 minutes or until wooden pick inserted in center comes out clean. Cool in pans on wire racks 5 minutes; remove from pans, and let cool completely on wire racks.

Place 1 cake layer on serving plate, praline side up; spread evenly with half of Whipped Cream Topping. Top with remaining layer, praline side up, and spread remaining Whipped Cream Topping over top of cake. Sprinkle evenly with ½ cup toasted pecans. Store, covered, in refrigerator. **Yield:** 12 servings.

Whipped Cream Topping:

Prep: 5 min.

1¾ cups whipping cream
¼ cup powdered sugar
¼ tsp. vanilla extract

Beat cream at high speed with an electric mixer until soft peaks form. Add sugar and vanilla; beat until blended. **Yield:** 3½ cups.

editor's favorite

Coconut Sheet Cake

Prep: 15 min. Bake: 45 min. Freeze: 30 min.

3 large eggs
1 (8-oz.) container sour cream
⅓ cup water
1 (8.5-oz.) can cream of coconut
½ tsp. vanilla extract
1 (18.25-oz.) package white cake mix
Coconut-Cream Cheese Frosting

Beat eggs at high speed with an electric mixer 2 minutes. Add sour cream, ⅓ cup water, cream of coconut, and vanilla, beating well to combine. Add cake mix, beating at low speed just until blended. Beat at high speed 2 minutes. Pour batter into a greased and floured 13- x 9-inch pan (see note).

Bake at 325° for 40 to 45 minutes or until a wooden pick inserted in center comes out clean. Let cake cool completely in pan on a wire rack.

Cover pan with plastic wrap, and freeze cake 30 minutes. Remove from freezer.

Spread Coconut-Cream Cheese Frosting on top of chilled cake. Cover and store in refrigerator. **Yield:** 12 servings.

Note: If desired, bake cake in 1 greased and floured 15- x 10-inch jelly-roll pan for 30 to 32 minutes or until a wooden pick inserted in center comes out clean. Makes 15 servings.

Coconut-Cream Cheese Frosting:

This recipe yields a very thick frosting.

Prep: 15 min.

1 (8-oz.) package cream cheese, softened
½ cup butter, softened
3 Tbsp. milk
1 tsp. vanilla extract
1 (16-oz.) package powdered sugar, sifted
1 (7-oz.) package sweetened flaked coconut

Beat cream cheese and butter at medium speed with an electric mixer until creamy; add milk and vanilla, beating well. Gradually add powdered sugar, beating until smooth. Stir in coconut. **Yield:** 4 cups.

make ahead

Chocolate Roulade

This melt-in-your mouth "roulage," as many Southerners call it, delivers a decadent flavor. The spongy chocolate soufflé-like cake texture is complemented by a light and airy sweetened whipped cream.

Prep: 20 min. Bake: 15 min. Cool: 30 min. Chill: 1 hr.

1 cup semisweet chocolate chunks
¼ cup water
5 large eggs, separated
1 cup sugar, divided
3 Tbsp. unsweetened cocoa
1 cup whipping cream
Garnishes: red cinnamon candies, fresh rosemary sprigs, whipped cream, unsweetened cocoa

Microwave chocolate chunks and ¼ cup water in a large microwave-safe glass bowl at HIGH 1 minute or until chocolate chunks melt, stirring every 30 seconds.

Beat egg yolks and ¾ cup sugar at high speed with an electric mixer 3 minutes or until mixture is thick and pale yellow. Whisk into chocolate mixture.

Beat egg whites at high speed with an electric mixer until stiff peaks form; fold into chocolate mixture.

Line a lightly greased 15- x 10-inch jelly-roll pan with parchment paper. Lightly grease parchment paper. Pour batter evenly into prepared pan. Bake at 325° for 15 minutes or until puffed. Remove from oven, and cover cake in pan with a damp towel (photo 1). Let cool 30 minutes or until cake is completely cool.

Remove damp towel. Cut a 20- x 15-inch piece of parchment paper, and place on a cutting board or countertop. Dust cake with cocoa (photo 2), and invert onto parchment paper. Carefully peel top layer of parchment paper from cake, and discard (photo 3).

Beat whipping cream and remaining ¼ cup sugar at high speed with an electric mixer until stiff peaks form. Spread cream mixture over top of cake, leaving a 1-inch border on all sides. Lift and tilt parchment paper at 1 short side, and carefully roll up cake, jelly-roll fashion, using parchment paper as a guide (photo 4). Wrap rolled cake in parchment paper, and place on a baking sheet. Chill at least 1 hour or up to 8 hours. Transfer to a serving platter, seam side down; remove and discard parchment paper. Garnish, if desired. **Yield:** 10 servings.

Make-Ahead Note: Follow recipe directions to wrap in parchment paper, and chill at least 1 hour or up to 8 hours. Remove parchment paper; wrap tightly in plastic wrap, and freeze up to 1 month. Transfer to a serving platter while frozen, and allow to thaw, covered, in the refrigerator overnight. Garnish, if desired.

ROULADE STEP-BY-STEP

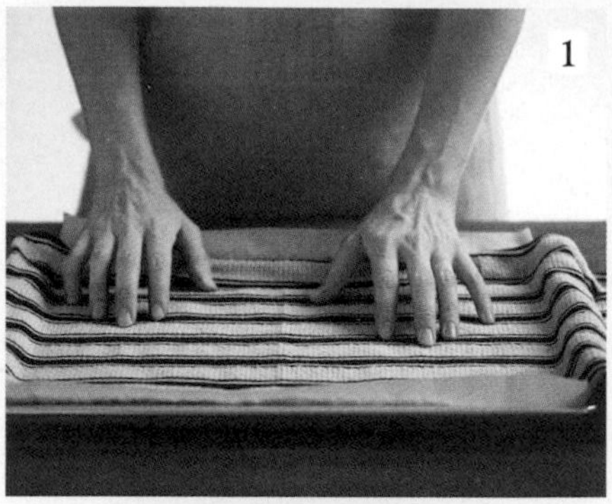

1

• Remove the cake from the oven, and immediately cover it with a damp kitchen towel until the cake is cool, about 30 minutes.

2

• Remove the kitchen towel from the cooled cake, and dust the surface with cocoa powder.

3

• Invert the cake onto a parchment paper-lined cutting board, and peel back the original piece of parchment paper.

4

• Spread sweetened whipped cream over the surface of the cake, and roll up, jelly-roll fashion, using the parchment paper as your guide.

Chocolate Roulade

Spiced Ginger Cake
With Candied Cream

editor's favorite

Spiced Ginger Cake With Candied Cream

Grated carrots add extra moistness to this dark, moist cake; cinnamon, allspice, and cloves give it a flavor boost.

Prep: 20 min. Bake: 50 min.

1¾ cups sugar
1½ cups vegetable oil
4 large eggs
3 large carrots, finely grated
1 cup minced fresh ginger (about ½ lb.)
2 cups all-purpose flour
2 tsp. baking powder
1½ tsp. baking soda
¾ tsp. salt
2½ Tbsp. ground ginger
2½ tsp. ground cinnamon
1 tsp. ground allspice
½ tsp. ground cloves
1½ cups chopped walnuts or pecans
Candied Cream
Garnish: fresh mint sprig, sugar

Beat sugar and oil at medium speed with an electric mixer 3 minutes or until smooth. Add eggs, 1 at a time, beating well after each addition. Beat in carrots and fresh ginger.

Combine flour and next 7 ingredients; gradually add to sugar mixture, beating at low speed until moistened. Stir in nuts.

Pour batter into a lightly greased 13- x 9-inch baking dish.

Bake at 350° for 45 to 50 minutes or until a wooden pick inserted in center comes out clean. Cool on a wire rack; serve with Candied Cream, and garnish, if desired. **Yield:** 12 servings.

Candied Cream:

Prep: 5 min.

1 cup whipping cream
2 Tbsp. powdered sugar
1 tsp. vanilla extract
⅓ cup chopped candied ginger

Beat whipping cream at high speed with an electric mixer until foamy; gradually add sugar and vanilla, beating until stiff peaks form. Stir in candied ginger. **Yield:** 2¼ cups.

Double Chocolate Cupcakes

These cupcakes offer rich chocolate flavor with minimal prep.

Prep: 20 min. Bake: 22 min.

1 (18.25-oz.) package devil's food cake mix
1⅓ cups water
4 large eggs
1 cup semisweet chocolate chunks
½ cup butter
27 paper baking cups
2 cups whipping cream
½ cup sugar
Red candy sprinkles

Beat first 3 ingredients at low speed with an electric mixer 30 seconds; beat at medium speed 1½ minutes.

Microwave chocolate chunks and butter in a medium microwave-safe glass bowl at HIGH 1 minute or until melted, stirring every 30 seconds. Add to cake mixture, and beat at low speed 30 seconds or until combined.

Place 27 paper baking cups in muffin pans; spoon batter into paper cups, filling two-thirds full.

Bake at 350° for 18 to 22 minutes or until a wooden pick inserted in center comes out clean. Remove cupcakes from pan, and let cool completely on wire racks.

Beat whipping cream and sugar at high speed with an electric mixer until stiff peaks form; spread generously on cupcakes, and top with sprinkles. **Yield:** 27 cupcakes.

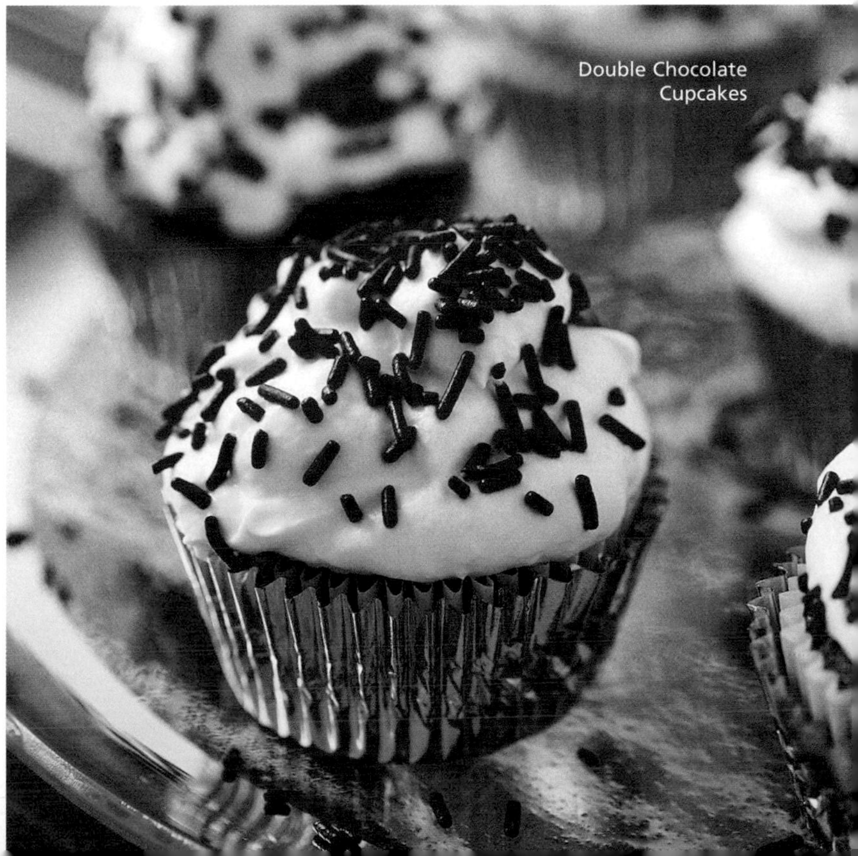

Double Chocolate Cupcakes

Red Velvet Miniatures

The cans that diced tomatoes come in work great for baking this recipe.

Prep: 30 min. Bake: 35 min. Cool: 15 min.

2 (14- or 14.5-oz.) empty cans
¼ cup butter, softened
¾ cup sugar
1 large egg
½ tsp. vanilla extract
1 Tbsp. red liquid food coloring
1¼ cups sifted cake flour
¼ tsp. salt
1 tsp. unsweetened cocoa
½ cup buttermilk
1½ tsp. white vinegar
½ tsp. baking soda
Cream Cheese Frosting
Sugar sprinkles or edible glitter (optional)

Place cans in a bowl of warm water to loosen and remove labels. Wash cans well with soap and water, and thoroughly dry. Grease and flour insides of cans, or spray evenly with cooking spray for baking. Set aside.

Beat butter at medium speed with an electric mixer until creamy. Gradually add sugar, beating at medium speed until well blended. Add egg and vanilla, beating until blended. Stir in food coloring, beating well. Set butter mixture aside.

Combine flour, salt, and cocoa in a bowl. Combine buttermilk, vinegar, and baking soda in 2-cup liquid measuring cup.

Add flour mixture to butter mixture alternately with buttermilk mixture, beating at low speed until blended, beginning and ending with flour mixture. Spoon batter evenly into prepared cans. Place on baking sheet.

Bake at 350° for 30 to 35 minutes or until a wooden pick inserted in center comes out clean.

Cool cakes in cans on wire rack 10 to 15 minutes. Remove from cans; cool completely on wire rack. Cut each cake in half. Frost with Cream Cheese Frosting, and decorate, if desired. **Yield:** 4 servings.

Red Velvet Cupcakes: To bake in muffin pans, spoon batter evenly into 12 greased and floured cups of muffin pans, filling two-thirds full. Bake at 350° for 23 to 25 minutes. Remove from pans immediately, and cool on wire racks. Spread evenly with Cream Cheese Frosting. **Yield:** 12 cupcakes.

Cream Cheese Frosting:

Prep: 5 min.

1 (3-oz.) package cream cheese, softened
¼ cup butter or margarine, softened
2 cups powdered sugar, sifted
½ tsp. vanilla extract

Beat cream cheese and butter at medium speed with electric mixer until creamy. Gradually add powdered sugar, beating until fluffy; add vanilla, beating until blended. **Yield:** about 1½ cups.

Coconut-Glazed Baby Bundt Cakes

(pictured on cover)

Prep: 30 min. Bake: 24 min. Cool: 10 min.

1 (18.25-oz.) package white cake mix*
2 large eggs
1 (8-oz.) container sour cream
½ cup water
⅓ cup vegetable oil
Cooking spray for baking
Powdered Sugar Glaze
¾ cup sweetened flaked coconut
2 Tbsp. white cake sparkles (edible glitter)

Beat first 5 ingredients at low speed with an electric mixer 30 seconds or just until moistened; beat at medium speed 2 minutes.

Pour batter evenly into 10 (1-cup) baby Bundt pans coated with cooking spray (about ½ cup batter per pan).

Bake at 350° for 22 to 24 minutes or until a wooden pick inserted in center comes out clean. Cool in pans on wire racks 10 minutes. Remove from pans, and cool completely on wire racks. Pour Powdered Sugar Glaze evenly over cakes; sprinkle with coconut and sparkles. **Yield:** 10 cakes.

*Spice, chocolate, or your favorite flavor cake mix may be substituted.

Powdered Sugar Glaze:

Prep: 5 min.

2 cups powdered sugar
3 to 4 Tbsp. milk
1 tsp. vanilla extract

Stir together powdered sugar, 3 Tbsp. milk, and vanilla, adding another 1 Tbsp. milk for desired consistency. **Yield:** about 1 cup.

Brown Sugar Pound Cake

editor's favorite

Brown Sugar Pound Cake

Don't preheat the oven for this scrumptious pound cake—it gets its start in a cold oven. To add a light dusting of powdered sugar, spoon a few tablespoons into a wire-mesh strainer, and gently shake over the cake's surface.

Prep: 20 min. Bake: 1 hr., 45 min. Cool: 15 min.

- 1 cup butter, softened
- ½ cup shortening
- 2 cups firmly packed brown sugar
- 1 cup granulated sugar
- 6 large eggs
- 3 cups cake flour
- 1 tsp. baking powder
- 1 cup evaporated milk
- 2 tsp. vanilla extract
- 2 cups chopped pecans, toasted

Beat butter and shortening at medium speed with an electric mixer until creamy. Gradually add sugars, beating until light and fluffy. Add eggs, 1 at a time, beating just until the yellow yolk disappears.

Sift together flour and baking powder; add to butter mixture alternately with milk, beginning and ending with flour mixture. Beat batter at low speed just until blended after each addition. Stir in vanilla and pecans. Pour batter into a greased and floured 12-cup tube pan. Place pan in a cold oven; set oven temperature at 300°.

Bake for 1 hour and 30 minutes to 1 hour and 45 minutes or until a long wooden pick inserted in center of cake comes out clean. Cool in pan on a wire rack 10 to 15 minutes. Remove from pan; cool completely on wire rack. **Yield:** 10 to 12 servings.

editor's favorite

Cream Cheese-Bourbon-Pecan Pound Cake

The bourbon gives this pound cake a wonderful aroma and flavor, but you may substitute an equal amount of milk, if desired.

Prep: 20 min. Bake: 1 hr., 35 min. Cool: 15 min.

- 1½ cups butter, softened
- 1 (8-oz.) package cream cheese, softened
- 3 cups sugar
- 6 large eggs
- 3 cups all-purpose flour
- ½ tsp. salt
- ¼ cup bourbon
- 1½ tsp. vanilla extract
- 1½ cups chopped pecans, toasted

Beat butter and cream cheese at medium speed with an electric mixer until creamy. Gradually add sugar, beating at medium speed until light and fluffy. Add eggs, 1 at a time, beating just until the yellow yolk disappears.

Sift together flour and salt; add to butter mixture alternately with bourbon, beginning and ending with flour mixture. Beat batter at low speed just until blended after each addition. Stir in vanilla and pecans. Pour batter into a greased and floured 12-cup tube pan.

Bake at 325° for 1 hour and 30 minutes to 1 hour and 35 minutes or until a long wooden pick inserted in center of cake comes out clean. Cool in pan on a wire rack 10 to 15 minutes. Remove from pan; cool completely on wire rack. **Yield:** 10 to 12 servings.

Cream Cheese-Coconut-Pecan Pound Cake: Substitute 1 cup chopped toasted pecans and ½ cup shredded coconut for 1½ cups chopped toasted pecans. Proceed with recipe as directed.

POUND CAKE PANACHE

Heaped high with a snowy drift of coconut, Cream Cheese-Coconut-Pecan Pound Cake is made all the more merry when trimmed with a wreath of sugared cranberries and rosemary. Any flavor of pound cake that pairs well with coconut can be decorated in a similar way using these easy instructions:

- Invert the completely cooled pound cake onto a serving plate or cake stand; spoon Powdered Sugar Glaze evenly over the cake.
- Toss together ¾ cup each of coconut chips (see note) and sweetened flaked coconut; sprinkle evenly over the cake. Sprinkle the coconut mixture evenly with 2 Tbsp. white cake sparkles (see note).
- Arrange Sugared Rosemary, Sugared Cranberries, and pecan halves around the bottom edge of the cake.

Note: Coconut chips can be found in the produce section of many supermarkets or ordered online from www.kalustyans.com. White cake sparkles (edible glitter) can be found in stores that carry cake-decorating supplies or ordered online from www.wilton.com.

Powdered Sugar Glaze: Stir together 2 cups powdered sugar, 3 Tbsp. milk, and 1 tsp. vanilla extract until smooth, adding another 1 Tbsp. milk, if necessary, for desired consistency. Makes about 1 cup.

Sugared Rosemary: Microwave ½ cup corn syrup at HIGH for 10 seconds or until warm. Brush 10 to 12 rosemary sprigs lightly with corn syrup; sprinkle evenly with granulated sugar. Arrange in a single layer on wax paper. Use immediately, or let stand at room temperature, uncovered, for up to 24 hours.

Sugared Cranberries: Bring ½ cup sugar, ½ cup water, and 1 cup fresh cranberries to a boil in a small saucepan, stirring often, over medium-high heat. (Do not overcook; cranberries should swell and just begin to pop.) Remove from heat, and drain, reserving liquid for another use. Toss cranberries with ¼ cup granulated sugar, and arrange in a single layer on wax paper. Use immediately, or let stand at room temperature, uncovered, for up to 24 hours.

Cream Cheese-Coconut-
Pecan Pound Cake

Lemon Curd Pound Cake

Prep: 20 min. Bake: 1 hr., 30 min. Cool: 15 min.

1 cup butter, softened
½ cup shortening
3 cups sugar
6 large eggs
3 cups all-purpose flour
½ tsp. baking powder
⅛ tsp. salt
1 cup milk
1 tsp. vanilla extract
1 tsp. lemon extract
Lemon Curd
Garnishes: fresh rosemary, Sugared Cranberries (see Pound Cake Panache box on page 230), lemon rind strips

Beat butter and shortening at medium speed with an electric mixer until creamy. Gradually add sugar, beating at medium speed until light and fluffy. Add eggs, 1 at a time, beating just until the yellow yolk disappears.

Sift together flour, baking powder, and salt. Add flour mixture to butter mixture alternately with milk, beginning and ending with flour mixture. Beat batter at low speed just until blended after each addition. Stir in vanilla and lemon extracts. Pour batter into a greased and floured 12-cup tube pan.

Bake at 325° for 1 hour and 30 minutes or until a long wooden pick inserted in center of cake comes out clean. Cool in pan on a wire rack 10 to 15 minutes. Remove from pan; carefully brush Lemon Curd over top and sides of cake. Cool completely on wire rack. Garnish, if desired. **Yield:** 10 to 12 servings.

Lemon Curd:

Prep: 10 min. Cook: 12 min.

⅔ cup sugar
1½ Tbsp. butter, melted
2 tsp. grated fresh lemon rind
2 Tbsp. fresh lemon juice
1 large egg, lightly beaten

Stir together first 4 ingredients in a small, heavy saucepan; add egg, stirring until blended.

Cook mixture, stirring constantly, over low heat, 10 to 12 minutes or until mixture thickens slightly (cooked mixture will have a thickness similar to unwhipped whipping cream) and begins to bubble around the edges. Remove from heat. (The curd should be brushed immediately over cake, as mixture will continue to thicken as it cools.) **Yield:** about ¾ cup.

editor's favorite
Noel Pound Cake Loaf

Prep: 20 min. Bake: 1 hr. Cool: 10 min.

1 (6-oz.) jar red maraschino cherries
1 (6-oz.) jar green maraschino cherries
½ cup butter, softened
1⅓ cups sugar
3 large eggs
1½ cups all-purpose flour
½ tsp. salt
⅛ tsp. baking soda
½ cup sour cream
½ tsp. vanilla extract

Drain cherries well, and finely chop. Press gently between paper towels to absorb excess moisture; set aside.

Beat butter at medium speed with an electric mixer until creamy. Gradually add sugar, beating until light and fluffy. Add eggs, 1 at a time, beating just until the yellow yolk disappears.

Sift together flour, salt, and baking soda; stir in chopped cherries. Add flour mixture to butter mixture alternately with sour cream, beginning and ending with flour mixture. Beat batter at low speed just until blended after each addition. Stir in vanilla. Pour batter into a greased and floured 9- x 5-inch loaf pan.

Bake at 325° for 1 hour or until a long wooden pick inserted in center of cake comes out clean. Cool in pan on a wire rack 10 minutes. Remove from pan; cool completely on wire rack. **Yield:** 6 to 8 servings.

editor's favorite • make ahead
Red Velvet Cheesecake

The cheesecake's deep red filling and snowy topping is wonderfully dramatic. Fresh mint sprigs add a pop of Christmas color.

Prep: 20 min. Bake: 1 hr., 25 min. Stand: 1 hr. Chill: 8 hr.

1½ cups chocolate graham cracker crumbs
¼ cup butter, melted
1 Tbsp. granulated sugar
3 (8-oz.) packages cream cheese, softened
1½ cups granulated sugar
4 large eggs, lightly beaten
3 Tbsp. unsweetened cocoa
1 cup sour cream
½ cup whole buttermilk
2 tsp. vanilla extract
1 tsp. distilled white vinegar
2 (1-oz.) bottles red food coloring
1 (3-oz.) package cream cheese, softened
¼ cup butter, softened
2 cups powdered sugar
1 tsp. vanilla extract
Garnish: fresh mint sprigs

Stir together graham cracker crumbs, melted butter, and 1 Tbsp. granulated sugar; press mixture onto bottom of a 9-inch springform pan.

Beat 3 (8-oz.) packages cream cheese and 1½ cups granulated sugar at medium-low speed with an electric mixer 1 minute. Add eggs and next 6 ingredients, mixing on low speed just until fully combined. Pour batter into prepared crust.

Bake at 325° for 10 minutes; reduce heat to 300°, and bake for 1 hour and 15 minutes or until center is firm. Run knife along outer edge of cheesecake. Turn oven off. Let cheesecake stand in oven 30 minutes. Remove cheesecake from oven; cool in pan on a wire rack 30 minutes. Cover and chill 8 hours.

Beat 1 (3-oz.) package cream cheese and ¼ cup butter at medium speed with an electric mixer until smooth; gradually add powdered sugar and vanilla, beating until smooth. Spread evenly over top of cheesecake. Remove sides of springform pan. Garnish, if desired. **Yield:** 8 to 10 servings.

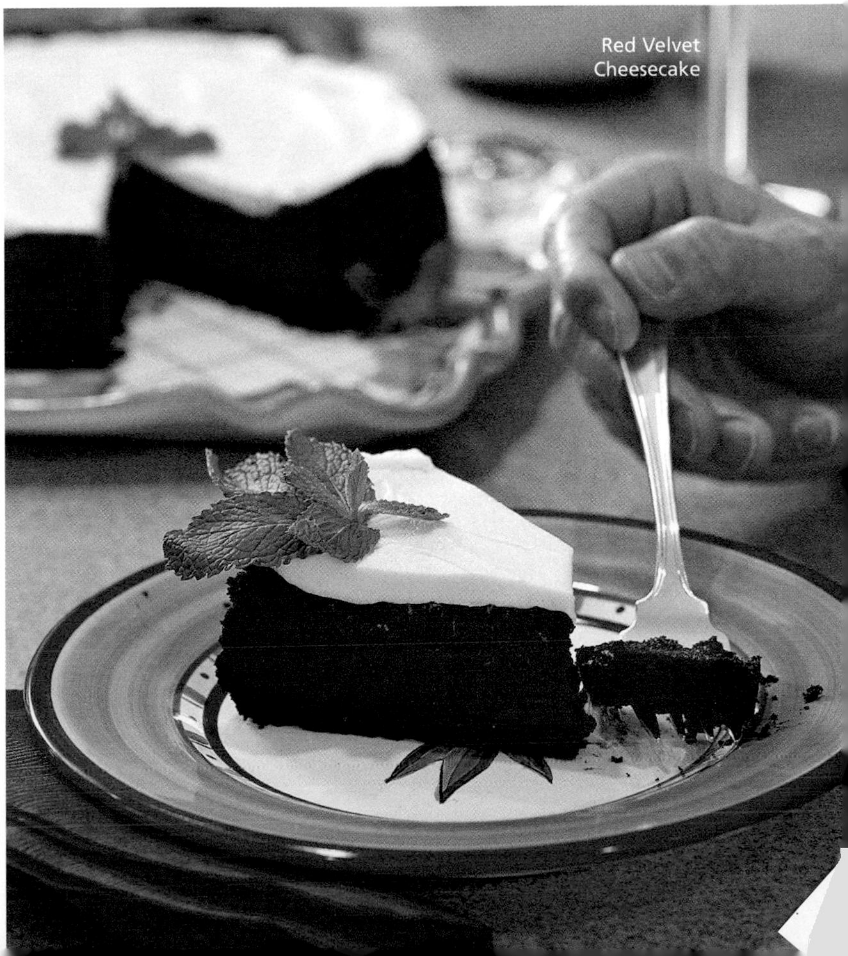
Red Velvet Cheesecake

Eggnog Cheesecake With Gingersnap Crust

Prep: 15 min. Bake: 1 hr. Stand: 1 hr. Chill: 8 hr.

12 oz. gingersnaps (about 48 cookies), finely crushed
¼ cup sugar
¼ cup melted butter
4 (8-oz.) packages ⅓-less-fat cream cheese
4 large eggs
2 cups refrigerated or canned eggnog, divided
2 cups powdered sugar
2 Tbsp. all-purpose flour
1 cup whipping cream

Stir together first 3 ingredients; press mixture onto bottom of a 10-inch springform pan.

Beat cream cheese at medium speed with an electric mixer until smooth; add eggs, 1 at a time, beating until blended after each addition. Add 1½ cups eggnog, and beat until blended. Fold in 2 cups powdered sugar and 2 Tbsp. flour; carefully pour cream cheese mixture into prepared pan.

Bake at 325° for 1 hour. Turn off oven. Let cheesecake stand in oven, with door closed, 1 hour. Remove to wire rack, and let cool completely. Cover and chill at least 8 hours.

Beat cream at high speed with an electric mixer until stiff peaks form; fold in remaining ½ cup eggnog. Spread mixture evenly over top of chilled cheesecake. **Yield:** 12 servings.

Chocolate Chunk Cheesecake

Prep: 35 min. Bake: 55 min. Stand: 20 min. Cool: 30 min. Chill: 8 hr., 30 min.

2 cups finely crushed cream-filled chocolate sandwich cookies (about 20 cookies)
2 Tbsp. butter, melted
4 (8-oz.) packages cream cheese, softened
1½ cups sugar
4 large eggs
2 tsp. vanilla extract
1 (11.5-oz.) package semisweet chocolate chunks, divided
1½ cups coarsely crushed cream-filled chocolate sandwich cookies (about 14 cookies)
⅓ cup whipping cream

Stir together 2 cups cookie crumbs and butter; press mixture into bottom and ½ inch up sides of a 9-inch springform pan.

Beat cream cheese and sugar at medium speed with an electric mixer until blended. Add eggs, 1 at a time, beating just until blended after each addition. Stir in vanilla, 1 cup chocolate chunks, and 1½ cups crushed cookies. Pour into prepared crust.

Bake at 325° for 55 minutes or until center is almost set. Turn off oven; let cheesecake stand in oven, with oven door partially open, 20 minutes. Remove cheesecake from oven, and cool in pan on a wire rack 30 minutes. Cover cheesecake, and chill 8 hours. Release sides of pan.

Microwave remaining ¾ cup chocolate and cream in a glass bowl at HIGH 1 minute; stir until chocolate melts. Chill 30 minutes. Pour evenly over cheesecake. **Yield:** 12 to 14 servings.

editor's favorite

Cranberry-Apple-Raisin Pie

Decorate the crust using extra dough and cookie-cutter shapes. To reheat, cover with aluminum foil; bake at 350° for 20 minutes.

Prep: 40 min. Bake: 1 hr. Stand: 30 min.

1½ (15-oz.) packages refrigerated piecrusts, divided
1 cup sugar, divided
2 Tbsp. cornstarch
1 tsp. ground cinnamon
3 large Golden Delicious apples, peeled and sliced
1 cup fresh cranberries
½ cup golden raisins
½ cup chopped pecans, toasted
3 Tbsp. butter, cut into pieces
1 large egg
1 Tbsp. water

Fit 1 piecrust into a 9-inch pieplate according to package directions, allowing excess crust to hang over edge; chill.

Stir together ¾ cup sugar, 2 Tbsp. cornstarch, and 1 tsp. ground cinnamon in a large bowl; add apple slices, cranberries, raisins, and chopped pecans, tossing to coat. Spoon into prepared piecrust; dot top of filling with butter.

Unroll another piecrust; place on top of apple mixture in pieplate. Fold excess crusts under, and seal by pressing edges with a fork. Cut an "X" into top of crust to allow steam to escape.

Unroll remaining piecrust. Cut with a 2-inch star-shaped cutter; arrange stars on top of pie.

Whisk together egg and 1 Tbsp. water; brush mixture evenly over top of pie. Sprinkle evenly with remaining ¼ cup sugar.

Bake at 400° for 20 minutes; reduce temperature to 350°, and bake 40 minutes, shielding edges with aluminum foil after 30 minutes to prevent excessive browning. Let stand 30 minutes. Serve warm, or cool completely on a wire rack. **Yield:** 8 servings.

Cranberry-Apple-Raisin Pie

editor's favorite • freezer friendly • make ahead

Mocha-Pecan Mud Pie

Round out your meal with a slice of decadent ice-cream pie. Drizzled with chocolate syrup and sprinkled with crumbled chocolate sandwich cookies, this dessert is so rich, your guests will never know it was lightened.

Prep: 15 min. Bake: 10 min. Freeze: 8 hr., 10 min.

½ cup chopped pecans
Vegetable cooking spray
1 tsp. sugar
1 pint light coffee ice cream, softened (see note)
1 pint light chocolate ice cream, softened (see note)
1 cup coarsely chopped reduced-fat cream-filled chocolate sandwich cookies, divided (about 10 cookies)
1 (6-oz.) ready-made chocolate crumb piecrust (see note)
2 Tbsp. light chocolate syrup

Place pecans in a single layer on a baking sheet coated with cooking spray; sprinkle evenly with sugar.

Bake at 350° for 8 to 10 minutes or until lightly toasted. Cool.

Stir together ice cream, ¾ cup cookie chunks, and ⅓ cup pecans; spoon into piecrust. Freeze 10 minutes. Press remaining cookie chunks and pecans evenly on top. Cover with plastic wrap, and freeze 8 hours. Drizzle individual slices evenly with chocolate syrup. **Yield:** 9 servings.

Note: For testing purposes only, we used Häagen-Dazs Light Coffee Ice Cream, Häagen-Dazs Light Dutch Chocolate Ice Cream, and Keebler Chocolate Ready Crust.

Maple-Pecan Tartlets

Flavoring the cream cheese pastry with ground cinnamon makes these petite pies something special.

Prep: 40 min. Chill: 1 hr. Bake: 25 min.

1 (3-oz.) package cream cheese, softened
⅓ cup butter, softened
1 cup all-purpose flour
¼ tsp. ground cinnamon
¾ cup firmly packed brown sugar
¼ cup maple syrup
1 large egg, lightly beaten
1 Tbsp. butter, melted
⅛ tsp. salt
¾ cup finely chopped pecans, toasted
Garnishes: fresh rosemary sprigs, fresh raspberries

Beat cream cheese and butter at medium speed with an electric mixer until creamy. Gradually add flour and cinnamon, beating at low speed just until blended. Wrap dough in plastic wrap, and chill 1 hour.

Divide dough in half. Divide each dough half into 12 balls. Press dough balls on bottoms and up sides of lightly greased miniature (1¾-inch) muffin pans, shaping each into a shell.

Whisk together brown sugar and next 4 ingredients in a medium bowl until blended. Stir in pecans. Spoon filling evenly into pastry shells.

Bake at 325° for 25 minutes or until set. Cool slightly. Remove from pans, and cool completely on wire racks. Garnish, if desired. **Yield:** 2 dozen.

make ahead

Mascarpone Pecan Pie

This recipe offers a twist on a Southern favorite with the addition of a sweet, creamy layer.

Prep: 15 min. Bake: 1 hr. Chill: 6 hr.

1 (15-oz.) package refrigerated piecrusts
1 (8-oz.) package cream cheese, softened
1 (8-oz.) package mascarpone cheese*
1½ cups sugar, divided
1 tsp. lemon juice
5 large eggs, divided
1 cup light corn syrup
1½ cups chopped pecans

Fit 2 piecrusts into 2 separate 9-inch pieplates according to package directions; fold edges under, and crimp.

Beat cheeses, 1 cup sugar, and lemon juice at medium speed with an electric mixer until smooth. Add 2 eggs, 1 at a time, blending well after each addition. Spread cheese mixture evenly into crusts.

Whisk together remaining ½ cup sugar, remaining 3 eggs, and corn syrup in a medium bowl. Stir in pecans. Gently pour pecan mixture evenly over cheese mixture in pieplates.

Bake at 350° for 20 minutes; reduce heat to 325°, and bake 40 minutes more or until set. Cool to room temperature; cover and chill pies at least 6 hours or overnight. **Yield:** 16 servings.

*1 (8-oz.) package cream cheese, softened, may be substituted for mascarpone cheese.

Maple-Pecan Tartlets

editor's favorite

Sweet Potato-Apple Cobbler

This fall-friendly recipe makes a scrumptious finale to a fine meal.

Prep: 20 min. Bake: 1 hr., 45 min.

4 medium-size sweet potatoes
2 Granny Smith apples, peeled and thinly sliced
1½ cups orange juice
½ cup granulated sugar
¼ cup firmly packed dark brown sugar
3 Tbsp. all-purpose flour
½ tsp. ground cinnamon
¼ tsp. ground nutmeg
¼ tsp. salt
½ cup butter or margarine, divided
1 cup chopped pecans, toasted
1 (15-oz.) package refrigerated piecrusts
2 tsp. granulated sugar
Bourbon Whipped Cream (optional)

Pierce sweet potatoes several times with a fork, and place on an aluminum foil-lined baking sheet.

Bake at 400° for 1 hour or until done; cool slightly. Peel and cut crosswise into ¼-inch-thick slices.

Place apple slices in an even layer in a lightly greased 13- x 9-inch baking dish; top with sweet potato slices.

Stir together 1½ cups orange juice and next 6 ingredients. Pour over sweet potato mixture. Dot with 6 Tbsp. butter.

Sprinkle ½ cup chopped pecans on a cutting board. Unfold 1 piecrust, and place on pecans; gently roll piecrust dough into pecans. Cut with a leaf-shaped cookie cutter; place leaves over sweet potato mixture. Repeat procedure with remaining ½ cup chopped pecans and piecrust.

Microwave remaining 2 Tbsp. butter in a 1-cup glass measuring cup at HIGH 20 to 30 seconds or until melted. Brush butter over crust, and sprinkle with 2 tsp. granulated sugar.

Bake at 400° for 45 minutes or until golden. Serve warm with Bourbon Whipped Cream, if desired. **Yield:** 12 servings.

Bourbon Whipped Cream:

Prep: 5 min.

1 cup whipping cream
2 Tbsp. granulated sugar
1 Tbsp. bourbon

Beat whipping cream and sugar at medium speed with an electric mixer until stiff peaks form; stir in bourbon. **Yield:** about 2 cups.

Quick Apple Dumplings

Quick Apple Dumplings

Refrigerated piecrusts make quick work of these pastry-wrapped treats.

Prep: 25 min. Cook: 15 min. Bake: 45 min.

1½ cups sugar
2 cups water
½ tsp. ground cinnamon, divided
½ tsp. ground nutmeg, divided
¼ cup butter or margarine
⅔ cup sugar
2 (15-oz.) packages refrigerated piecrusts
8 medium Braeburn apples, peeled and cored*
3 Tbsp. butter or margarine, cut up
Vanilla ice cream (optional)

Bring 1½ cups sugar, 2 cups water, ¼ tsp. cinnamon, and ¼ tsp. nutmeg to a boil in a saucepan over medium-high heat, stirring constantly; reduce heat to low, and simmer, stirring occasionally, 10 minutes. Remove pan from heat, and stir in ¼ cup butter. Set syrup aside.

Combine ⅔ cup sugar, remaining ¼ tsp. cinnamon, and remaining ¼ tsp. nutmeg.

Cut piecrusts in half, and roll into eight 8-inch circles. Place 1 apple in center of each circle. Sprinkle each evenly with cinnamon-sugar mixture; dot evenly with 3 Tbsp. butter.

Fold dough over apples, pinching to seal. Place in a lightly greased 13- x 9-inch baking dish. Drizzle with syrup.

Bake dumplings at 375° for 40 to 45 minutes. Serve with vanilla ice cream, if desired. **Yield:** 8 servings.

*Golden Delicious or Granny Smith apples may be substituted.

Praline Sweet Potatoes and Apples

Serve this dish as a replacement for your classic sweet potato pie recipe.

Prep: 10 min. Cook: 20 min.

¼ cup butter
2 lb. sweet potatoes, peeled and cut into ¼-inch-thick slices (about 2 large)
2 apples, peeled and cut into ¼-inch-thick slices
¼ cup granulated sugar
¼ cup firmly packed brown sugar
¼ cup pecans, chopped
¼ tsp. ground cinnamon
⅛ tsp. salt
2 Tbsp. water

Melt butter in a large skillet over medium heat. Add sweet potatoes; cover and cook over medium heat 5 minutes or until golden. Turn potato slices over. Reduce heat to low, cover and cook 5 minutes more.

Remove potatoes from skillet. Add apples; cook 5 minutes on each side or until tender and golden.

Return potatoes to skillet. Add granulated sugar and next 4 ingredients, tossing to coat. Add 2 Tbsp. water, stirring to loosen particles from bottom of skillet. Cook 5 minutes or until potatoes and apples are glazed and tender. **Yield:** 4 servings.

Layered Almond-Cream Cheese Bread Pudding With Amaretto Cream Sauce

Prep: 30 min. Chill: 30 min. Bake: 1 hr.

1 (16-oz.) loaf honey white bread, divided
1 (8-oz.) package cream cheese, softened
9 large eggs, divided
¼ cup sugar
3 tsp. vanilla extract, divided
1¼ cups almond filling (see note)
1 cup butter, melted and divided
2½ cups half-and-half
Dash of salt
2 Tbsp. almond filling
2 Tbsp. sugar
1 egg yolk
¼ cup slivered almonds
Amaretto Cream Sauce

Arrange 4½ bread slices in a lightly greased 13- x 9-inch pan, cutting slices as necessary to fit pan.

Beat cream cheese, 1 egg, ¼ cup sugar, and 1 tsp. vanilla at medium speed with an electric mixer until smooth. Spread half of cream cheese mixture over bread.

Whisk together 1¼ cups almond filling and ½ cup melted butter. Spread half of almond mixture over cream cheese mixture. Repeat layers once, using 4½ bread slices, remaining cream cheese mixture, and remaining almond mixture.

Cut remaining bread slices into 1-inch cubes, and sprinkle over almond mixture.

Whisk together remaining 8 eggs, remaining 2 tsp. vanilla, half-and-half, and salt; pour over bread cubes. Cover and chill 30 minutes or until most of egg mixture is absorbed.

Whisk together remaining ½ cup melted butter, 2 Tbsp. almond filling, 2 Tbsp. sugar, and egg yolk until blended. Drizzle evenly over bread pudding; sprinkle with almonds.

Bake at 325° for 1 hour or until set. Serve warm or chilled with Amaretto Cream Sauce. **Yield:** 12 servings.

Note: For testing purposes only, we used Solo Almond Filling.

Amaretto Cream Sauce:

Prep: 5 min. Cook: 10 min.

½ cup amaretto liqueur
2 Tbsp. cornstarch
1½ cups whipping cream
½ cup sugar

Combine amaretto liqueur and cornstarch, stirring until smooth.

Cook 1½ cups whipping cream in a heavy saucepan over medium heat, stirring often, just until bubbles appear; gradually stir in amaretto mixture. Bring to a boil over medium heat, and boil, stirring constantly, 30 seconds. Remove mixture from heat; stir in ½ cup sugar, and let cool completely. **Yield:** about 2½ cups.

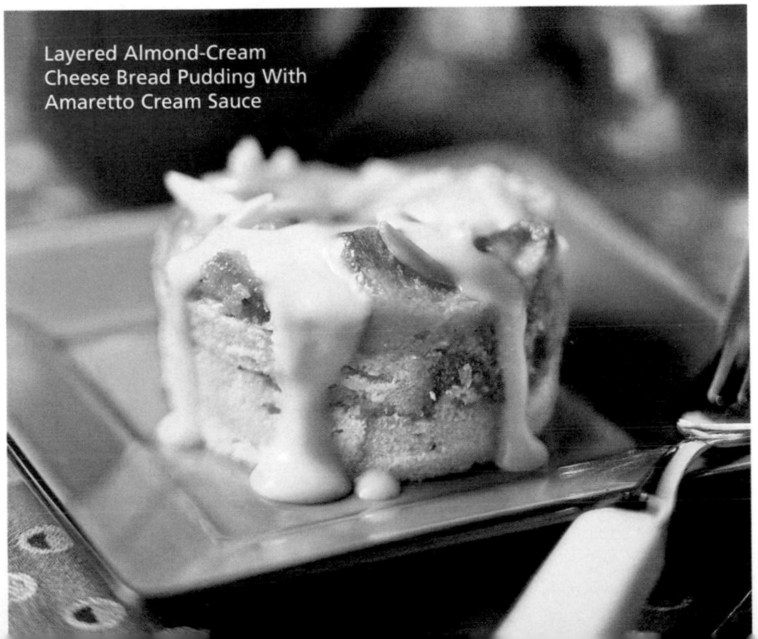
Layered Almond-Cream Cheese Bread Pudding With Amaretto Cream Sauce

make ahead

Espresso Crème Brûlée

We recommend a small kitchen torch for crowning the custards with burnt-sugar shells. Using a torch is easy, as well as faster than the stovetop method also given. This dessert is best made 1 to 2 days ahead.

Prep: 10 min. Cook: 40 min. Stand: 30 min. Bake: 25 min. Chill: 4 hr.

2 cups 2% reduced-fat milk
1 cup whole espresso coffee beans
¾ cup instant non-fat dry milk
3 Tbsp. sugar, divided
1 tsp. vanilla extract
Dash of salt
4 large egg yolks
¼ cup sugar, divided

Combine 2% milk, espresso beans, dry milk, and 2 Tbsp. sugar in a medium saucepan. Heat mixture over medium heat to 180° or until tiny bubbles form around edge, stirring occasionally. (Do not boil.) Remove milk mixture from heat. Cover and steep 30 minutes.

Strain mixture through a sieve into a bowl; discard solids. Stir in vanilla.

Combine remaining 1 Tbsp. sugar, salt, and egg yolks in a medium bowl, stirring well with a whisk.

Add milk mixture to egg mixture gradually, stirring constantly with a whisk. Divide the mixture evenly among 4 (4-oz.) ramekins, custard cups, or shallow baking dishes. Place ramekins in a 13- x 9-inch baking pan, and add hot water to a depth of ½ inch.

Bake at 300° for 25 minutes or until center barely moves when ramekin is touched. Remove ramekins from pan; cool completely on a wire rack. Cover and chill at least 4 hours or overnight.

Sift 1 Tbsp. sugar evenly over each custard. Holding a kitchen blow torch about 2 inches from the top of each custard, heat the sugar, moving the torch back and forth, until sugar is completely melted and caramelized (about 1 minute; see note). Serve immediately or within 1 hour. **Yield:** 4 servings.

Note: If you don't have a kitchen blow torch (available at kitchen-supply stores), you can make the sugar topping on the stovetop. Place ¼ cup sugar and 1 Tbsp. water in a small, heavy saucepan. Cook over medium heat 5 to 8 minutes or until golden. (Resist the urge to stir, since doing so may cause the sugar to crystallize.) Immediately pour the sugar mixture evenly over cold custards, spreading to form a thin layer.

Espresso Crème Brûlée

editor's favorite • make ahead

White Chocolate Panna Cotta With Dark Chocolate Sauce

Panna cotta is a delicate eggless custard. Serve it in stemmed glasses for an updated presentation or classically molded in ramekins.

Prep: 10 min. Stand: 5 min. Cook: 4 min. Chill: 24 hr.

1 (¼-oz.) envelope unflavored gelatin
1½ cups cold milk, divided
1 cup whipping cream
½ cup white chocolate morsels
¼ cup sugar
Dark Chocolate Sauce
Garnishes: fresh mint sprigs, chocolate shavings

Sprinkle gelatin over ¼ cup milk in a small bowl; stir until moistened. Let stand 5 minutes. (Mixture will be lumpy.)

Cook whipping cream, chocolate morsels, and sugar in a saucepan over medium-low heat, stirring occasionally, 4 minutes or until morsels are melted and sugar is dissolved. Remove from heat, and add gelatin mixture, stirring until mixture is dissolved. Stir in remaining 1¼ cups milk.

Pour mixture evenly into 4 to 6 stemmed glasses or 6 (8-oz.) ramekins. Cover and chill 24 hours. Serve with Dark Chocolate Sauce. Garnish, if desired. **Yield:** 4 to 6 servings.

Dark Chocolate Sauce:

Prep: 5 min.

1 (3-oz.) dark chocolate baking bar, chopped
¾ cup heavy cream

Microwave chocolate and cream in a small microwave-safe bowl at HIGH 1½ minutes or until melted and smooth, stirring every 30 seconds. **Yield:** about 1 cup.

White Chocolate Panna Cotta

editor's favorite • make ahead

Turtle Trifle

This trifle requires no baking; just assemble, and then chill.

Prep: 20 min. Chill: 1 hr.

8 oz. mascarpone cheese, softened*
1½ cups whipping cream
1½ tsp. vanilla extract
1 (2-lb.) frozen pecan pie, thawed and cut into 1-inch cubes (see note)
⅓ cup chocolate fudge topping (see note)
⅓ cup caramel topping (see note)
½ cup chopped pecans, toasted

Beat mascarpone cheese, whipping cream, and vanilla in a large bowl at medium speed with a heavy-duty electric stand mixer, using the whisk attachment, 2 to 3 minutes or until smooth and firm.

Place half of pie cubes in bottom of a 4-qt. trifle dish or tall, clear 4-qt. glass bowl. Spread half of whipped cream mixture over pie cubes. Drizzle with half each of chocolate fudge topping and caramel topping. Sprinkle with half of chopped pecans. Repeat layers.

Cover and chill at least 1 hour or up to 8 hours. **Yield:** 10 servings.

*1 (8-oz.) package cream cheese may be substituted.

Note: For testing purposes only, we used Edwards Georgia Pecan Pie, Smucker's Chocolate Fudge Topping, and Smucker's Caramel Flavored Topping.

Holiday Pavlova

This dessert gets its delicate sweetness from amaretto cookies, lemon curd, and assorted fruits atop a billowy cloud of meringue.

Prep: 50 min. Bake: 2 hr.

Basic Meringue
12 amaretto cookies, coarsely crushed
1 (12-oz.) jar lemon curd
Assorted fresh fruits
Garnish: fresh mint sprigs

Line a baking sheet with parchment paper; draw a 9-inch circle on paper.

Spoon or pipe Basic Meringue onto parchment paper, covering entire circle. Spoon or pipe a 2-inch border around outside edge of circle.

Bake at 200° for 1 hour; reduce oven temperature to 150°, and bake 1 more hour. Cool completely on a wire rack.

Place meringue on a serving platter, and sprinkle with crushed cookies. Spread lemon curd over cookies. Layer fresh fruits over curd. Garnish, if desired. **Yield:** 8 servings.

Basic Meringue:

Prep: 8 min.

¾ cup water
2 Tbsp. meringue powder (see note)
1⅓ cups granulated sugar
1 tsp. lemon juice
½ cup powdered sugar

Add ¾ cup water slowly to meringue powder in a metal mixing bowl, and beat at low speed with an electric mixer until foamy, using clean, dry beaters. Add 1⅓ cups granulated sugar, 1 Tbsp. at a time, beating 2 to 4 minutes until stiff peaks form. Add lemon juice, beating until blended.

Fold ½ cup powdered sugar gently into egg white mixture. **Yield:** 1 (9-inch) pavlova.

Note: Look for meringue powder in local cake-decorating and crafts stores.

Holiday Pavlova

editor's favorite

Chocolate-and-Almond Macaroons

For easy cleanup, put wax paper under the wire rack to catch the excess as you drizzle chocolate on the cookies.

Prep: 15 min. Bake: 17 min. per batch

¾ cup sweetened condensed milk
1 (14-oz.) package sweetened flaked coconut
¼ to ½ tsp. almond extract
⅛ tsp. salt
24 whole unblanched almonds
½ cup dark chocolate morsels

Stir together first 4 ingredients. Drop dough by lightly greased tablespoonfuls onto parchment paper-lined baking sheets. Press an almond into top of each cookie.

Bake at 350° for 15 to 17 minutes or until golden. Remove to wire racks to cool.

Microwave ½ cup chocolate morsels in a microwave-safe bowl at HIGH 1 minute and 15 seconds or until melted and smooth, stirring at 30-second intervals and at end. Transfer to a 1-qt. zip-top plastic freezer bag; cut a tiny hole in 1 corner of bag. Pipe melted chocolate over cooled cookies by gently squeezing bag. **Yield:** 2 dozen.

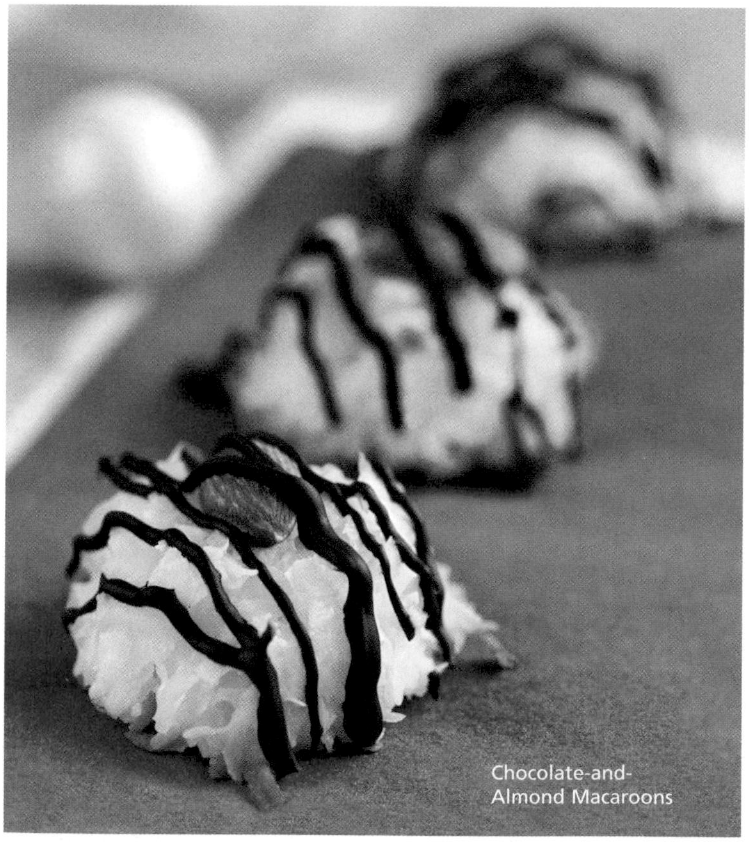

Chocolate-and-Almond Macaroons

big batch • editor's favorite

Chocolate Chunk-Mocha Cookies

These amazing frosted cookies received our highest rating.

Prep: 25 min. Bake: 12 min. per batch Cool: 32 min.

2¼ cups all-purpose flour
⅔ cup unsweetened cocoa
1 tsp. baking soda
¼ tsp. salt
1 cup butter, softened
¾ cup granulated sugar
⅔ cup firmly packed brown sugar
1 tsp. vanilla extract
2 large eggs
1 (11.5-oz.) package semisweet chocolate chunks
Mocha Frosting
Powdered sugar (optional)

Combine flour and next 3 ingredients in a bowl.

Beat butter and next 3 ingredients at medium speed with an electric mixer until creamy. Add eggs, 1 at a time, beating just until blended after each addition. Gradually add flour mixture, beating at low speed until blended. Stir in chocolate chunks.

Drop dough by heaping tablespoonfuls onto parchment paper-lined baking sheets.

Bake at 350° for 10 to 12 minutes or until puffy. Cool on baking sheets 2 minutes; remove to wire racks, and let cool 30 minutes or until completely cool. Spread cookies with Mocha Frosting. Dust evenly with powdered sugar, if desired. **Yield:** 3 dozen.

Mocha Frosting:

Prep: 10 min.

¼ cup unsweetened cocoa
¼ cup hot strong brewed coffee
¼ cup butter, melted
1 tsp. vanilla extract
3½ cups powdered sugar, sifted

Stir together first 4 ingredients until smooth. Gradually add powdered sugar, stirring until creamy. **Yield:** about 3 cups.

big batch • editor's favorite

Mississippi Mud Cookies

Dough containing sticky ingredients, such as marshmallows and toffee bits, are best baked on parchment paper-lined baking sheets.

Prep: 25 min. Bake: 12 min. per batch

1 cup semisweet chocolate morsels
½ cup butter, softened
1 cup sugar
2 large eggs
1 tsp. vanilla
1½ cups all-purpose flour
1 tsp. baking powder
½ tsp. salt
1 cup chopped pecans
½ cup milk chocolate morsels
1 cup plus 2 Tbsp. miniature marshmallows

Microwave semisweet chocolate morsels in a small microwave-safe glass bowl at HIGH 1 minute or until smooth, stirring every 30 seconds.

Beat butter and sugar at medium speed with an electric mixer until creamy; add eggs, 1 at a time, beating until blended after each addition. Beat in vanilla and melted chocolate.

Combine flour, baking powder, and salt; gradually add to chocolate mixture, beating until well blended. Stir in chopped pecans and ½ cup milk chocolate morsels.

Drop dough by heaping tablespoonfuls onto parchment paper-lined baking sheets. Press 3 marshmallows into each portion of dough.

Bake at 350° for 10 to 12 minutes or until set. Remove to wire racks. **Yield:** about 3 dozen.

Mississippi Mud Cookies

big batch • editor's favorite • freezer friendly

Easy Chocolate Fudge Cookies

As the batter cools, the later batches of cookies will take longer to bake than the earlier ones.

Prep: 10 min. Cook: 5 min. Bake: 10 min. per batch

¼ cup butter or margarine
1 (12-oz.) package semisweet chocolate morsels
1 (14-oz.) can sweetened condensed milk
1 tsp. vanilla extract
1 cup all-purpose flour
1 cup chopped pecans

Combine first 3 ingredients in a heavy saucepan. Cook over low heat, stirring constantly, 5 minutes or until chocolate morsels are melted. Remove from heat. Stir in vanilla and flour until well blended. Fold in pecans.

Drop immediately by level tablespoonfuls onto a lightly greased baking sheet (see note).

Bake at 350° for 7 to 10 minutes. Cool on baking sheets; remove to wire racks to cool completely. **Yield:** 4 dozen.

Make-Ahead Note: Dough may be frozen up to 1 month or refrigerated up to 2 days. Let stand at room temperature before baking as directed.

big batch

Grandmom's Orange Crispies

Prep: 15 min. Bake: 10 min. per batch

1 cup granulated sugar
1 cup shortening
1 large egg
1½ tsp. orange extract
1½ cups all-purpose flour
¾ tsp. salt
Powdered sugar (optional)

Beat granulated sugar and 1 cup shortening at low speed with an electric mixer until creamy. Add egg and orange extract, beating until blended. Gradually add flour and salt, beating until light and fluffy after each addition.

Drop mixture by rounded teaspoonfuls, 2 inches apart, onto ungreased baking sheets.

Bake at 375° for 10 minutes or just until edges begin to brown; remove to wire racks to cool. Dust warm cookies with powdered sugar, if desired. **Yield:** about 6 dozen.

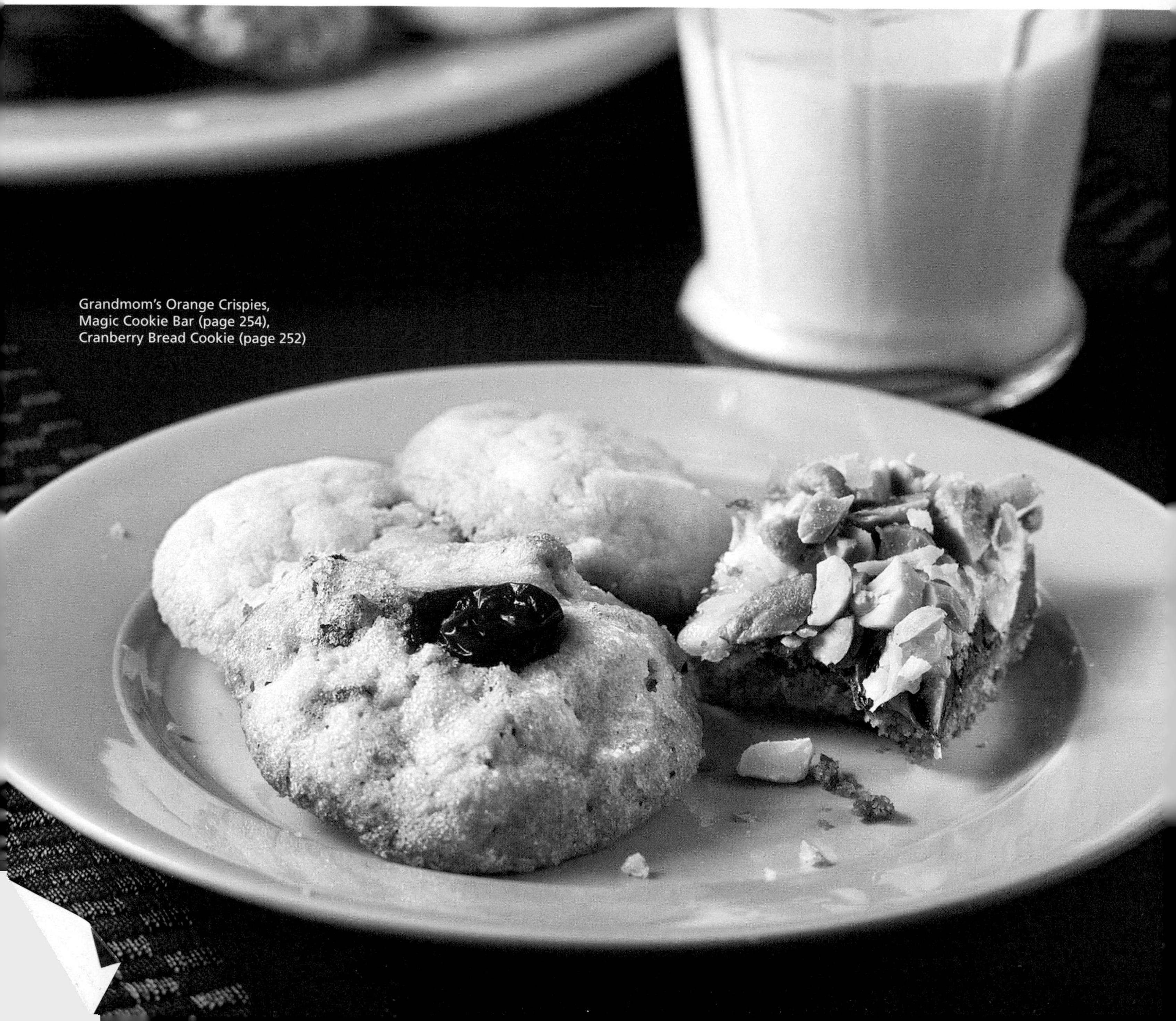

Grandmom's Orange Crispies, Magic Cookie Bar (page 254), Cranberry Bread Cookie (page 252)

big batch • editor's favorite

Lemon-Basil Snaps

Chilling the dough will help these cookies hold their shape while baking. We don't recommend substituting dried basil in this recipe, which comes to us from the Charlotte Herb Guild in North Carolina.

Prep: 15 min. Chill 1 hr. Bake: 12 min. per batch

¾ cup butter, softened
¾ cup sugar
1 large egg
1 Tbsp. grated fresh lemon rind
1 Tbsp. fresh lemon juice
⅓ cup minced fresh lemon basil leaves*
2 cups all-purpose flour
½ tsp. baking soda
¼ tsp. salt
⅓ cup finely chopped pistachio nuts
3 Tbsp. sugar

Beat butter at medium speed with electric mixer until fluffy; add ¾ cup sugar, beating well. Add egg and next 3 ingredients, beating until blended.

Combine flour, baking soda, and salt; gradually add to butter mixture, beating until blended. Cover and chill 1 hour.

Combine nuts and 3 Tbsp. sugar in a shallow bowl.

Shape dough into 1-inch balls; roll in nut mixture, and place 2 inches apart on ungreased baking sheets. Flatten slightly with hands or bottom of a glass.

Bake at 350° for 10 to 12 minutes or until golden brown. Remove to wire racks to cool. **Yield:** 3 dozen.

*Fresh sweet basil may be substituted.

big batch • editor's favorite

Peanut Butter Snowballs

Prep: 25 min. Bake: 15 min. per batch Cool: 5 min. per batch

1 cup butter, softened
⅔ cup granulated sugar
⅔ cup chunky peanut butter
2½ cups all-purpose flour
¼ tsp. salt
¾ cup powdered sugar, sifted
White edible glitter (optional; see note)

Beat softened butter at medium speed with an electric mixer until creamy; gradually add granulated sugar, beating well. Stir in chunky peanut butter until blended.

Lemon-Basil Snaps

Combine flour and salt; gradually add to peanut butter mixture, beating until well blended.

Roll dough into 60 (1-inch) balls; place 1 inch apart on parchment paper-lined baking sheets.

Bake at 350° for 12 to 15 minutes. Cool on baking sheets on wire racks 5 minutes. Roll warm cookies in powdered sugar. Dust with white edible glitter, if desired. **Yield:** about 5 dozen.

Note: Edible glitter can be found at local crafts stores.

Winter Mitten

editor's favorite
Winter Mittens

Prep: 30 min. Bake: 10 min. per batch

½ (18-oz.) package refrigerated sugar cookie dough
1 (16-oz.) container ready-to-spread vanilla frosting
Blue food coloring gel
White edible glitter (see note)
Garnish: powdered sugar

Roll refrigerated sugar cookie dough to ⅛-inch thickness on a lightly floured surface; cut with a (3- x 5-inch) mitten cookie cutter, and place dough on parchment paper-lined baking sheets.

Bake cookies at 350° for 8 to 10 minutes or until edges are lightly browned. Cool cookies completely on wire racks.

Tint half of ready-to-spread vanilla frosting with blue food coloring gel to desired shade. Spread frosting evenly on cookies.

Spoon remaining half of frosting into a 1-qt. zip-top plastic bag. (Do not seal.) Snip a tiny hole in 1 corner of bag, and pipe decorative designs on cookies. Sprinkle with edible glitter. Garnish, if desired. **Yield:** 8 cookies.

Note: Edible glitter can be found at local crafts stores.

big batch
Snickerdoodles

Prep: 20 min. Bake: 13 min. per batch

½ cup butter or margarine, softened
1½ cups all-purpose flour
1 cup sugar
1 large egg
½ tsp. vanilla
¼ tsp. baking soda
¼ tsp. cream of tartar
2 Tbsp. sugar
1 tsp. ground cinnamon

Beat butter at medium speed with an electric mixer 30 seconds. Add ¾ cup flour, 1 cup sugar, and next 4 ingredients, beating until well blended. Add remaining ¾ cup flour, beating until blended. Set aside.

Stir together 2 Tbsp. sugar and 1 tsp. cinnamon.

Shape dough into 1-inch balls; roll in cinnamon mixture. Place 2 inches apart on ungreased baking sheets.

Bake at 375° for 11 to 13 minutes or until edges are golden. Cool on wire rack. **Yield:** about 30 cookies.

big batch
Sugarplum Thumbprints

Decorating cookies is as much fun as eating them. Let the kids help measure ingredients and choose shapes and colors. (also pictured on page 99)

Prep: 15 min. Chill: 30 min. Bake: 12 min. per batch

1 cup butter, softened
1 cup powdered sugar
1 tsp. vanilla extract
2 cups all-purpose flour
¼ tsp. salt
⅔ cup ready-to-spread cream cheese frosting
Gumdrops
Colored edible glitter (see note)
Powdered sugar

Beat butter at medium speed with an electric mixer until creamy. Gradually add powdered sugar and vanilla, beating well. Add flour and salt, mixing until well combined. Cover and chill 30 minutes.

Roll dough into 48 (¾-inch) balls, and place on parchment paper-lined baking sheets. Press thumb in center of each cookie to make an indention.

Bake at 350° for 10 to 12 minutes or until lightly browned on edges. Cool completely on wire racks.

Dollop cream cheese frosting into cookie indentions; top each cookie with a gumdrop. Sprinkle with edible glitter, and dust with powdered sugar. **Yield:** about 4 dozen.

Note: Edible glitter can be found at local crafts stores.

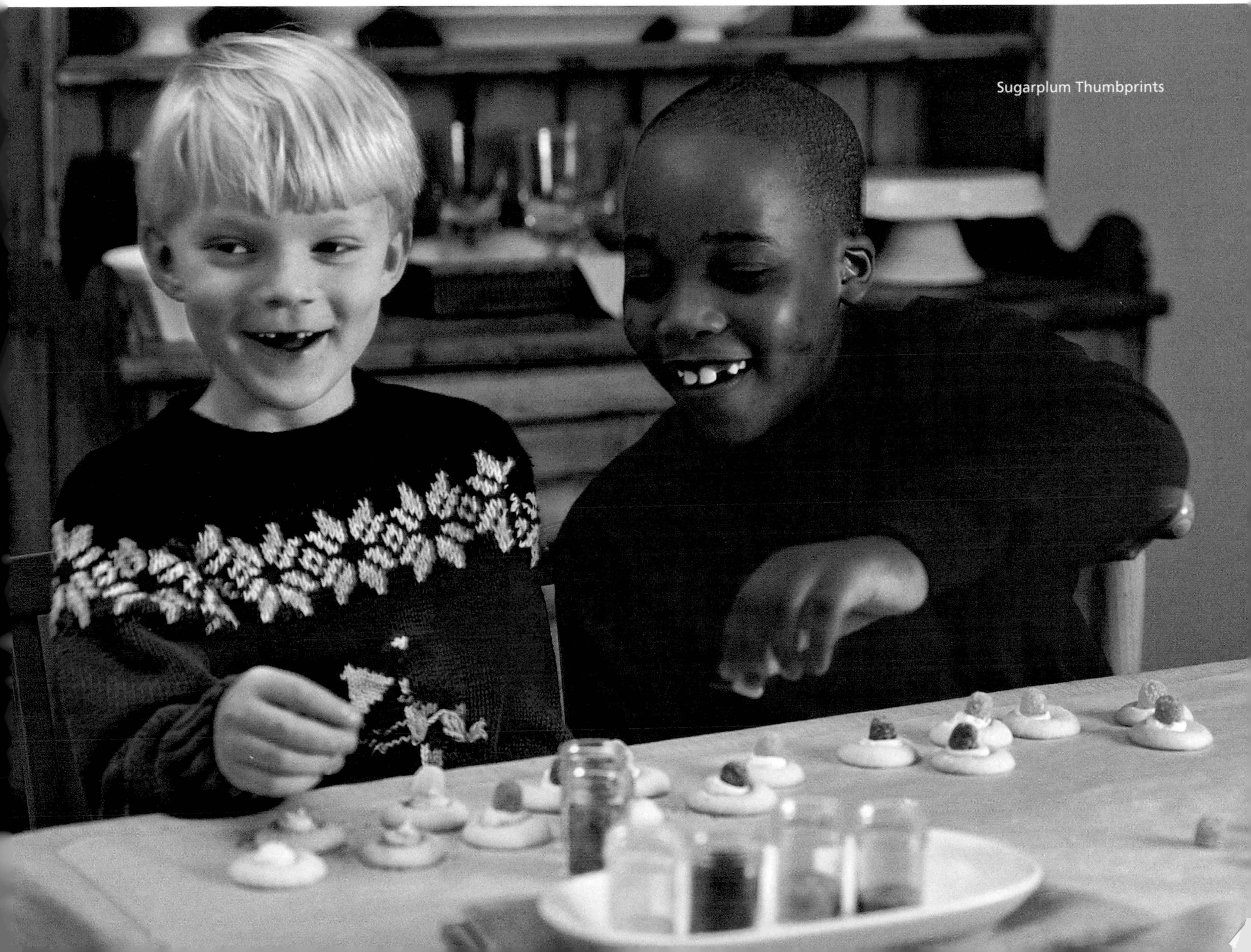

Sugarplum Thumbprints

big batch • freezer friendly

Coconut-Pecan Cookie Tarts

These tarts are very similar to pecan tassies but with a thicker, cookie-type crust.

Prep: 45 min. Chill: 1 hr. Bake: 25 min. Cool: 10 min.

1 cup butter, softened
2 (3-oz.) packages cream cheese, softened
1 cup sweetened flaked coconut
2 cups all-purpose flour
Pecan Filling

Beat butter and cream cheese at medium speed with an electric mixer until creamy; stir in coconut. Gradually add flour to butter mixture, beating at low speed after each addition.

Shape dough into 36 balls; chill 1 hour. Place dough balls in lightly greased miniature muffin pans, shaping each into a thick shell. Spoon Pecan Filling evenly into tart shells.

Bake at 350° for 15 minutes; reduce heat to 250°, and bake 10 minutes more or until filling is set. Cool tarts in pan on wire rack 10 minutes. Remove tarts from pan; cool completely on wire rack. **Yield:** 3 dozen.

Pecan Filling:

Prep: 5 min.

¾ cup firmly packed brown sugar
½ cup chopped pecans, toasted
1 large egg, lightly beaten
1 Tbsp. butter, melted
½ tsp. vanilla extract
⅛ tsp. salt

Whisk together all ingredients together until well blended. **Yield:** about 1 cup.

big batch • freezer friendly

Cranberry-Pecan Rugalach

Prep: 45 min. Chill: 8 hr. Bake: 20 min.

1 cup butter, softened
1 (8-oz.) package cream cheese, softened
½ cup granulated sugar
2¾ cups all-purpose flour
½ tsp. salt
Cranberry-Pecan Filling
1 large egg, lightly beaten
½ cup sparkling sugar (see note)

Beat butter and cream cheese at medium speed with an electric mixer until creamy; gradually add granulated sugar, beating until fluffy. Stir in flour and salt. Divide dough into 8 equal portions; flatten each portion into a disk; wrap each disk separately in plastic wrap. Chill 8 hours.

Roll 1 portion of dough at a time into an 8-inch circle on a lightly floured surface. Spread with 3 Tbsp. Cranberry-Pecan Filling, leaving a ½-inch border around edge. Cut circle into 8 wedges; roll up wedges, starting at wide end, to form a crescent shape. Place, point side down, on a lightly greased baking sheet. Brush gently with egg; sprinkle evenly with sparkling sugar. Repeat procedure with remaining dough and filling.

Bake at 350° on a lightly greased baking sheet for 20 minutes or until golden brown. Remove to wire racks to cool completely. **Yield:** 64 pastries.

Note: Sparkling sugar is available at stores that sell cake-decorating supplies.

Cranberry-Pecan Filling:

Prep: 10 min.

¾ cup sugar
⅔ cup chopped pecans, toasted
⅔ cup finely chopped sweetened dried cranberries*
½ cup butter, melted
1½ tsp. ground cinnamon
¾ tsp. ground allspice

Stir together all ingredients until blended. **Yield:** about 1½ cups.
*⅔ cup finely chopped dried cherries or apricots can be substituted.

Coconut-Pecan Cookie Tarts,
Cranberry-Pecan Rugalach

big batch

Cranberry Bread Cookies

This dough becomes soft and sticky as it reaches room temperature, so work with one portion at a time; chill remaining dough until ready to use. To prevent the cranberries on top from bleeding, you can press the fruit into the cookies after they've baked for 7 minutes, and then return the cookies to the oven. *(pictured on page 246)*

Prep: 35 min. Chill: 8 hr. Bake: 16 min. per batch

½ cup shortening
½ cup butter, softened
2½ cups sugar, divided
2 large eggs
3⅓ cups all-purpose flour
1½ cups chopped walnuts
1½ cups chopped fresh cranberries
2 Tbsp. grated fresh orange rind
1 tsp. baking powder
1 tsp. salt
1 tsp. cream of tartar
¼ cup fresh orange juice
1 cup fresh cranberries

Beat ½ cup shortening and ½ cup butter at low speed with an electric mixer until fluffy; add 1½ cups sugar, beating until blended. Add eggs, 1 at a time, beating mixture until blended after each addition.

Stir together flour and next 6 ingredients; add flour mixture to butter mixture, beating at medium speed until blended. Add orange juice, beating until blended. Cover and chill 8 hours.

Shape dough into 1-inch balls; roll balls in remaining 1 cup sugar. (Dampen hands with water if dough is sticky.)

Place on lightly greased baking sheets. Press 1 fresh cranberry into top of each dough ball.

Bake at 350° for 14 to 16 minutes or just until edges begin to brown. Cool on baking sheets 1 minute. Remove to wire racks to cool completely. **Yield:** about 6 dozen.

Chewy Raspberry-Streusel Bars

After preparing the batter, make sure to spread it in an even layer (to ensure consistent baking) in a pan that's the correct size. Using a smaller pan will make the bars gummy, while a larger pan will produce dry bars.

Prep: 15 min. Bake: 45 min.

1 cup all-purpose flour
1 cup uncooked regular oats
¼ tsp. baking powder
⅛ tsp. salt
½ cup butter, softened
½ cup sugar
2 Tbsp. milk
⅛ tsp. almond extract
¾ cup seedless raspberry fruit spread (see note)

Combine first 4 ingredients in a small bowl.

Beat butter and sugar at medium speed with an electric mixer until well blended. Reduce speed to medium-low; gradually add flour mixture, beating until mixture is crumbly and begins to stick together. Add milk and almond extract, beating just until blended.

Remove and reserve ¾ cup flour mixture. Press remaining mixture evenly and firmly in bottom of a lightly greased 8-inch square pan.

Bake at 350° for 15 minutes. Remove pan from oven. Spread raspberry fruit spread evenly over crust. Sprinkle evenly with reserved ¾ cup flour mixture, pressing gently into fruit layer.

Bake 25 to 30 minutes more or until edges are lightly browned. Cool completely in pan on a wire rack. Cut into 16 (2-inch) squares. **Yield:** 16 bars.

Note: For testing purposes only, we used Polaner All Fruit Raspberry Spreadable Fruit.

Chewy Apricot-Streusel Bars: Add ¼ tsp. ground cinnamon to flour mixture. Substitute ¼ tsp. vanilla extract for ⅛ tsp. almond extract and apricot fruit spread for raspberry fruit spread. Prepare recipe as directed.

freezer friendly • make ahead

Gingerbread Bars With Lemon-Cream Cheese Frosting

If you decide to freeze these bars, do not frost before freezing. Add the frosting to partially thawed bars, and then cut them into shapes.

Prep: 20 min. Bake: 25 min.

1¾ cups all-purpose flour
2 tsp. ground cinnamon
2 tsp. ground ginger
½ tsp. baking soda
¼ tsp. salt
1 cup butter, softened
½ cup granulated sugar
½ cup firmly packed light brown sugar
1 large egg
⅓ cup molasses
3 Tbsp. milk
Lemon-Cream Cheese Frosting
Garnish: grated fresh lemon rind

Combine first 5 ingredients in a small bowl; set aside.

Beat butter at medium speed with an electric mixer until creamy. Gradually add sugars, beating until well blended. Add egg, beating until blended. Reduce speed to low; gradually add flour mixture, beating just until blended. Add molasses and milk, beating just until blended. Spread batter evenly in a lightly greased 13- x 9-inch pan.

Bake at 350° for 25 minutes or until a wooden pick inserted in center comes out clean. Cool completely in pan on a wire rack. Spread evenly with Lemon-Cream Cheese Frosting (see note). Cut into bars. If desired, cut each bar in half, forming 2 triangles, and garnish. **Yield:** 2 to 3 dozen.

Make-Ahead Note: Frosted bars may be stored in an airtight container in the refrigerator 5 to 7 days.

Lemon-Cream Cheese Frosting:

Prep: 10 min.

2 (3-oz.) packages cream cheese, softened
2 Tbsp. butter, softened
¼ cup lemon curd
1 tsp. grated fresh lemon rind
2½ cups powdered sugar

Beat cream cheese and butter at medium speed with an electric mixer until creamy. Add lemon curd and lemon rind, beating until blended. Gradually add powdered sugar, beating until smooth. **Yield:** about 2 cups.

CUT-AND-FREEZE GINGERBREAD BARS

To keep up with holiday gift giving, follow these simple steps to cut and freeze your baked goodies ahead of time:

- Line a baking pan with heavy-duty aluminum foil, allowing several inches to extend over the sides (photo 1); lightly grease the foil. Spread the batter in the pan, bake and cool according to recipe directions.
- Lift the baked bars from the pan, using the foil sides as handles (photo 2).
- Lining the pan with foil also creates a no-fail way to cut the bars. After lifting the bars from pan, place on a hard surface, and press the foil sides down. Cut into the desired sizes and shapes. It's actually much easier to make clean cuts into partially frozen bars, so you might place the uncut baked bars in the freezer until partially frozen (about 30 to 40 minutes if you're planning to serve them without freezer storage).
- A 13- x 9-inch pan will yield about 36 (2¼- x 1½-inch) bars or about 24 (2¼-inch square) bars.
- To freeze, lift the baked bars from the pan (do not cut), and wrap the foil sides over the top (photo 3); wrap with additional foil to tightly seal, or place in a large zip-top plastic freezer bag and seal the bag. Freeze the bars up to 2 months, if desired. Before cutting, let them thaw at room temperature 1 to 2 hours or until partially thawed.

1

2

3

big batch
Magic Cookie Bars

(pictured on page 246)

Prep: 10 min. Bake: 30 min. Chill: 1 hr.

2 cups graham cracker crumbs
½ cup butter, melted
1 (14½-oz.) can sweetened condensed milk
1 cup semisweet chocolate morsels
1 cup peanut butter chips
1 (7-oz.) package sweetened flaked coconut
1 cup chopped peanuts

Stir together crumbs and melted butter, and press evenly into bottom of a 13- x 9-inch pan (see note).

Pour sweetened condensed milk over crust; sprinkle evenly with chocolate morsels and remaining ingredients. Gently press mixture to a uniform thickness with a fork.

Bake at 350° for 30 minutes or until coconut is lightly browned. Cool in pan on a wire rack. Cover and chill 1 hour. Cut into 1½- x 2½-inch bars. **Yield:** 30 bars.

Note: Line the baking pan with heavy-duty aluminum foil; this makes it easier to remove bars from the pan.

Brittle Fondue

Prep: 5 min.

1 (12-oz.) package semisweet chocolate morsels
¾ cup whipping cream

Microwave chocolate morsels and whipping cream in a medium microwave-safe glass bowl at HIGH 1 minute, whisking once after 30 seconds. Whisk until smooth. Transfer to fondue pot. Serve with peanut or pecan brittle (see note). **Yield:** 8 servings.

Note: While peanut brittle is readily available at most grocery stores, you might have to search a little harder to find pecan brittle. But don't worry—the Internet is a great resource for this product. Start your search with www.lalagniappe.com, ww.lcandy.com, or www.paulineshandmadebrittle.com.

Coffee Penuche

These morsels have a fudgelike texture with a brown-sugar flavor.

Prep: 10 min. Cook: 28 min. Cool: 1 hr., 30 min. Beat: 10 min.

3 cups firmly packed light brown sugar
1 cup brewed coffee
2 Tbsp. light corn syrup
2 Tbsp. butter
1 tsp. vanilla extract
⅛ tsp. salt
1 cup chopped pecans

Cook first 3 ingredients in a large heavy saucepan over low heat, stirring until sugar dissolves, about 10 minutes. Cover and cook over medium heat 2 to 3 minutes to wash down sugar from sides of pan. Uncover and cook, about 15 minutes, without stirring, until candy thermometer registers 238° (soft ball stage).

Remove from heat, and add butter, vanilla, and salt. (Do not stir.) Cool to 175°, about 1 hour. Stir in pecans, and beat about 10 minutes with a wooden spoon until mixture thickens and begins to lose its gloss. Spread into a buttered 8-inch square pan. Cool 30 minutes or until firm. Cut into 1-inch squares. Store in airtight containers. **Yield:** 2 lb. or 5⅓ dozen squares.

White Chocolate-Peanut Butter Crunch

Prep: 10 min. Cook: 2 min. Stand: 15 min.

8 (2-oz.) vanilla bark coating squares
2 Tbsp. creamy peanut butter
2 cups miniature marshmallows
2 cups crisp rice cereal
2 cups dry-roasted peanuts

Microwave bark coating in a large glass bowl at HIGH 2 minutes or until melted, stirring every 30 seconds. Stir in peanut butter until smooth. Stir in marshmallows, cereal, and peanuts.

Drop by teaspoonfuls onto wax paper. Let stand 15 minutes or until firm. Store in airtight containers. **Yield:** 1¾ lb.

Hazelnut-Chocolate Truffles

Hazelnut-Chocolate Truffles

For an impressive presentation, stack truffles on a platter, and drizzle with chocolate syrup. Serve with coffee or sparkling wine.

Prep: 20 min. Chill: 2 hr. Bake: 10 min.

¾ cup whipping cream
1 cup finely chopped bittersweet chocolate
1 Tbsp. unsalted butter
2 Tbsp. hazelnut liqueur
¾ cup hazelnuts
1 (3-oz.) dark chocolate bar, chopped*

Bring cream to a boil in a medium saucepan over medium-high heat; whisk in bittersweet chocolate, butter, and hazelnut liqueur until well combined. Chill at least 2 hours.

Place hazelnuts on a baking sheet. Bake at 350° for 10 minutes or until hazelnuts are toasted. Place warm hazelnuts in a dish towel, and rub vigorously to remove skins.

Process toasted hazelnuts in a food processor until ground. Place in a shallow dish.

Shape chocolate mixture into 1-inch balls. Melt chopped dark chocolate bar in a small saucepan over low heat. Roll each ball in 1 tsp. melted dark chocolate, and immediately roll in toasted, ground hazelnuts until lightly coated.

Cover and chill truffles until ready to serve. **Yield:** 20 truffles.
*½ cup semisweet morsels may be substituted for dark chocolate bar. For testing purposes only, we used Ghirardelli Dark Chocolate for dark chocolate bar.

editor's favorite

Traditional Peanut Brittle

If you're a fan of peanut brittle, be sure to try one of the variations below for a flavorful twist. Prepare this recipe on a sunny day; damp weather can cause the candy to be chewy.

Prep: 5 min. Cook: 10 min. Stand: 5 min.

1 cup sugar
½ cup light corn syrup
⅛ tsp. salt
1 cup dry-roasted or shelled raw peanuts
2 Tbsp. butter
1 tsp. baking soda
2 tsp. vanilla extract

Cook first 3 ingredients in a 2-qt. heavy saucepan over medium heat, stirring constantly, until mixture starts to boil. Cover and boil, without stirring, 2 minutes. Uncover and boil, without stirring, 3 minutes more or until a candy thermometer reaches 310° (photo 1).

Stir in peanuts gently, and cook 1 to 2 minutes more or until mixture is golden brown (photo 2). Remove from heat, and stir in butter and remaining ingredients.

Pour mixture into a buttered 15- x 10-inch jelly-roll pan; spread thinly (photo 3).

Allow to stand at room temperature 5 minutes or until hardened. Break into pieces. Store in an airtight container. **Yield:** 1 lb.

Microwave Brittle: Combine first 3 ingredients in a large microwave-safe bowl. Microwave at HIGH 5 to 6 minutes or until a candy thermometer registers 310° (do not microwave thermometer). Add peanuts; microwave at HIGH 1½ to 2 minutes more in a 1,000-watt microwave or until mixture is golden. Microwave at HIGH 4 minutes more if using a 700-watt microwave. Stir in butter and remaining ingredients. Pour into a buttered 15- x 10-inch jelly-roll pan; spread thinly. Allow to stand at room temperature 5 minutes or until hardened; break into pieces. Store in an airtight container.

Pecan Brittle: Substitute 1 cup chopped pecans for peanuts.

Chocolate-Dipped Peanut Brittle: Prepare peanut brittle as directed. Melt 2 (2-oz.) chocolate bark coating squares; dip pieces into chocolate. Place on wax paper; let harden.

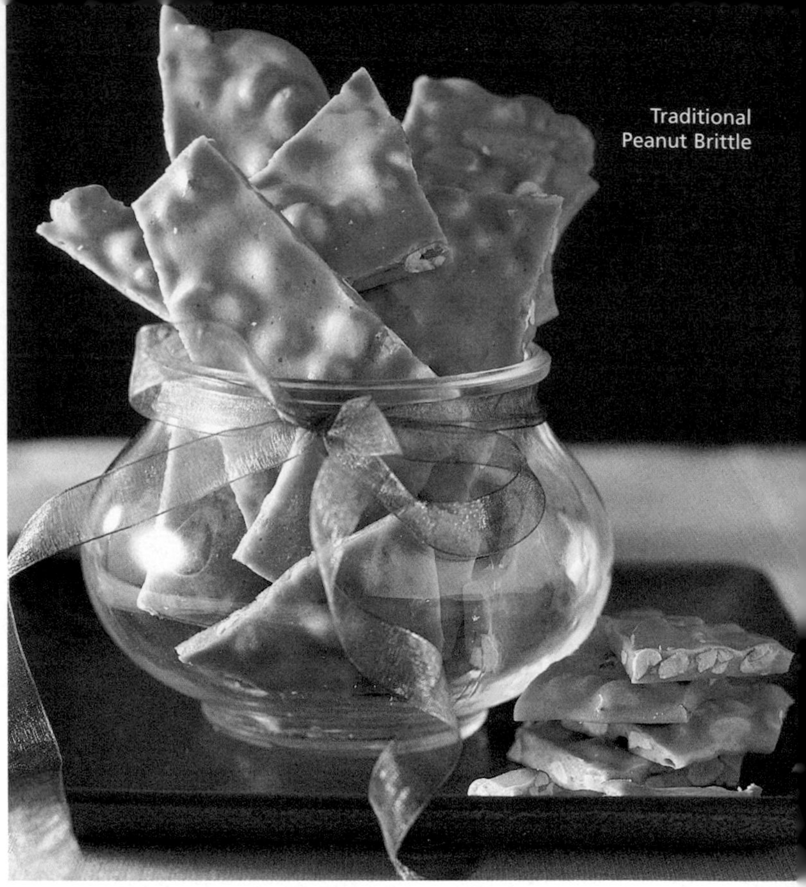
Traditional Peanut Brittle

TRADITIONAL PEANUT BRITTLE STEP-BY-STEP

1

- Cook the mixture, without stirring, until the candy thermometer registers 310°.
- Gently stir in the peanuts, and cook until the mixture is golden brown.
- Immediately pour the mixture into a buttered pan, spreading it thinly.

2

3

Pecan Toffee

Prep: 10 min. Cook: 20 min. Chill: 1 hr.

1½ cups chopped pecans, toasted and divided
1 cup sugar
1 cup butter
1 Tbsp. light corn syrup
¼ cup water
1 cup semisweet chocolate morsels

Spread 1 cup pecans into a 9-inch circle on a lightly greased baking sheet.

Bring sugar and next 3 ingredients to a boil in a heavy saucepan over medium heat, stirring constantly. Cook until mixture is golden brown and a candy thermometer registers 290° to 310° (about 15 minutes). Pour sugar mixture over toasted pecans on baking sheet.

Sprinkle with morsels; let stand 30 seconds. Spread melted morsels evenly over top; sprinkle with remaining ½ cup chopped pecans. Chill 1 hour. Break into bite-size pieces. Store in an airtight container. **Yield:** about 1½ lb.

Pecan Toffee

PECAN TOFFEE STEP-BY-STEP

- Bring the sugar mixture to a boil over medium heat (photo 1).
- Continue cooking until the sugar mixture reaches 290° to 310° on a candy thermometer. The color will change to a deep golden brown, and the mixture will get slightly thicker (photo 2).
- Carefully pour the sugar mixture over the nuts that have been spread into a 9-inch circle on a baking sheet lightly greased with vegetable cooking spray (photo 3).
- Sprinkle morsels evenly on top, and let stand for 30 seconds or until the morsels are totally melted. Spread the melted morsels over the surface (photo 4).
- Sprinkle chopped toasted nuts over the chocolate, and chill until firm (photo 5).
- Break the toffee into small pieces before storing in airtight containers (photo 6).

big batch

Homemade Marshmallows

These lighter-than-air homemade confections take time to prepare but are more than worth the effort. Lightly coat scissors with cooking spray to cut precise marshmallow shapes and to keep scissors from getting sticky.

Prep: 45 min. Stand: 5 min. Cook: 15 min. Chill: 8 hr.

- 3½ (.25-oz.) envelopes unflavored gelatin (2 Tbsp. plus 2½ tsp.)
- ½ cup cold water
- 2 cups granulated sugar
- ½ cup light corn syrup
- ½ cup water
- ½ tsp. salt
- 2 tsp. powdered egg whites
- ¼ cup water
- 10 drops red liquid food coloring (optional)
- 1 tsp. vanilla extract
- 1 cup powdered sugar, divided

Sprinkle gelatin over ½ cup cold water in a medium mixing bowl; stir to blend gelatin, and let stand 5 minutes.

Whisk together granulated sugar and next 3 ingredients in a medium-size heavy saucepan. Cook over medium-low heat, stirring constantly, 3 minutes or until sugar dissolves. Bring to a boil over medium heat; cook, without stirring, 12 minutes or until a candy thermometer registers 240° (soft ball stage). Remove from heat; add to gelatin mixture, stirring until gelatin dissolves. Beat at high speed with an electric mixer 8 minutes or until thick and tripled in size.

Combine powdered egg whites and ¼ cup water in a small mixing bowl. Add food coloring, if desired. Beat at high speed with an electric mixer 6 minutes or until stiff peaks form. Fold egg whites and vanilla into sugar mixture.

Pour mixture into a lightly greased 13- x 9-inch pan coated with powdered sugar. Sprinkle with ¼ cup powdered sugar. Cover and chill 8 hours or overnight.

Run a knife around edge of pan to loosen. Invert marshmallows onto a cutting board, and cut into 1-inch squares or desired shapes. Dredge marshmallows in remaining powdered sugar. **Yield:** 9 dozen.

Toasted Coconut Marshmallows: Substitute coconut extract for vanilla. After cutting shapes, coat in 5 cups toasted, sweetened flaked coconut.

Chocolate-Peanut Butter Marshmallows: Prepare marshmallows according to directions. Fold in ½ cup melted creamy peanut butter into sugar mixture along with egg whites and vanilla. Pour into pan coated with 2 Tbsp. powdered sugar. Sprinkle with ½ cup chopped dry roasted peanuts, pressing into marshmallow mixture. Chill as directed. After cutting shapes, drizzle with ¾ cup melted semisweet chocolate morsels. Let stand until hardened.

HOMEMADE MARSHMALLOWS STEP-BY-STEP

• Boil the syrup mixture over medium heat until a candy thermometer registers 240°. Add the syrup to the gelatin mixture; beat until the mixture is thick and tripled in size.

• Beat the egg whites until stiff peaks form. Fold the whipped egg whites and vanilla into the sugar mixture.

• Pour the mixture into a pan coated with powdered sugar; sift additional sugar on top.

Homemade Marshmallows,
Toasted Coconut Marshmallows

FAST & *Festive*

Spiced Cider Mix
(page 268)

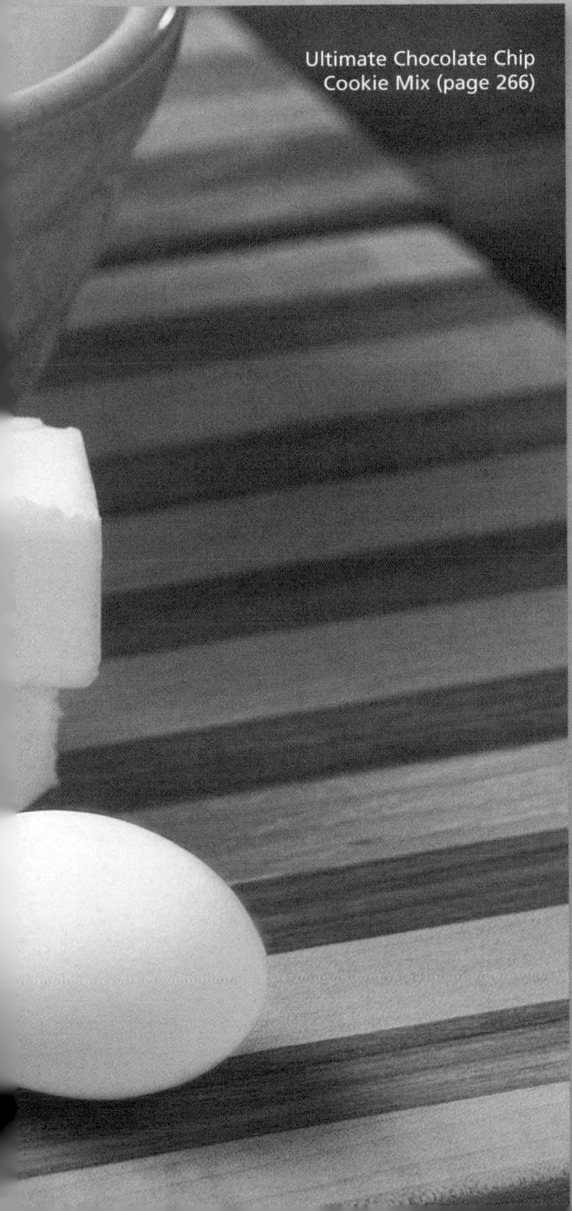

Ultimate Chocolate Chip Cookie Mix (page 266)

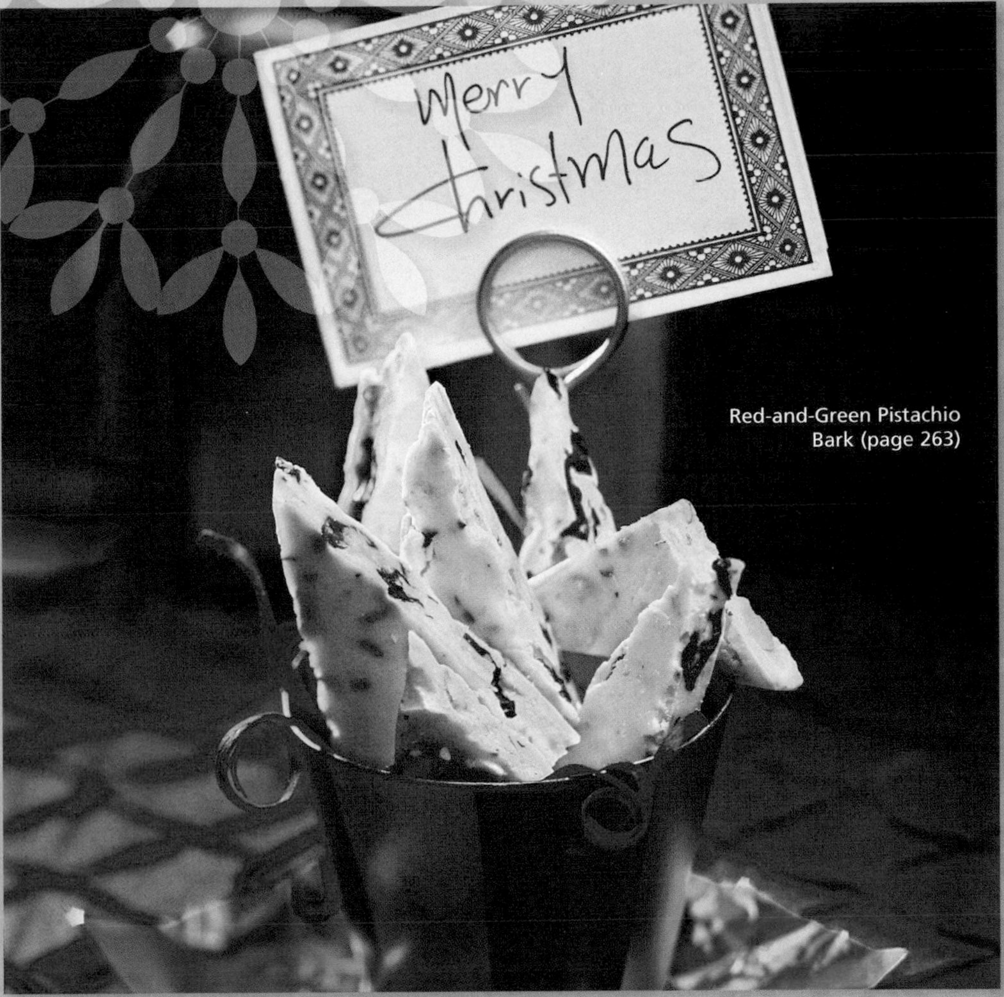

Red-and-Green Pistachio Bark (page 263)

Peanutty Turtle Shortbread Bars (page 268)

THESE TWELVE KITCHEN-FRESH GIFT IDEAS ARE DELIGHTFULLY QUICK AND EASY TO MAKE.

Red-and-Green
Pistachio Bark

5 INGREDIENT 15 MINUTE
Gifts from the Kitchen

How wonderful to complete your holiday shopping at the grocer's! With these recipes—which have only 5 ingredients, take just 15 minutes to prepare, or both—you will have a heartwarming, homemade gift from the kitchen for each person on your list.

editor's favorite • make ahead

Red-and-Green Pistachio Bark

Vanilla bark coating squares can be found on the baking aisle at your grocery store.

Prep: 10 min. Cook: 10 min. Chill: 1 hr.

1¼ cups dried cherries, chopped
2 Tbsp. water
2 (12-oz.) packages white chocolate morsels
6 (2-oz.) vanilla bark coating squares
1¼ cups chopped green pistachios

Microwave cherries and 2 Tbsp. water in a small glass bowl at HIGH 2 minutes; drain.

Melt morsels and bark coating in a heavy saucepan over low heat. Remove from heat; stir in cherries and pistachios. Spread into a wax paper-lined 15- x 10-inch jelly-roll pan.

Chill 1 hour or until firm. Break into pieces, and store in an airtight container. **Yield:** 3½ lb.

editor's favorite • make ahead

Minted Hot Chocolate Mix

Prep: 10 min.

3 (4½-inch) soft peppermint candy sticks (see note)
1 cup sugar
¾ cup instant nonfat dry milk
¾ cup powdered nondairy coffee creamer
½ cup unsweetened cocoa

Place peppermint sticks in a zip-top plastic freezer bag; seal bag, and crush candy with a mallet.

Combine crushed candy and remaining ingredients in an airtight container, and store at room temperature up to 1 month. **Yield:** 3 cups dry mix (about 16 servings).

Note: For testing purposes only, we used King Leo Peppermint Sticks.

Attach These Directions: Stir about 2½ to 3 Tbsp. Minted Hot Chocolate Mix into 1 cup hot milk, stirring until dissolved. Top with marshmallows, if desired. Makes 1 serving.

Fruited Rice Mix

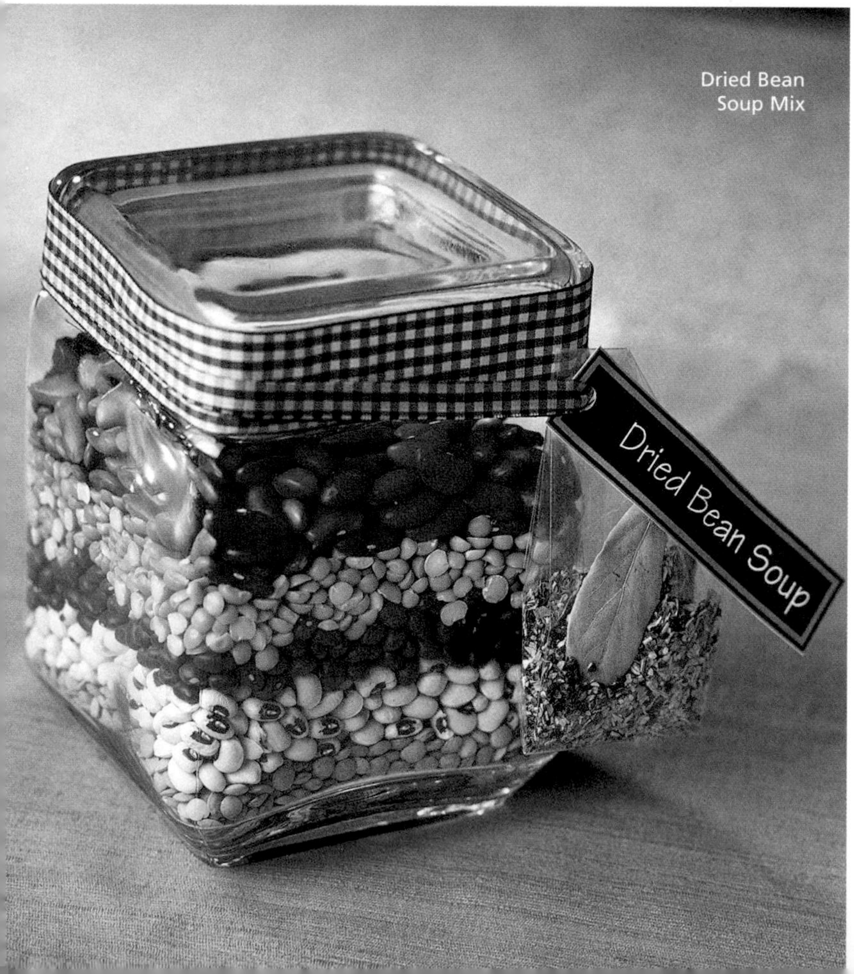

Dried Bean Soup Mix

make ahead

Fruited Rice Mix

Prep: 10 min.

3 cups uncooked quick-cooking brown rice
1 (6-oz.) package dried fruit bits
1 (2.25-oz.) package sliced almonds, toasted
1 tsp. chicken bouillon granules
1 tsp. curry powder

Divide all ingredients evenly between 2 (2-cup) clear containers with airtight lids, creating desired layers. Seal. **Yield:** 2 gifts.

Attach These Directions: Bring 1 cup water and ¾ cup orange juice to a boil; stir in rice mix. Cover, remove from heat, and let stand 5 minutes. Makes 4 servings.

make ahead

Dried Bean Soup Mix

Prep: 15 min.

1 lb. dried lentils
1 lb. dried black-eyed peas
1 lb. dried black beans
1 lb. dried green split peas
1 lb. dried kidney beans
2½ tsp. salt
2½ tsp. dried basil
2½ tsp. dried rosemary
2½ tsp. dried marjoram
2½ tsp. freshly ground black pepper
1¼ tsp. dried crushed red pepper
5 packages ham bouillon (each package 1 tsp.)
5 bay leaves

Divide first 5 ingredients into 5 equal portions. Layer evenly between 5 (2½-cup) clear containers with lids; seal.

Combine salt and next 6 ingredients in a bowl. Divide spice mix into 5 equal portions; place each portion in small plastic bags. Add 1 bay leaf to each bag; tie 1 bag to each jar. **Yield:** 5 gifts.

Attach These Directions: Sort and wash soup mix; place in a large Dutch oven. Cover beans with water; soak 8 hours. Drain beans. Add beans and 8 cups water to Dutch oven; bring to a boil. Add 1 small onion, chopped; 1 (14.5-oz.) can diced tomatoes; and spice mix. Cover, reduce heat, and simmer 2 hours. Uncover; simmer 1 hour. Discard bay leaf. Makes 8 cups.

editor's favorite • make ahead

Sweet-Hot Honey Mustard

This condiment is a delicious complement to holiday ham and turkey. Spread it on a grilled chicken sandwich or over the crust of a quiche before adding the filling. Straight from the jar, it makes a spicy dip for egg rolls. Look for bargains on packets of dry mustard at wholesale clubs and specialty markets, or order online at www.penzeys.com.

Prep: 5 min. Cook: 12 min.

2 cups sugar
1½ cups dry mustard
2 cups white vinegar
3 large eggs, lightly beaten
½ cup honey

Whisk together sugar and mustard in a heavy 3-qt. saucepan; gradually whisk in vinegar and eggs until blended.

Cook mustard mixture over medium heat, whisking constantly, 10 to 12 minutes or until smooth and thickened. Remove from heat, and whisk in honey. Let cool, and store in airtight containers in the refrigerator for up to 1 month. **Yield:** 4 cups.

Cranberry-Pecan Chicken Salad: Stir together 8 cups chopped cooked chicken; 3 celery ribs, diced; 5 green onions, thinly sliced; 1½ cups chopped, toasted pecans; 1 (6-oz.) package sweetened dried cranberries; 1 cup mayonnaise; and ½ cup Sweet-Hot Honey Mustard. Season with salt and pepper to taste. Cover and chill up to 3 days. Yield: 6 to 8 servings.

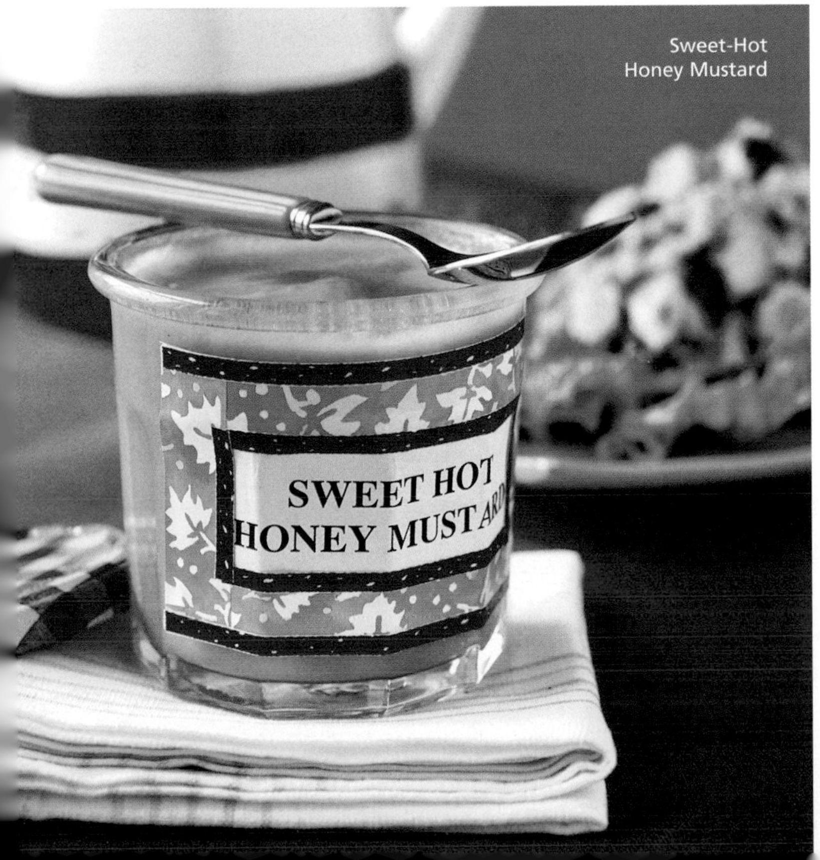

Sweet-Hot Honey Mustard

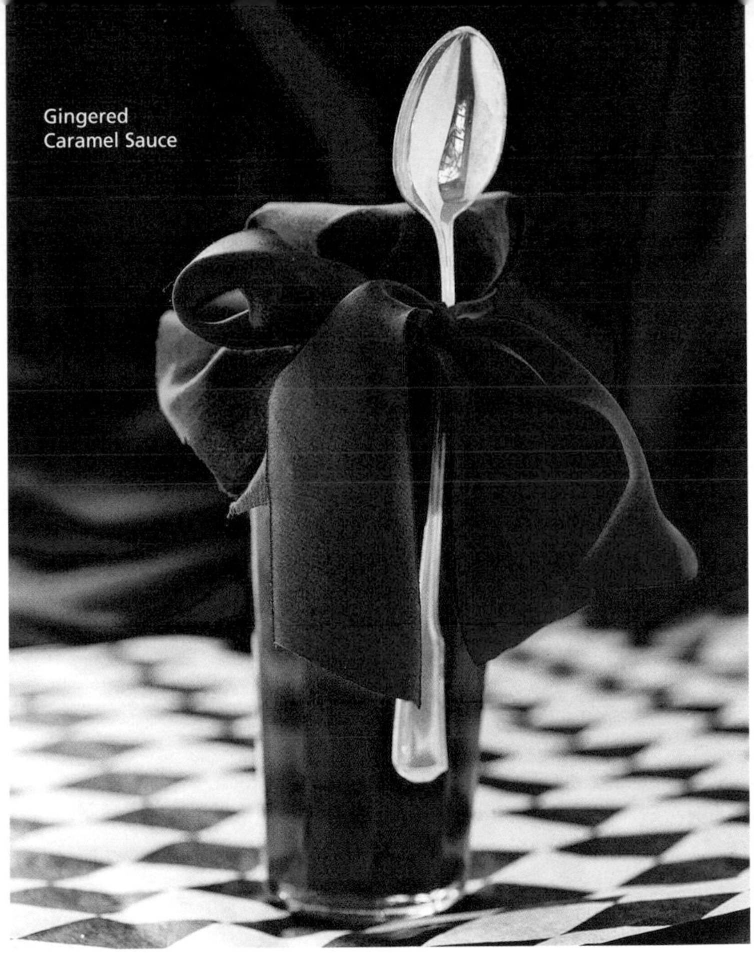
Gingered Caramel Sauce

make ahead

Gingered Caramel Sauce

Include this note on the gift tag: "This sauce is terrific over ice cream, pound cake, or pumpkin pie. Keep refrigerated."

Prep: 5 min. Cook: 10 min.

1 (1-inch) piece fresh ginger, sliced
1 cup whipping cream
1½ cups firmly packed light brown sugar
½ cup water
¼ cup butter
1 tsp. vanilla extract

Bring ginger and cream to a simmer in a large saucepan over medium heat, stirring occasionally. Remove from heat, and cool.

Bring brown sugar and ½ cup water to a simmer over medium heat, stirring occasionally. Cover and increase heat to medium-high; cook 2 minutes. Uncover and cook, stirring occasionally, about 5 minutes, or until mixture is golden brown. Remove from heat. Stir in cream mixture, butter, and vanilla. Cool. Store in an airtight container in refrigerator. **Yield:** 2 cups.

Lemon-Caramel Sauce: Substitute 1 Tbsp. grated fresh lemon rind for ginger. Proceed with recipe as directed.

editor's favorite • make ahead

Ultimate Chocolate Chip Cookie Mix

Prep: 15 min.

1¼ cups all-purpose flour
¼ cup granulated sugar
½ tsp. baking soda
¼ tsp. salt
½ cup semisweet chocolate morsels
½ cup white chocolate morsels
½ cup milk chocolate morsels
½ cup light brown sugar

Layer all ingredients in order listed above in a 1-qt. clear container with an airtight lid. (Pack each layer before adding another by lightly tapping bottom of container on countertop.) Seal; store in a cool, dry place. **Yield:** 1 gift.

Attach These Directions: Beat ½ cup softened butter at medium speed with an electric mixer until creamy. Add 1 large egg and 1 tsp. vanilla extract, beating until blended. Add Ultimate Chocolate Chip Cookie Mix, and stir with a spoon. Drop by tablespoonfuls onto baking sheets. Bake at 350° for 9 to 10 minutes or until golden brown. Cool on baking sheets 1 min. Transfer to wire racks; cool completely. Makes 2½ dozen.

make ahead

Cinnamon-Glazed Almonds

Prep: 5 min. Cook: 20 min.

½ cup water
½ tsp. ground cinnamon
1 cup sugar
2 cups whole blanched almonds
1 tsp. vanilla extract

Combine water, cinnamon, and sugar in a large cast-iron skillet. Bring to a boil over medium heat, stirring constantly, 2 minutes. Add almonds, and reduce heat to medium. Stir until sugar turns to soft crystals, about 17 minutes. Remove from heat; stir in vanilla, and pour onto a baking sheet. Separate almonds into pieces. Cool completely. Store in airtight containers. **Yield:** 3½ cups.

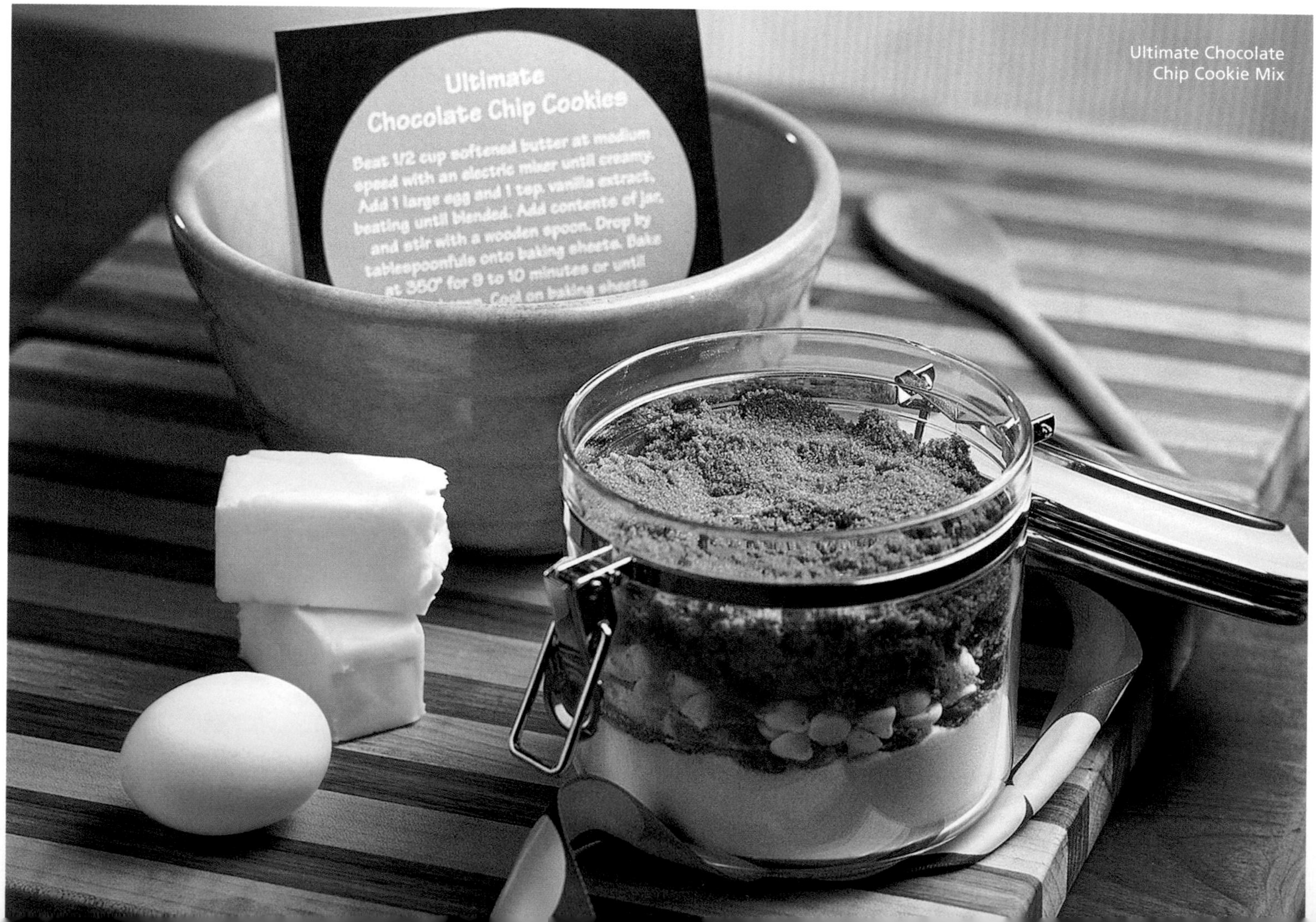

Ultimate Chocolate Chip Cookie Mix

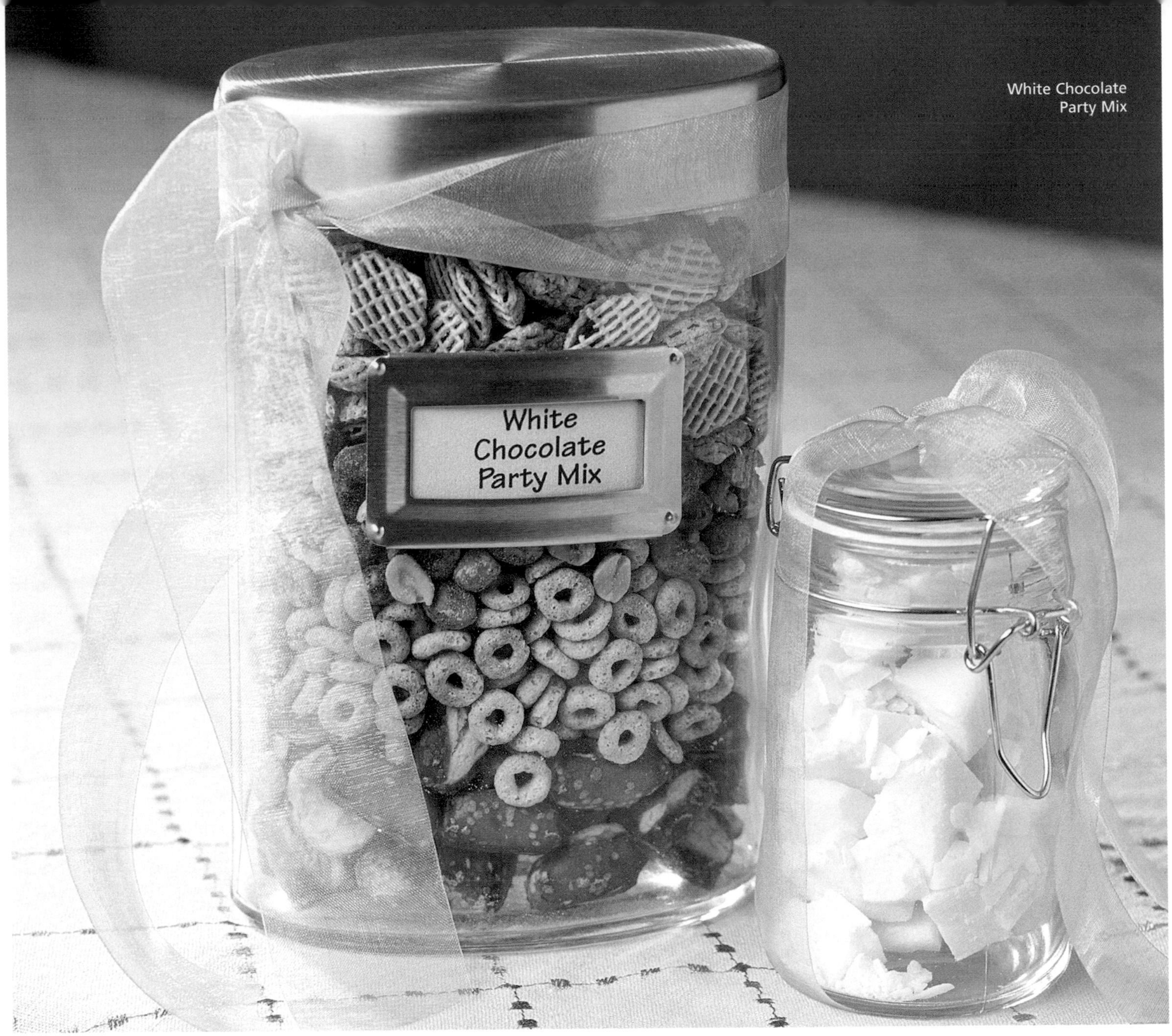

White Chocolate Party Mix

make ahead

White Chocolate Party Mix

Prep: 10 min.

1 (9-oz.) package butter-flavored pretzels (see note)
6 cups toasted oat O-shaped cereal (see note)
6 cups crispy corn cereal (see note)
2 (7-oz.) packages salted peanuts
1 (24-oz.) package almond bark candy coating

Divide first 4 ingredients into 6 equal portions, keeping each ingredient separate. Layer portions evenly between 6 (3-cup) clear containers with airtight lids. Seal; store in a cool, dry place.

Place 6 candy coating squares, chopped, in each of 6 small jars or bags to accompany each jar of party mix. **Yield:** 6 gifts.

Note: For testing purposes only, we used Snyder's of Hanover Snaps Pretzels, Cheerios, and Corn Chex.

Attach These Directions: Remove candy coating squares from jar. Microwave candy coating in a large microwave-safe dish at HIGH 1 min., stirring once. Microwave at HIGH for 1 more min.; stir until coating is smooth. Pour contents from other container into melted coating, stirring to combine. Spread White Chocolate Party Mix onto wax paper; cool 30 min. Break apart, and store in an airtight container.

make ahead

Peanutty Turtle Shortbread Bars

(pictured on page 261)

Prep: 15 min. Cook: 7 min. Bake: 25 min. Stand: 3 min. Chill: 1 hr.

2 cups all-purpose flour
1¾ cups firmly packed light brown sugar, divided
1½ cups butter, softened and divided
1½ cups coarsely chopped cocktail peanuts
1 cup semisweet chocolate morsels

Beat first 3 ingredients at medium-low speed with an electric mixer until mixture resembles coarse meal. Press firmly in bottom of an ungreased 13- x 9-inch pan. Sprinkle with peanuts.

Stir together remaining ¾ cup brown sugar and 1 cup butter in a 2-qt. saucepan over medium heat; cook 3 minutes or until bubbles form around edges. Cook, stirring constantly, 4 more minutes; pour evenly over peanuts in pan.

Bake at 350° for 22 to 25 minutes or until bubbly. Remove pan from oven; sprinkle evenly with chocolate morsels. Let stand 3 minutes or until morsels are softened. Swirl chips gently over surface of bars with a knife, creating a marble effect. Cool completely in pan on a wire rack. Cover and chill 1 hour or until chocolate is set. Cut into bars. **Yield:** 2 to 3 dozen.

make ahead

Toasted Pecan Clusters

Prep: 20 min. Cook: 15 min. Bake: 25 min. Cool: 2 min.

3 Tbsp. butter or margarine
3 cups coarsely chopped pecans
12 oz. chocolate bark coating squares

Melt butter in a 15- x 10-inch jelly-roll pan in a 300° oven. Add pecans to pan; toss with butter until coated. Spread pecans into a single layer. Bake at 300° for 25 minutes, stirring every 10 minutes.

Melt bark coating in a heavy saucepan over low heat, stirring occasionally. Remove from heat, and cool 2 minutes. Stir in pecans. Drop by rounded teaspoonfuls onto wax paper. Cool. Store in an airtight container. **Yield:** about 5 dozen.

Microwave Directions: Place butter in a 1-qt. glass bowl; microwave at HIGH 30 seconds or until melted. Add pecans; toss to coat. Microwave at HIGH 3 to 5 minutes or until toasted, stirring at 1-minute intervals. Place bark coating in a 1-qt. glass bowl. Microwave at MEDIUM (50% power) 2 to 3 minutes or until softened; stir until smooth. Cool 2 minutes; proceed as directed.

make ahead

Spiced Cider Mix

Tie a bag of red cinnamon candies with a pretty ribbon, and attach to each gift along with a gift card.

Prep: 15 min.

2 tsp. ground cinnamon
2 tsp. ground cloves
2 tsp. ground allspice
1 (21.1-oz.) container orange breakfast drink mix
2 cups sugar
2 cups instant tea
1 (19-oz.) package sweetened lemonade drink mix
2 cups red cinnamon candies

Stir together first 3 ingredients. Layer ¾ tsp. spice mixture and ¼ cup each orange drink mix, sugar, instant tea, and lemonade drink mix between 8 (1½-cup) containers with airtight lids; seal. Reserve remaining drink mixes for another use. (Pack each layer before adding another by lightly tapping bottom of containers on countertop.)

Place ¼ cup red cinnamon candies in 8 (3-oz.) bags. Tie 1 bag to each container. **Yield:** 8 gifts.

Attach These Directions: Shake contents of container to combine. Combine Spiced Cider Mix, cinnamon candies, and 1 cup boiling water in a mug. Stir well. Makes about 1 cup.

DISTINCTIVE PACKAGING *doubles the charm* OF THESE TASTY TREATS.

Spiced
Cider

ENTERTAINING *Ideas*

TURN TO THESE PAGES FOR PARTY DECORATING IDEAS AND TIPS, AS WELL AS A DOZEN ALL-OCCASION MENUS.

Fruit Stand

Insert a chopstick or skewer about 1 inch into fruits, such as apples or pears, to make openings for flowers, such as roses. Push the stem of a flower into each hole. If blooms are small, as with spray roses, you may want to insert more than one stem. Arrange several fruits with flowers atop a cake stand, and scatter others around the base of the stand.

GET READY FOR

Holiday Gatherings

Whether you're serving family and close friends or entertaining a crowd, here are some easy table decorations that you can master in minutes.

START WITH WHAT YOU HAVE

You don't have to spend a fortune to decorate your table for holiday parties. Use everyday items in creative ways:

- Arrange flowers in pitchers, creamers, and gravy boats, and line them down the center of the dining table.
- Place votive candles and jingle bells in wineglasses, and display them on top of a mirrored place mat.
- Use a long fabric remnant as a table runner. Simply turn under and press the raw edges along the ends of the fabric.
- Fill small glass vases or jelly jars with candies in bright holiday colors. Hang candy canes on the rims of wine and martini glasses.
- Fill clear hurricane globes or large vases with richly colored ornaments. Scatter individual ornaments around the vases and down the middle of the table.

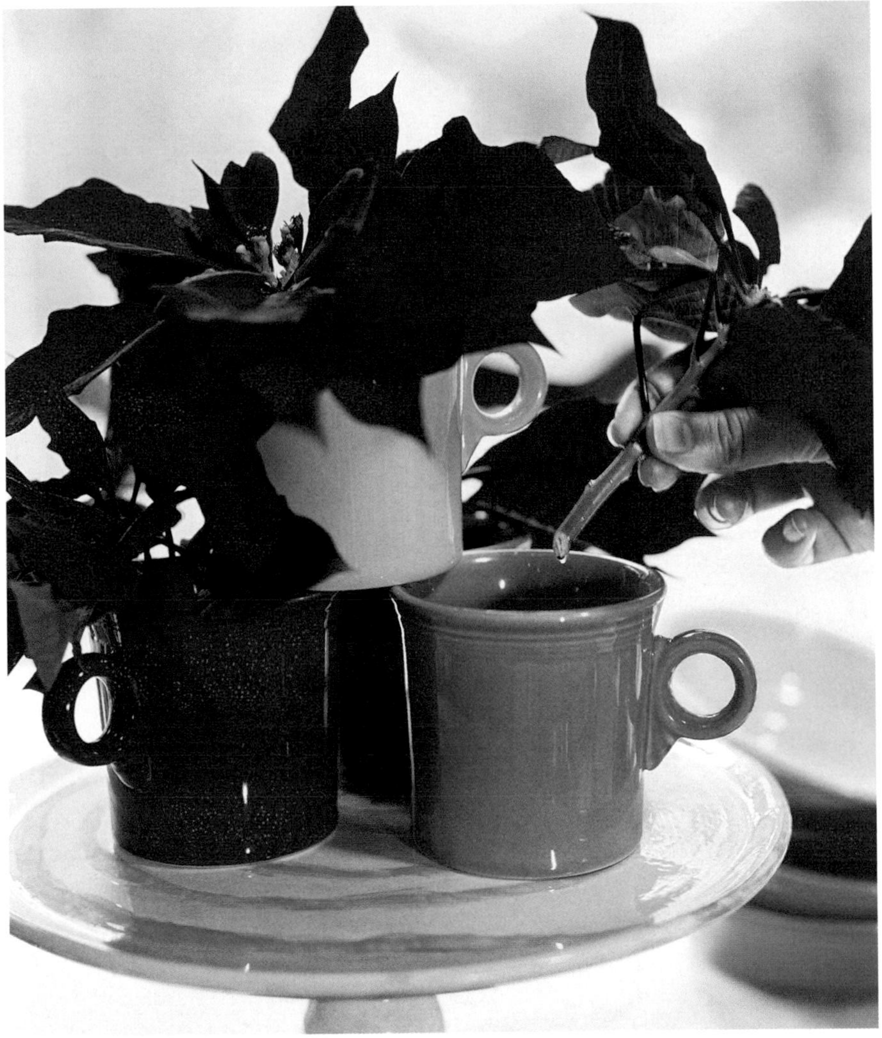

Mug Magic

Stack coffee mugs on a cake stand, fill with water, and place poinsettia blooms inside for a table topper that's ready in a snap. To make cut poinsettias last, cut each stem and sear it quickly by holding it over a lit pillar candle for several seconds. Place seared stems in tepid water with a floral preservative added to condition and extend the life of the blossoms.

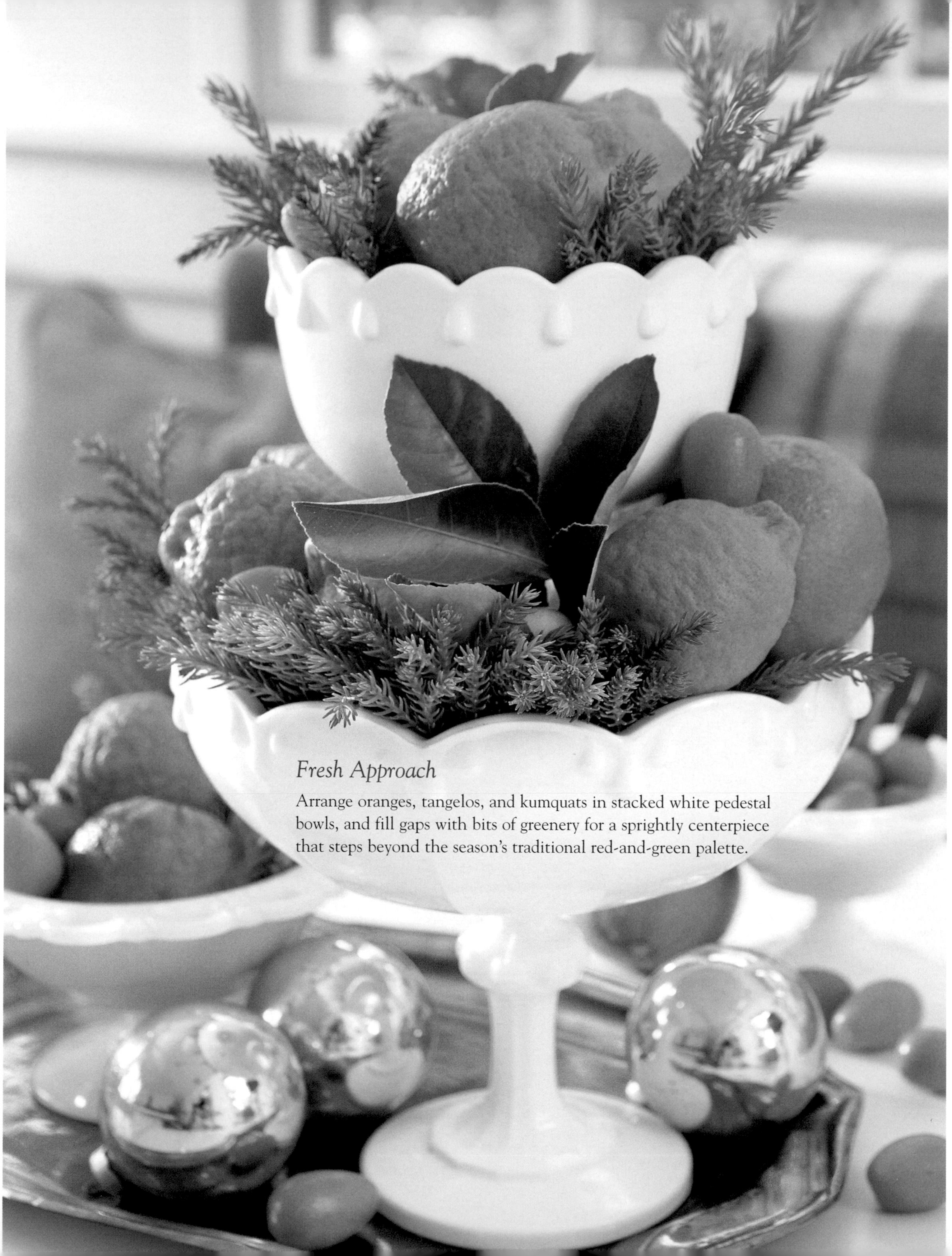

Fresh Approach

Arrange oranges, tangelos, and kumquats in stacked white pedestal bowls, and fill gaps with bits of greenery for a sprightly centerpiece that steps beyond the season's traditional red-and-green palette.

Simple Style

No need to buy special holiday centerpiece containers. Snow-white lilies in decorative white vases are perfect for Yuletide tables. Look for flower stems that have one bloom open and several others beginning to unfurl. Clip the flowers from the stem, and place them in a vase. Add water daily, and the flowers should last for a week.

Easy Choice

Use a couple of complementary flowers for a quick display. Here, euphorbia and star-of-Bethlehem pair for an arrangement that's simply beautiful. Strip leaves off flower stems below the waterline for a clean look.

1

2

3

4

PLACE SETTINGS *With Style*

Place cards easily address the prevailing question that weighs on every dinner guest's mind: Where do I sit? Here are some decorative ways to answer.

PLACE CARD PANACHE

Re-create place cards like the ones at left and right, or use the images as inspiration for your own designs.

- Write a guest's name on a rectangle of heavy paper, and punch a hole in the paper. Slide stems of flowers or berries through the hole, and push them into a florist's plastic water vial. Prop atop a dinner plate (photo 1).
- Personalize place settings by tying guests' initials to stemmed glasses. Find metal letters at crafts stores (photo 2).
- Use mini picture frames as place cards that also serve as party favors. Inscribe names on paper, and slip them inside the frames (photo 3).
- Greet dinner guests with initialed, clove-studded oranges. Use a pen to sketch an initial on each orange, and then press whole cloves into the orange following the marked letter. Let guests take home their fragrant pomanders, which should last about a week (photo 4).
- Surprise dinner guests by enlisting serving pieces to create whimsical place cards. For each, fill a mint julep cup with moist florist foam and a small bundle of hypericum berries or fresh flowers. Push a fork into the foam, and insert a place card between the tines (photo at right).

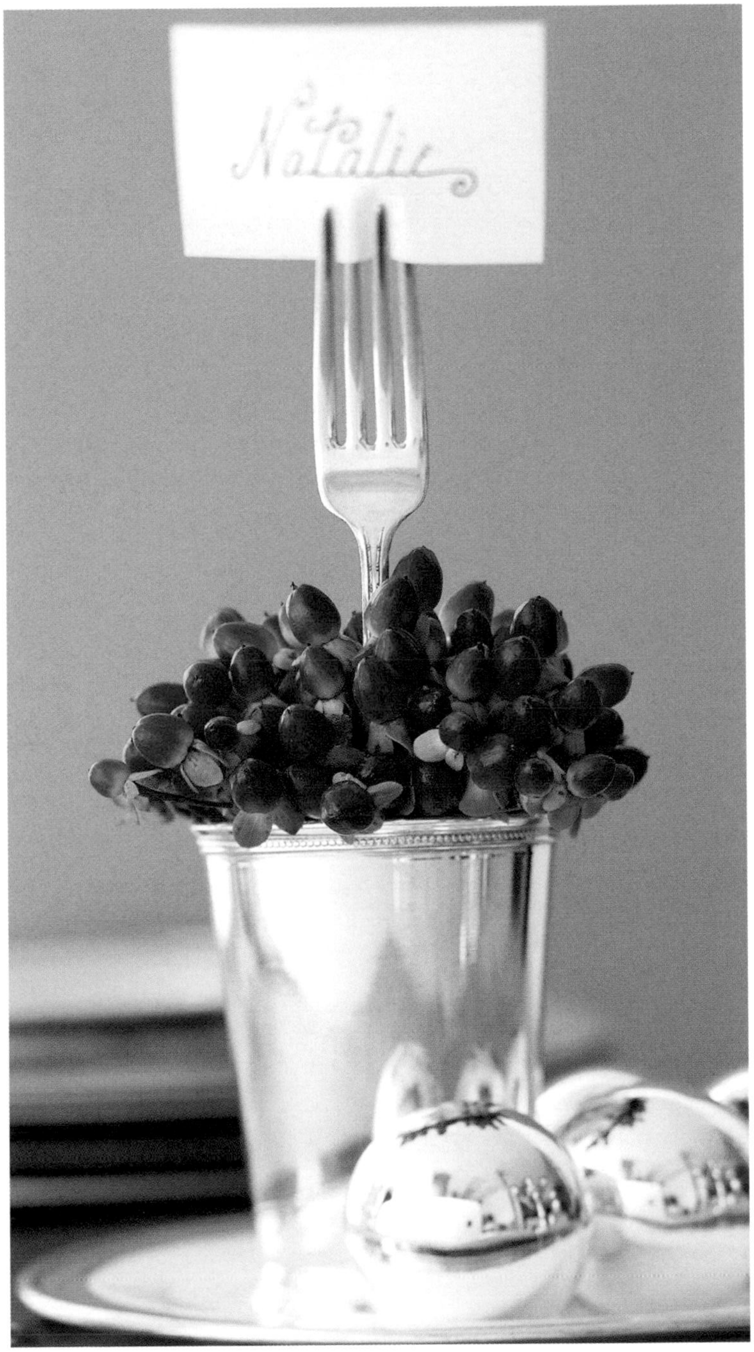

BE A *Savvy Hostess*

You know what they say—always expect the unexpected. With these tips, you'll always be ready for any entertaining eventuality.

Party Tips To Save the Day

A little prep work goes a long way. Before guests arrive, uncork all the wine bottles, light candles, and put coffee and water in your coffeemaker.

Double-check that you have plenty of extra hangers in your coat closet. Or use a spare bedroom to store guests' coats, hats, and handbags.

Think about parking. Too many extra cars on the street can be dangerous. Check with your neighbors to see if their driveways may be available.

If it rains on your parade, keep a few extra umbrellas handy so your friends won't get soaked while running to their cars.

Ask friends to arrive with a few of their favorite CDs so you have an eclectic music collection from which to choose.

If someone asks to help, don't be shy about taking that person up on the generous offer.

Should someone spill red wine, be prepared with your favorite stain remover. We love Wine Away, available through www.drugstore.com.

Make It a Wine-and-Cheese Affair

Having friends come over for cheese and wine? Limit cheese choices to three or four for a small group and five or six for a larger crowd.

Not sure which cheese to serve? One popular method is to serve a mild, a sharp, and a pungent cheese (or two of each). For example, try an Edam or Brie, an aged Cheddar or Manchego, and a blue cheese such as Maytag Blue or Roquefort. Alternately, you could serve a cheese (or two) made from each milk type: cow, goat, and sheep. Goat and sheep's milk cheeses tend to be tangy. Roquefort and Pecorino Romano are examples of sheep's milk cheeses.

A good rule of thumb is to buy 4 or 5 oz. of cheese per person. A 750-milliliter bottle of wine will yield five to six glasses; plan on one or two glasses of wine per person.

Serve each cheese on its own wooden cutting board, plate, or piece of marble instead of placing all of it on one platter. If you must use a single serving tray, separate the cheeses as much as possible so a mild cheese such as Brie won't taste like a pungent cheese such as Asiago or Taleggio.

Always serve cheeses at room temperature (around 70°) to taste their full flavor. Remove them from the refrigerator an hour before the gathering. Serve hard cheeses first, and then move to soft ones. Save the blues for last. If you have any left over, wrap it in fresh plastic wrap to get a good seal.

GUEST GIFTS

Kids of all ages (and that includes adults) love take-home treats. Here are some party-favor ideas that are sure to be well received.

Name Game

Write guests' names on wineglasses using a paint pen. Decorate each glass with simple shapes, such as dots or stars. Look for paint pens at crafts stores. Hand washing is recommended for painted glassware.

Play Tag

Put a signature touch on party favors. Tie ribbons around bottles of coffee syrup. Apply rub-on transfer initials to decorative papers, and pin a guest's initial to each bottle. Look for rub-on transfer initials at crafts stores.

Pretty Packaging

Place a box of chocolates under a small garden cloche at each place setting for a gourmet presentation.

Secrets to Casual Entertaining

Keep your table settings simple by starting with tableware that you have on hand, including everyday dishes and glasses, casual place mats, and colorful napkins. Then use these elements in unexpected ways. Turn place mats lengthwise, allowing them to hang over the edge of the table. Tuck the other end slightly under the table runner so the place mats don't detract from the centerpiece. Mix patterns, stripes, and solids to achieve an up-to-the-minute look.

Provide inviting spots for dining, and let guests serve themselves. Set out food on a buffet stacked with dinner plates. Have a separate area designated for drinks, complete with glasses, beverages, and ice. Place napkin-wrapped flatware at each place setting at your dining and breakfast room tables. If you need extra seating, set up a few small tables in the family room and place a small decoration on each table. And don't forget the little ones: They love to have their own table. Go with melamine, plastic, or paper dishes, and tuck a violet in a basket for a mini-version of the grown-ups' centerpiece.

Rather than stack dirty dishes in the sink, find another convenient place to put them. Partially fill a large cooler with soap and water, and carefully slide the dishes in (no sharp knives, please!). Close the lid, and dirty dishes are out of sight and out of mind until after guests leave.

CONSIDER *buffet entertaining* TO SERVE A LARGE NUMBER OF GUESTS. THIS *easygoing approach* ALLOWS YOU TO MINGLE WITH YOUR GUESTS AND REPLENISH SERVING CONTAINERS AS NEEDED.

YEAR-ROUND *All-Occasion Menus*

This at-a-glance planner offers a dozen menus based on recipes in the book.

Cozy Fireside Meal
serves 6 to 8
Mandarin-Almond Salad (page 21)
Cheesy Vegetable Chowder (page 151)
Peppery Cheese Bread (page 208)
Magic Cookie Bars (page 254)

Elegant Winter Repast
serves 6
Champagne and Cranberries (page 60, make 6 recipes)
Marinated Cornish Hens (page 37)
Fruited Rice Pilaf (page 191)
Honey-Glazed Carrots (page 177)
Chocolate Roulade (page 224)

Laid-back Supper
serves 6
Pizza Spaghetti Casserole (page 162)
green salad
Garlic Bread (page 208)
S'mores Sundaes (page 27, double recipe)

Easter Dinner
serves 8 to 10
Peach Holiday Ham (page 34)
Out-of-This-World Scalloped Potatoes (page 12)
Garlic Green Beans (page 31, double recipe)
Carrot Soufflé (page 177)
Grand Oranges and Strawberries (page 191)
Coconut Layer Cake (page 24)

Lunch in the Garden
serves 6 to 8
Cherry-Tarragon Chicken Salad (page 165)
Asparagus Amandine (page 175)
Dill Mini-Muffins (page 56)
Lemon-Basil Snaps (page 247)

Mother's Day Breakfast
serves 10
Champagne Shimmers (page 129)
Mini Sausage-and-Egg Casseroles (page 106)
fresh strawberries
Peaches-and-Cream Cinnamon Rolls (page 101)

Dinner for Four
serves 4
Baked Pecan Chicken (page 141)
Rosemary Baked Vegetables (page 188)
hot dinner rolls
Cranberry-Apple-Raisin Pie (page 234)

Special Birthday Dinner
serves 6
Perfect Prime Rib (page 138)
Broccoli With Orange Sauce (page 176)
Carrot Soufflé (page 177)
bakery rolls
Lemon-Coconut Cake (page 218)

Mediterranean-Style Menu
serves 8
Herbed Turkey Strips With Roasted Peppers and Beans (page 148)
Roasted Garlic-and-Cheese Risotto (page 192)
green salad
Lemon-Basil Snaps (page 247)

Tailgate Picnic
serves 8 to 10
Toffee-Apple Dip (page 16)
Hip Snack Mix (page 114)
Over-the-Border BLT Wraps (page 159)
Snickerdoodles (page 248)

Weeknight Comfort Food
serves 6 to 8
Turnip Greens Stew (page 157)
Creamy Apple-and-Pecan Salad (page 194)
Black-eyed Pea Cornbread Cakes With Jalapeño Sour Cream (page 90)
Gingerbread Bars With Lemon-Cream Cheese Frosting (page 253)

One-Dish Dinner
serves 8
Shrimp Casserole (page 167)
sliced fruit
French bread

HOLIDAY *Notes*

Use this space as a reminder of your favorite recipes and party ideas.

METRIC *Equivalents*

The recipes that appear in this cookbook use the standard U.S. method for measuring liquid and dry or solid ingredients (teaspoons, tablespoons, and cups). The information on this chart is provided to help cooks outside the United States successfully use these recipes. All equivalents are approximate.

Metric Equivalents for Different Types of Ingredients

A standard cup measure of a dry or solid ingredient will vary in weight depending on the type of ingredient. A standard cup of liquid is the same volume for any type of liquid. Use the following chart when converting standard cup measures to grams (weight) or milliliters (volume).

Standard Cup	Fine Powder (*ex. flour*)	Grain (*ex. rice*)	Granular (*ex. sugar*)	Liquid Solids (*ex. butter*)	Liquid (*ex. milk*)
1	140 g	150 g	190 g	200 g	240 ml
¾	105 g	113 g	143 g	150 g	180 ml
⅔	93 g	100 g	125 g	133 g	160 ml
½	70 g	75 g	95 g	100 g	120 ml
⅓	47 g	50 g	63 g	67 g	80 ml
¼	35 g	38 g	48 g	50 g	60 ml
⅛	18 g	19 g	24 g	25 g	30 ml

Useful Equivalents for Liquid Ingredients by Volume

¼ tsp	=							1 ml		
½ tsp	=							2 ml		
1 tsp	=							5 ml		
3 tsp	=	1 Tbsp	=			½ fl oz	=	15 ml		
	=	2 Tbsp	=	⅛ cup	=	1 fl oz	=	30 ml		
	=	4 Tbsp	=	¼ cup	=	2 fl oz	=	60 ml		
	=	5⅓ Tbsp	=	⅓ cup	=	3 fl oz	=	80 ml		
	=	8 Tbsp	=	½ cup	=	4 fl oz	=	120 ml		
	=	10⅔ Tbsp	=	⅔ cup	=	5 fl oz	=	160 ml		
	=	12 Tbsp	=	¾ cup	=	6 fl oz	=	180 ml		
	=	16 Tbsp	=	1 cup	=	8 fl oz	=	240 ml		
	=	1 pt	=	2 cups	=	16 fl oz	=	480 ml		
	=	1 qt	=	4 cups	=	32 fl oz	=	960 ml		
						33 fl oz	=	1000 ml	=	1 l

Useful Equivalents for Dry Ingredients by Weight

(To convert ounces to grams, multiply the number of ounces by 30.)

1 oz	=	1⁄16 lb	=	30 g
4 oz	=	¼ lb	=	120 g
8 oz	=	½ lb	=	240 g
12 oz	=	¾ lb	=	360 g
16 oz	=	1 lb	=	480 g

Useful Equivalents for Length

(To convert inches to centimeters, multiply the number of inches by 2.5.)

1 in					=	2.5 cm		
6 in	=	½ ft			=	15 cm		
12 in	=	1 ft			=	30 cm		
36 in	=	3 ft	=	1 yd	=	90 cm		
40 in					=	100 cm	=	1 m

Useful Equivalents for Cooking/Oven Temperatures

	Fahrenheit	Celsius	Gas Mark
Freeze Water	32° F	0° C	
Room Temperature	68° F	20° C	
Boil Water	212° F	100° C	
Bake	325° F	160° C	3
	350° F	180° C	4
	375° F	190° C	5
	400° F	200° C	6
	425° F	220° C	7
	450° F	230° C	8
Broil			Grill

INDEX